DARE TO
INSPIRE

Allison Holzer • Sandra Spataro
Jen Grace Baron

DARE TO
INSPIRE

SUSTAIN THE
FIRE *of* INSPIRATION
IN WORK *and* LIFE

LIFE
LONG

Da Capo Lifelong Books
Hachette Book Group
1290 Avenue of the Americas, New York, NY 10104
www.hachettebooks.com
@HachetteBooks

Printed in the United States of America

First Edition: November 2019

Published by Da Capo Lifelong Books, an imprint of Perseus Books, LLC, a subsidiary of Hachette Book Group, Inc. The Da Capo Lifelong Books name and logo is a trademark of the Hachette Book Group.

The Hachette Speakers Bureau provides a wide range of authors for speaking events. To find out more, go to www.hachettespeakersbureau.com or call (866) 376-6591.

The publisher is not responsible for websites (or their content) that are not owned by the publisher.

Print book interior design by Amy Quinn.

ISBNs: 978-0-7382-8572-6 (hardcover); 978-0-7382-8573-3 (ebook)

Library of Congress Control Number: 2019947237

LSC-C

10 9 8 7 6 5 4 3 2 1

We dedicate this book to our incredible InspireCorps team—your passion, dedication, and commitment to making a difference in the world of work inspires us every day.

"A mighty flame followeth a tiny spark."

Dante Alighieri

CONTENTS

PART IV: SCALING INSPIRATION

PART I

UNDERSTANDING INSPIRATION

Our story as friends, business partners, and authors is a story about inspiration—how we spark it in ourselves and one another, how we are sustaining it over time, and how we translate it into positive impact in our work and lives.

We founded our company InspireCorps in 2013, but its roots were planted years earlier.

One of our earliest collective memories is meeting over Google Hangouts to talk about "our positive change model." We came from vastly different industries and backgrounds: Jen from leadership development in Fortune 500 companies, Sandy from Silicon Valley and academia with a PhD in organizational behavior, and Allison from emotional intelligence and coaching within education. Despite our different perspectives, one common passion connected us.

Given that the average person will spend more than ninety thousand hours at work in a lifetime,[1] it is a travesty that so many lack a meaningful connection to their work, unable to use personal skills and talents to have a positive impact, unable to feel fulfilled in their work. It's a lost opportunity to make a positive difference in the world. It's a lost opportunity to feel fulfilled and excited in those ninety thousand hours of our lives.

We recognized early on that our common passion is to remedy this for individuals, teams, and organizations. And we had good ideas for the shape and content of the remedy. But we didn't know, at first, what to call it. We talked about it as that magic thing that happens when

- your performance and impact are at their absolute best, or
- teams collaborate in sync and together create incredible impact, or
- organizations innovate and delight the world with positive change and extraordinary results, both internally and in their business.

Through ongoing conversations, we wrestled with trying to pinpoint the key concept that captured our vision. We talked it through until finally, one day in August of 2012, we had a conversation where we punched through the wall. Allison, with her MFA in fine arts and visual memory, remembers exactly where she was sitting at that moment—on the phone in the kitchen of a small historic home her parents were renting for the summer in Essex, Connecticut.

We realized that day that the key concept we had been searching for was inspiration—inspiring individuals, inspiring teams, inspiring organizations. There is little research on it in the areas we came from, so it eluded us at first. But when we landed on it, we knew.

With renewed clarity about our focus, we started researching what is known about inspiration. Our digging confirmed that, while a few academics have studied the abstract concept, very little is known about how it actually works, especially in the workplace. Thus began our quest to understand inspiration: how to create and replicate it and how to harness it as a resource that leads to extraordinary directed actions and results.

Our own research on inspiration began by consolidating insights and observations from our work with more than 320 senior leaders and then, starting in 2016, by embarking on focused, original data collection on inspiration through interviews with leaders across industries and levels about inspiration in their lives and work. We have conducted live and video interviews with nearly seventy-five leaders across a variety of industries, experiences, generations, and backgrounds, which confirmed and expanded on the considerable secondary research (i.e., positive psychology, emotional intelligence, motivation theory, and organizational behavior) that we conducted on the topic. We have analyzed these interviews qualitatively, identifying themes and insights that are the foundation for the frameworks we introduce in this book. This work is at the frontier of a new field of exploration that will continue to evolve and unfold. As we continue these interviews, we are already recognizing new and important ways to reinvent work around inspiration.

From this research, we learned that inspiration can be more than a fleeting emotion that feels good—it can and should be a daily practice, a deliberate orientation, and a mindset of staying connected to what inspires you. Our mission became clear with these core insights. In our work with clients, what makes the difference for them individually and collectively is sustainable inspiration directed toward positive impact. We are committed to building a corps of individuals who spark and sustain their own inspiration.

The truth is, we are lifelong learners excited to continue learning (and sharing about) how inspiration works. For now, we are thrilled to share the fundamentals with you in this book.

Inspiration is a most critical resource
to be managed in modern work.

We have learned that inspiration is a most critical resource to be managed in modern work. It is *the* intangible that generates extraordinary results. What inspires us is that *you* have the ability to harness it in ways we can't even imagine.

Our wish for you as you read this book is that you take command of how inspiration works specifically and uniquely in your life and work. Each chapter offers tools, strategies, and examples of how to make inspiration happen and last. And each chapter concludes with a Work It section that invites you to engage in the chapter's material with a designed activity. The first three parts of the book focus on your individual experience of sparking and sustaining inspiration. As you master this, you will also learn, in Part IV, how to share inspiration with others and to harness inspiration on teams and within organizational cultures to make your greatest contribution.

CHAPTER ONE

WHAT IS INSPIRATION AND WHY DOES IT MATTER?

We all know of India's famed Taj Mahal, the breathtaking white marble shrine inspired by Emperor Shah Jahan's favorite wife, Mumtaz Mahal. The massive mausoleum complex where Mahal is buried took twenty thousand workers and one thousand elephants more than twenty years to construct.[1] It is a reflection of a great inspiration that started with an initial spark of an idea that was sustained over time and through obstacles until completion. An initiative of such magnitude required more than the initial flash of an idea and a robust checkbook. It began with a promise—a promise Jahan made to his wife as she lay dying.

Their story began nearly twenty-four years earlier, when Jahan had first spotted Mahal,[2] then named Arjumand Banu Begum, a Muslim Persian princess, while walking through a bazaar with an entourage. He was fourteen and she fifteen. He was so taken with her beauty that he went home and announced to his father that he wanted to marry her. After five years, they were married, and she was renamed Mumtaz Mahal, "Jewel of the Palace."[3]

Mumtaz became Emperor Shah Jahan's constant companion, even accompanying him on military campaigns. Although he had other wives, as was the tradition, she was his soul mate. But her life was cut short due to complications from childbirth, as she bore Jahan's fourteenth child. On her deathbed she made Jahan promise two things: "that he would never remarry" and that he would build a monument to their love.[4]

Her dying request was the spark that inspired the project that became his personal mission—constructing a building as a symbol of his enduring love for his late wife. He required his court to go into mourning for two years, during which he began working on plans to build a beautiful mausoleum over her grave.[5] Jahan was known for commissioning impressive structures throughout Northern India, so this tribute was in keeping with previous projects. Erecting ornate mausoleums in memory of royal family members was a tradition of the Mughal people.

The Taj Mahal complex was situated across the Yamuna River from Jahan's Red Fort at Agra and "was constructed of white marble inlaid with semi-precious stones such as jade, crystal, lapis lazuli, amethyst, and turquoise, forming intricate designs in a design known as pietra dura. Its central dome reached a height of 240 feet and was surrounded by four smaller domes; four slender towers, or minarets, stood at the corners . . . the real sarcophagus containing her actual remains lay below, at garden level."[6] The final cost was more than $6.3 million, in seventeenth-century money, and is now worth more than $1 billion.[7]

Clearly, the building of the Taj Mahal reflects an act of inspiration sustained over decades. We offer this as an illustration of the immense power of one individual's sustainable inspiration to fuel extraordinary results rather than to advocate the building process itself (which included some unethical practices by modern standards). In the same way that inspiration fueled the building of the Taj Mahal, inspiration can be a powerful driver of extraordinary results in our work today. When we observe phenomenal leaders, teams, organizations, and endeavors in the world, we see that inspiration is not only an essential element in the spark of a novel idea, but it is also the fuel that feeds motivation over time to realize their achievements. What little research there is on inspiration in the workplace bears this out. Eric Garton and Michael Mankins show in their research that an inspired employee is more than twice as productive as a satisfied employee and more than three times as productive as a dissatisfied employee.[8] The problem, and the opportunity, is that only one in eight employees today is inspired in his or her work.[9] To explore the opportunity further, we must start with understanding what inspiration is and how it works.

WHAT IS INSPIRATION?

Traditionally, inspiration is defined as an ephemeral experience, where a situation, event, or person sparks new possibilities, capabilities, and actions. The Latin roots of the word *inspiration* mean, literally, "to breathe in" or "to take a breath"—imagine experiencing that moment as a gasp or infusion that gives new life and excitement to the project at hand.[10] Typically, the experience is fast, like being overcome with a burst of positive energy—*like a spark*. That burst of energy makes one feel full of ideas and potential along with freedom from constraints that can hinder progress. Sometimes this spark of energy wanes over time, sometimes it translates into action—such as Emperor Shah Jahan's spark of inspiration from his late wife's last request that propelled him to engineer one of the greatest and most beautiful architectural feats that exist today.

> We define the initial moment
> of inspiration—the spark—as
> the intersection of possibility
> and invincibility.

We define the initial moment of inspiration—the spark—as the intersection of *possibility* and *invincibility*. **Possibility** expands the boundary of what could be, it extends beyond our normal limits of what is possible or current conceptions of what may "work." Possibility is firmly rooted in hope—it introduces new ways of thinking about things and a new capacity to visualize, create, analyze, and foresee. It's what allowed Jahan to conceive of a monument that far surpassed anything done prior.

Invincibility is the confident energy that complements possibility in the spark of inspiration and translates it into action. Some people may hear the word *invincibility* as an abandonment of all common sense and regard for safety. Instead, within the experience of inspiration, invincibility operates as a heightened confidence and courage that leads to taking action toward a goal in ways that are rational but bold. In Jahan's case, invincibility showed up in his ability to mobilize tremendous numbers of people and resources, over decades, to realize the project.

As an example of this: one participant in our original research on inspiration, the chief executive of a not-for-profit organization, explained the feeling of inspiration as a combination of possibility and invincibility. He is neither a fighter, nor a race car driver, nor a cyclist, but he described the feeling of inspiration as: "I felt like I could do anything. I could walk out of the room and knock anyone out. I could get into a car and win the Indy 500; I could get on a bicycle and win the Tour de France."[11] We see possibility in this executive's vision of himself fighting or driving or cycling, all of which are outside his normal activities. And we see invincibility in his confidence to conquer all these areas, despite his lack of experience in them. What is important here is the opening up of his perspective and options for the future, whether or not he decides to pursue these lofty goals or achieves them.

The flipside of inspiration, as most
of us have experienced, is burnout.

The flipside of inspiration, as many of us have experienced, is *burnout*. Christina Maslach, a pioneer of research on burnout, explains her most current research with Michael Leiter[12] on burnout as the simultaneous presence of three states: (1) physical exhaustion; (2) professional inefficacy, defined as lack of confidence in your own abilities; and (3) cynicism, defined as irritability, withdrawal, and loss of hope. Many who are caught in burnout long to recapture inspiration.

The way Jennifer Tombaugh, president of Tauck, a family-owned travel and leisure company, described inspiration to us illustrates how it contrasts with burnout: "Inspiration for me is about hope. It's about wanting something better, more—not in a greedy way, but in a way that makes you (or a family, or a company) feel more fulfilled and complete. You're looking for individuals, experiences, or stories that provide a sense of: 'I can do it.' There is that sense of confidence and aspiration of knowing that you can raise your game, that things can get better, that we can be more. There are these moments and converging points of optimism, positivity, and desire to make yourself and the world a better place."[13]

The spark of inspiration can transform our mindsets: it makes the impossible seem possible. It can change how we see our own capacity; it can even change the way we see the world. The result can be major revelations, even revolutionary ones: inventions, the creation of new industries, markets, and produtcs, new careers or partnerships never before thought possible.

Joe Gebbia, one of the cofounders and chief product officer of Airbnb, was unemployed and struggling with a recent increase in rent when he and his roommate at the time, Brian Chesky, came up with the idea for their business in 2007. Joe Gebbia, a designer himself, knew that a major design conference was going on over the weekend and quickly set up a website for artists to stay with them in their apartment. In his TED Talk,[14] he speaks fondly about that weekend when a few guests paid twenty dollars each to sleep on an air mattress on the floor. Gebbia and Chesky hosted them, made them feel at home, and went out of their way to make their guests' stays memorable. This experience led to their revolutionary idea to create a new possibility, a way for people to share their homes with strangers and the founding of Airbnb.

Possibility is not always about new ideas; sometimes it shows up as recognizing future trends and forces. In his book *The Purpose Economy*, Aaron Hurst writes about his belief that we are in the early stages of a fourth economy, a purpose economy. He explains that millennials are demanding purpose through a more localized economy and are moving away from consumption and toward the enjoyment of relationships, connection, and experiences.[15]

Coworking is a perfect example. In coworking, people who are self-employed, have different employers, or have different work arrangements share a common, independent work space. While it has been around for a while, coworking is now a fast-growing way of work; the number of people participating in a cowork situation has grown from less than one hundred in 2007 to a projected five million in 2023.[16] Adam Neumann saw possibility in the integration of these existing trends and launched WeWork in 2007, which now includes almost 250 global workspace locations where people rent the use of private and shared space as their place of work.[17] Neumann likens it to a gym membership—you pay your fee and have access to the equipment.

But Neumann did not stop at just providing work spaces. Instead, he saw greater possibility in light of people aspiring to purpose and connection; he believed that at the heart of WeWork was creative community. Neumann brings people together with workplace amenities like snacks, baristas, foosball tables, networking and learning events, and happy hours. He even offers coliving spaces where workers actually make their homes at, or very near, the coworking space. Neumann aspires to help redesign entire cities to increase connection and community. Meeting the opportunity to provide workspace for millions of workers was a new idea, but going the extra mile to create community, connection, and purpose for their members, supporting the *whole* worker and not just their need for a table and chair, is the visionary idea. It reflects creating a greater possibility; and it demonstrates a sense of invincibility in transforming expectations for what work is and can be in our modern world.

THE PROBLEM WITH INSPIRATION: SPARKS FLAME OUT

We have described inspiration in the previous section as a powerful, and even potentially transformative, moment that combines feelings of possibility and invincibility. The problem is the intense, heightened experience of inspiration can be fleeting. Further, we often think about it happening *to* us, and we don't know when it will happen again. In other words, inspiration isn't something you can control, create, sustain, or replicate on demand.

But what if you could?

There are two aspects to making inspiration a reliable tool to fuel our endeavors: first, we have to be able to make it happen on demand; and second, we have to be able to make it last. The spark of inspiration is much like the artist's muse—an external force or being that brings about new ideas and approaches. However, once you seek out, observe, and know the kinds of situations and people that spark your inspiration, you can actively pursue moments of inspiration so they happen more frequently and in new or different ways.

This ability to be self-aware and actively engage in creating more inspiration in your life is at the foundation of how we aim to reinvent inspiration as you know it through this book. We will do this by providing readers with a blueprint of eighteen **engines of inspiration**—actions that will reliably spark feelings of invincibility and possibility—that emerged from our observation and interviews of business leaders across myriad industries and life circumstances. These engines of inspiration and how to activate them in your life comprise Part II of this book. In providing this framework of engines, we give you an opportunity to know what sparks you and learn about new engines you can actively pursue to find that initial spark of inspiration.

With engines to fuel the initial spark of inspiration, the question then becomes, How do you make the spark last?

The Taj Mahal was surely not just a fleeting idea that came up on Mumtaz Mahal's deathbed. The initial idea grew into a vision, then a plan, which was sustained over a long period of time and through many obstacles along the way. Clearly, Jahan was able to make his initial spark of inspiration from his wife's deathbed request last roughly two decades, dedicating tremendous resources and commitment to the completion of this endeavor. In this case, the spark of an idea to memorialize his wife led to Jahan's life's work, which kept him connected to her memory. Today, millions of people a year travel to the Taj Mahal to be inspired by this shrine to love, which English poet Sir Edwin Arnold describes as "Not a piece of architecture, as other buildings are, but the proud passion of an emperor's love wrought in living stones."[18]

THE PRACTICE OF SUSTAINABLE INSPIRATION

Jahan's inspiration is only one example of lasting, sustained inspiration. It is a tangible, historically important illustration of what inspiration can do, which serves now as a source of inspiration for many who visit and admire the architectural feat. But inspiration happens on smaller scales all the time in important and impactful ways. Individuals across myriad industries—from health care to the automotive industry, education, government, market research, think tanks, and start-up companies—and throughout all levels of an organization thrive in today's changing world when they are inspired to achieve collective goals and have greater impact in their work. Our great opportunity is to increase how—and how many—employees are inspired in their work. The current rate of only 1 in 8 is tragic.[19]

In our firm's work with clients, and based on our research on the topic across numerous industries, we've seen individuals who can sustain their inspiration in their life and work over time and in the face of obstacles. They have demonstrated that inspiration need not be just a fleeting, intense burst of momentary brilliance.

> Inspiration can be actively sought
> after and sustained over time.

Inspiration can be actively sought after and sustained over time. The key, we've found, is knowing what inspires you, understanding that you can choose it and generate it, and then making an intentional practice of it.

Like other intentional practices for thriving in life (i.e., exercise, time management, meditation), you get to choose to sustain inspiration, own how you practice it, and maintain it in a way that is your own. When inspiration is a practice, it can be sparked and resparked through intentional action, leading to an *enduring* sense of possibility and invincibility in areas that are meaningful. It is more than a passing thought or idea. It is also more than creativity and innovation. It is a resource that can provide ongoing support and guidance toward greater effectiveness.

Carefully designed intentional practice cultivates a habit of inspiration. Like a muscle you work at the gym, access to and regeneration of sustainable inspiration gets stronger and easier the more you exercise it. When you practice sustainable inspiration, you shape yourself in new ways. What is key to intentional practice, which is different from habit formation, is that it entails actively designing a portfolio of activities and experiences to support inspiration. Whereas a habit is rooted in repetition, intentional practice is steeped in thoughtful design and action.

Just as the bodies of athletes perform differently than less-fit ones, individuals practicing sustainable inspiration are qualitatively different from those that are uninspired. Fit bodies operate in new ways—the metabolism speeds up, blood pressure drops, and the resting heart rate falls, among other changes. Some people, once in shape, actually crave exercise; they notice when they are not active. In that same way, we can train ourselves to experience and sustain inspiration more often. The more inspiration is exercised, the easier sparks come, the longer the flame shines, and the more frequently they occur. We notice when we feel inspired and when we don't, and we crave it more often in our lives.

So, how do you intentionally practice inspiration in order to sustain it? This will be the focus of Part III in the book. We talk about ways to sustain inspiration through managing your energy, emotions, and mindset, boosting your inspiration through support, accountability, and success, and intentionally resparking the engines of inspiration more often.

THE ADVANTAGES OF SUSTAINABLE INSPIRATION

The advantages of sustainable inspiration show up vividly in our daily lived experience. Overall, we're more optimistic, creative, confident, and open when we're inspired. We make richer connections to people, we infuse interactions with more substance and value, and we enjoy our lives more. Being inspired has its own rewards in and of itself.

In addition, and equally as important, sustaining inspiration over time leads to success in your endeavors. The Taj Mahal was an incredible feat resulting from one individual's sustained inspiration. Imagine the results compounded within organizations comprised of many individuals sustaining inspiration in their work every day, integrating inspiration into their teams and the culture of their organization.

Our research looked at the advantages of inspiration at both the individual and organizational levels.

In addition to just feeling better and enjoying life more, when individuals sustain inspiration, they have a tremendous advantage in overall performance, with an opportunity to expand that impact to their teams and organizations. Sustainable inspiration yields important **individual advantages**, including (1) visionary and strategic thinking, (2) better performance and results, (3) stronger connections and community, and (4) purpose-driven and calling-oriented people.

1. **Visionary and strategic thinking** emerges from business leaders who foresee what most of us cannot even imagine. Because inspiration is a heightened positive emotion, it opens up neurological

pathways to thinking bigger, broadening our ideas, and seeing into the future.[20] Individuals are less likely to get stuck ruminating about the problem and more likely to see possibilities and solutions.[21]

2. Inspiration includes both possibility and invincibility, or confidence to take action in new ways, often leading to **better performance and results**. One example: inspired Starbucks baristas inventing new drinks that boost sales.[22]

3. Positive emotions like inspiration create neurological resonance (rather than dissonance), which leads to stronger relationships and collaboration.[23] Simply put, when individuals feel inspired, they are more inclined to **build stronger connections and community** with others, as software technology leader Andrea Goulet (CEO, Corgibytes) illustrates. Inspired leaders, like Goulet, are more open to and more appreciative of others and their contributions. Corgibytes is a firm that specializes in using software remodeling techniques to address problems in legacy code bases. Rather than conforming to a traditional software coding house culture of individual contribution from heads-down coders, Goulet intentionally cultivates a relationship-based culture. She invests regularly in efforts and initiatives designed to foster empathy, connection, collaboration, and rapport within her inspiring software coding team. She explains the importance of these connections as follows: "Empathy is the glue that holds a vision and the fuel that drives a team to achieve it."[24]

4. Finally, inspired individuals often **are more oriented to purpose and calling**, which leads to taking purposeful action. Many know the story of entrepreneur Blake Mycoskie, founder of TOMS, a company that designs and markets shoes, who traveled to Argentina for a much-needed respite from the hard-driving days of building four companies in a row.[25] While there, he learned that many children didn't own shoes, preventing them from attending school and walking to get water for their families and exposing

them to disease. He was inspired by the opportunity to put shoes on these children's feet, fueling his sense of invincibility. He loved the local canvas shoe, called *alpargatas*.[26] The question became how to act on this inspiration. The obvious path would be to organize a giving campaign, as many would feel compelled to help out. But he was inspired by a different possibility. Mycoskie recognized that a sustainable business model offered far more contributions than a giving campaign, so he began looking for a way to combine his business skills with this inspiration. Through his inspiration, he found a higher sense of fulfillment in developing his "give one, get one" model for shoes. Hence was born the company he named TOMS, for Tomorrow's Shoes.[27]

Altogether, these individual advantages show how inspiration blossoms into disproportionately positive actions and results. Inspired individuals, through their sense of possibility and invincibility, do great things in the world and experience great success.

It is not surprising, then, that teams and organizations led by inspired leaders and comprised of inspired employees also have disproportionately positive outcomes. Leaders scale inspiration through radical, innovative people strategies and cultures. They institutionalize inspired strategies and encourage intentional practice by making them part of the rituals, norms, and processes that comprise everyday life in their organizations. The result is that **inspired teams and organizations are** (1) more innovative and agile, (2) driven to produce results, (3) more collaborative and rich in information sharing, and (4) better at attracting and retaining top talent (we call this talent magnetism). Inspiration is therefore one of the greatest opportunities, and a most critical resource, to be managed in modern work.

1. **More innovation and agility in response to shifting markets** is an outcome of inspired teams and organizations. One of the most agile ventures around, Amazon is being inspired by shifts

in market demand and new opportunities presented by partnerships to be more efficient in their delivery to consumers.[28] From Seller Flex, which gives Amazon control over how its individual marketplace sellers ship orders out, to Amazon Key, which allows Amazon employees to deliver orders inside customers' houses, even putting away groceries in their kitchen cupboards, Amazon makes its entire enterprise more agile by taking control of the shipping process.[29]

2. Inspired teams and organizations generate **extraordinary business results**. Global manufacturing technology provider Barry-Wehmiller[30] is a case in point. Rather than focusing on using manufacturing equipment and technology to yield process improvements through speed and efficiency, Barry-Wehmiller focuses on achieving excellent results by having an inspired workforce. The company is known for its human approach and culture of compassion.[31] In turn, employees are inspired to give the company and its clients their best. The result is "significant cost-savings and competitive advantages" for their clients.

3. At the heart of inspired teams and organizations is often an ease of **information sharing** across data, perspectives, and ideas. And the likelihood of coming in contact with new perspectives is greater when people work together. As described by Ed Catmull, former president of Pixar Animation and Disney Animation, in his book *Creativity, Inc.: Overcoming the Unseen Forces That Stand in the Way of True Inspiration*, whenever the creative team needs new ideas, a greater sense of possibility, they call a meeting, which consists of watching a movie and then brainstorming about how to make it better. Additionally, every morning, he said they have a "daily," a meeting in which anyone can show their work-in-progress and ask for feedback to improve it. The trust exhibited here underlies the sense of invincibility—each person is fully confident in his or her quest to make the work as good as it can be. The idea is to learn from and inspire one another through

the exchange of ideas. Catmull notes that "dailies are designed to promote everyone's ability to be open to others, in the recognition that individual creativity is magnified by the people around you. The result: We see more clearly."[32]

4. Finally, inspiring teams and organizations also **have an easier time attracting, developing, and retaining top talent**. Just look at SAS, which designs business analytic tools. The company enjoys one of the lowest turnover rates in the software industry at around 4 percent.[33] SAS engineers are encouraged to try new things, to not be afraid of failure. The company's leadership boosts their sense of invincibility with rewards that confound the leaders of many publicly held companies, from a limit on hours worked—37.5 weekly—to free food in a number of onsite cafeterias, to getting your own private office, to being able to skip out during the day to run errands without having to make up a story.[34] At the end of the day, employees feel valued and trusted. The resulting sense of *possibility* and *invincibility* in SAS employees explains why very few ever want to leave.

The bottom line is that the benefits of sustainable inspiration are many. Jahan proved this through the monument he erected to honor the love between himself and his wife. And people in business prove it every day. Inspired individuals feel more fulfilled and valued and are driven to deliver great performance that benefits their employer. Organizations focused on inspiring employees to do their best work are then enriched by superior effort and inspired thinking. Inspired people drive success. This book is dedicated to helping you engineer and share sustainable inspiration.

WORK IT
Recognizing Inspiration in Yourself

Think of a time when you felt inspired and it led to a positive outcome or change for you. It may have been from your youth, in your current work, with your family—any time or place.

What was it that inspired you?

What did it feel like?

In what sense did you experience greater possibility or feelings of invincibility or confidence? What did that look like to you?

What happened? What were you inspired to do?

How did you end up acting on the inspiration?

Were you able to make it last?

What was the result (on you, the situation, those around you)?

Getting in touch with what sparks you and how inspiration operates within you is the first step toward building the self-awareness that is key to sparking and sustaining inspiration in your life.

CHAPTER TWO

TRUTHS ABOUT INSPIRATION

Despite the importance of inspiration to all of us and the great opportunity it presents, surprisingly little is known about what it is and how it works, especially in the workplace.

We have interviewed business executives, thought leaders, inspirational figures, creatives, trailblazers, and entrepreneurs across a wide swath of industries and business models to find out what inspires them, how inspiration works in their lives and business, and, most important, how they sustain inspiration over time and through challenges.

This research uncovered five truths about inspiration that help us understand how it works and how to have more of it in our lives.

These truths come to life in the story of Captain Barrington Irving, an aviator and educator who accomplished great feats as a young pilot—including being the youngest person and first African American to fly around the world.[1] He went on to develop an organization called Experience Aviation to expose children to flight and to educate and inspire them to explore careers in STEM+ (science, technology, engineering, math, and the arts).

Born in Kingston, Jamaica, in 1983, Irving moved with his family to Miami, Florida, when he was six. His parents ran a Christian bookstore, where he helped out in his spare time. When he was fifteen, a chance encounter with a Jamaican United Airlines pilot named Captain Gary Robinson, who was shopping in the store, changed the course of Irving's life forever. In our interview with Captain Irving, he said: "I pursued a career I never thought possible because of a chance meeting with this inspiring man."[2]

When they met, Robinson asked Irving if he'd ever considered being an airline pilot. Irving told us that at that point in his life, he was disinterested in school and focused on athletics; the future he imagined for himself was playing football, one day in college and perhaps professionally.

The conversation with Robinson opened up new possibilities for Irving. Robinson offered to give Irving a tour of the airport and of the cockpit of an airplane he flew—a Boeing 777—"and just like that I was hooked."[3] The many possibilities that flight introduced to Irving fueled his pursuit.

Earning a private pilot license cost six thousand dollars back then, which Irving did not have at the time. Exercising *invincibility* in the face of challenge, he began picking up odd jobs, like cleaning pools, bagging groceries, washing planes, and helping out around the hangar, to pay for it.[4] Another pilot, Robert Girdler, offered Irving the chance to fly his Cessna 172 every other week, and his free time was soon filled with work, studying, and practicing on a forty-dollar computer-based flight simulator at home.[5]

A standout high school football player, Irving's coaches were flabbergasted when he turned down a college football scholarship to the University of Florida in order to pursue his dream of becoming a pilot. He ultimately earned a full scholarship to Florida Memorial University after being noticed by the director of aviation at the school who saw him make an impassioned presentation at an aviation event (his 4.49 high school grade point average probably didn't hurt either).[6]

It was at Florida Memorial that he decided his next goal was to fly around the world solo, an almost unimaginable possibility. No one his age had yet done so. His goal was to exponentially replicate the inspiration that Robinson had sparked in him to consider aviation by reaching children all over the world. "I simply wanted to inspire others," he explained.[7]

His round-the-globe aspirations were costly—around $1 million—but that didn't deter Irving. He began knocking on the doors of sponsors, trying to raise the money needed to buy a single-engine Lancair Columbia 400 and cover his travel costs. Turned down by more than fifty potential sponsors over the next two and a half years, Irving finally landed enough support to build the plane and take off. A junior in college at that point, Irving took flight in March 2007 from Florida's Miami-Opa Locka Executive Airport in his plane aptly named *Inspiration* with thirty dollars in his pocket.[8]

Over the next ninety-seven days of travel, Irving sustained his inspiration by staying in touch with nearly three hundred thousand students and educators who followed his thirty-thousand-mile flight via the Internet. In doing so, he became the youngest pilot and first African American to fly around the world. One teacher who used a Sharpie and a shower curtain with a map of the earth on it to follow Irving with her class, wrote a letter to Irving saying: "Thank you for inspiring them . . . but I need you to empower them." Irving said this message stuck with him for years and moved him to found his organization Experience Aviation,[9] a nonprofit organization created to introduce students to aviation and STEM-based careers. Shortly thereafter, he created the Build & Soar program, which challenged sixty high school students to build an experimental plane in ten weeks, which he then flew—a plane he named *Inspiration 2*.

His next venture was the Flying Classroom, an interactive STEM+ experiential learning adventure that took place while he flew around the world again in a Hawker corporate jet to teach the fundamentals of science, engineering, and technology. Between September and November 2014, he conducted sixteen ground, sea, and air expeditions, exploring real-life applications of STEM topics as well as history, geography, social studies, and language arts.

Now, Irving continues his efforts to inspire middle and high school students, including underprivileged youth, to pursue careers in engineering and aviation, frequently speaking at schools and events nationwide. He says that "inspiration is a common denominator," where economic status, race, and other factors disappear. "You can inspire a child to do anything," he says, as he recalls building race cars and hovercrafts with children from all backgrounds and skill sets. When children are inspired to do something, they don't ask the question, How much math do I have to learn to do this? They just learn it. Children previously discouraged from learning or disinterested in the classroom suddenly show interest and are fully engaged in learning.[10]

He encourages children to set lofty goals and strive to achieve them by telling them: "They told me I was too young. They told me I didn't have enough money . . . They told me I'd never come back home. Well, guess what?"[11]

To this day, he has traveled to more than fifty countries, conducted thirty STEM expeditions and is constantly on the lookout for ways to push students to reach for their dreams, as he did. And he still stays in touch with Gary Robinson, his original inspiration, now mentor.

THE TRUTHS OF INSPIRATION

We looked closely at Captain Irving's story and other examples to understand the **truths of inspiration**, including

- **Inspiration is highly personal and evolves over time.** What inspires us is as unique as our fingerprints and is often determined by or traced back to a seminal event from early in our lives.
- **We have agency and choice about inspiration in our own lives.** Through intentional practice, we can take steps to spark and sustain inspiration when we need it. It is within our control to a large degree.

- **There are reliable engines that spark inspiration.** Inspiration engines vary by individual and can be sparked by the people we surround ourselves with or by the circumstances or environment we put ourselves in.
- **Inspiration can be sustained over time.** By consciously activating and using it, like a muscle, you can evoke inspiration more often, more readily. You'll also be able to make bursts of inspiration last longer.
- **Inspiration is contagious.** As with other emotions, you can become inspired by others' inspiration, just as they can be inspired by yours.[12]

TRUTH 1: INSPIRATION IS HIGHLY PERSONAL AND EVOLVES OVER TIME

What inspires each of us is highly personal and unique. In some cases, what inspires us can be traced to an event that occurred early in our lives.

Captain Irving's decision to pursue a career in aviation grew out of curiosity with planes and flying that was sparked by a chance conversation with a United Airlines pilot in his parents' store during his teens. Other teens may have had similar conversations with pilots—even Captain Robinson—and yet not had the same spark of curiosity that Irving did.

Likewise, filmmaker Steven Spielberg's viewing of the movie *Lawrence of Arabia*[13] during high school "set me on my journey," he says. "It just uplifted me . . . provoked me to know more about how movies are made . . . got me excited about making movies someday." It's almost universally understood that *Lawrence of Arabia* is a great movie, but few viewers are moved by it in the same way Spielberg was.

What sparks us can have an unexpected and lasting impact on who we are and who we become. Early experiences can fan the flames of curiosity, opening doors to opportunities we could never have imagined. These experiences—formal or chance encounters—have the power to transform us and to influence the decisions and career paths we choose as adults.

Research tells us that emotions attached to experiences can enhance our memories and details surrounding them.[14] The stronger the emotions associated with the experience, the more vivid the memory, presumably making it more likely to impact our subsequent thinking and choices.

Sources of inspiration are
unique to each person.

Although we all may recognize inspiration when we experience it, where it comes from and how it shows up in our lives is different for each of us. Sources of inspiration are unique to each person. In this way, the roots of inspiration are like a fingerprint: they are consistent, mostly stable over time, and individual. No two people have the same fingerprints—even identical twins—just as no two people are inspired consistently by the same thing.

"I equate inspiration with this phrase of being 'lit up.' Lit up for me means there is a moment of grace, a moment of ah-ha and I would even go as far to say a moment of euphoria. That is inspiration for me. It's powerful, who wouldn't want to be around that?"

—Claude Silver, Chief Heart Officer, VaynerMedia

Some are inspired by challenges, obstacles, and hardship, like trauma surgeon Dr. Shea Gregg, MD, who is inspired to perform at his best by seeing "low blood pressure, ongoing bleeding, or other signs of patient extremis," as it activates his urgency to mobilize his team to save a life, he told us.[15] Grieving the death of his son, Ryan, Dr. Joe Kasper tapped into his grief as a source of inspiration that led him to develop a model and platform to connect people who are grieving.[16] Devika Bulchandani, the newly installed president of McCann New York, said she is inspired by chaos.[17] Derek Ohly, COO of Peach, is inspired by the memory of his father painting every day: that drumbeat practice of his father provided insights that inform how he runs his company every day.[18]

Some people are inspired by silence or the quiet beauty found in nature, while others are energized and fueled by the hustle and bustle of city life. Some of us need community or other people, while other individuals are rejuvenated and more creative and find inspiration when given time to be alone with their thoughts.

Although inspiration is unique to each of us, and is often stable over time, what inspires us can also evolve over time. New experiences, new encounters with others, new exposure to ways of thinking or believing can all push what sparks us into new territory. Just as we grow and evolve as people, what inspires us evolves as well.

TRUTH 2: EACH OF US HAS AGENCY OR POWER TO CHOOSE INSPIRATION

Although many people think inspiration is something that happens to us—that we are suddenly struck by it, often out of the blue—the truth is that we can impact how often we are sparked by inspiration and how much we sustain it in our day-to-day lives.

Captain Irving, for example, is able to continuously reinspire himself and his love of flying through his work with an organization he founded that encourages young people to consider studying and pursuing careers in aviation. Irving shares his love of flying and is reinspired by the curiosity of the children who go through his program.

Intentionally choosing to become inspired leads to behavior and attitude changes. These choices include the things we do, perhaps even subconsciously, to give ourselves a boost—to make conditions more favorable for inspiration to occur. For example, professionals who work from home often opt to dress in professional attire rather than sit around in sweat clothes all day, to change their mindset about what they can get done that day, a concept called enclothed cognition.[19] Laying the groundwork for inspiration may include steps we take to lift our mood or to give ourselves a different perspective, to help us see things with a new perspective, such as fresh-cut flowers in a pretty vase, pushing a little harder than usual on your morning workout, or sharing your daily meditation with a friend. Every day, we can endeavor with hope and deliberate choice to bring more inspiration into our lives and affect our well-being.

Surely, our overall belief systems make a difference here. The extent to which inspiraton is accessible may be affected by our worldview. Jer Clifton, founding director of the Primals Initiative and one of our interviewees, studies our primal world beliefs as our most general impressions and expectations of reality. In our conversations with Clifton, he conveyed how those who have generally greater optimism about the world will likely find inspiration easier to access and sustain, while sustained pessimism might make inspiration harder to reach.[20]

Regardless of your worldview, first you make the choice to be inspired; second, you deliberately zero in on what inspires you. The power of choice is embodied in Jenna Bell, one of our interviewees, who told us about how she contracted a virus that led to a heart transplant. Bell was able to isolate for us the specific moment, presurgery, when she made a deliberate choice to do everything she could to maintain the little health and energy she had remaining and inspire herself to continue through what would turn out to be an almost two-month hospital stay. Without direction from her physicians, she walked hospital halls for four hours a day as part of her rehabilitation; she monitored her diet; she built family-like relationships with her nurses; she even decorated her hospital room in a way that made her feel more comfortable and inspired.[21]

Choosing a pathway to inspiration
starts with self-awareness.

Choosing a pathway to inspiration starts with self-awareness. We've witnessed aha moments—the realization that *yes, I can create inspiration in my life or work*—in many of our clients. As soon as clients accept that they can choose to be inspired, they are on a path toward it. When we asked interviewees about times in their lives they have actively chosen inspiration, their descriptions show great self-awareness. People know what inspires them. For example, Chuck Firlotte, president and CEO of Aquarion Water Company, made a conscious choice to spend more time meditating; he also talked about taking in the beauty and peace of wooded trails while exercising with his friend Charlie.[22] Keith Yamashita, cofounder of SYPartners, a creative firm that specializes in organizational transformation, created a ritual of buying and reading a stack of magazines and then carving out time to sit with them, clipping pictures and other inspiring excerpts to fuel his ongoing inspiration.[23] These are all examples of individuals recognizing the opportunity to inspire themselves and choosing to capitalize on it.

TRUTH 3: THERE ARE RELIABLE ENGINES THAT SPARK INSPIRATION

Once you've made the choice to be inspired, there are many ways to reliably generate sparks, including states of mind, behaviors, and interactions. Irving's inspiration to fly was sparked by meeting Captain Gary Robinson. Irving's inspiration to educate was and continues to be sparked by his realization that he could create opportunities for young people who might not otherwise have them; he could spark their interest in flying to rewrite possibilities in their lives. Joe Gebbia and Brian Chesky at Airbnb were inspired to create the company by reframing the way they looked at their own home—seeing it as a potential guest residence rather than just where they lived. Adam Neumann at WeWork was also sparked by seeing an existing space in a new way, specifically recognizing that shared work spaces could meet the needs of the increasing number of workers not affiliated with an organization but still seeking connection, community, and purpose.

Though the sparks of inspiration here are specific to the people and circumstances involved, they illustrate ways to spark inspiration that we've heard again and again in our research. There are reliable, repeatable methods to generate that critical initial spark of inspiration. We refer to these methods as the *engines of inspiration*. There are eighteen engines of inspiration that fall into three categories: sparked by you, sparked by others, and sparked by situations.

While these engines are born out of our research and our work with clients, they are also consistent with roughly twenty years of research in the field of positive psychology. This field, as originated by Dr. Martin Seligman in 1998, concerns itself with human thriving and flourishing.[24] Positive psychology uses PERMA, which stands for the five domains and pathways through which people create well-being: positive emotions, engagement, relationships, meaning, and achievement.[25] The PERMA framework helps us understand how and why many of the engines inspire us.

TRUTH 4: INSPIRATION CAN BE SUSTAINED OVER TIME

> "Inspiration takes work. It doesn't always come naturally, and I find as a leader I have to work at it. I have to be conscious, I have to push at it. But it's so worth it."
>
> —Cliff Bogue, MD, Chair of Pediatrics, Yale School of Medicine and Chief Medical Officer, Yale New Haven Children's Hospital

As we have discussed, the initial spark of inspiration need not be a fleeting emotion. Just like you can take action to spark inspiration, you can take action to sustain it.

Our research expands on this concept, combining the ecstatic feelings of invincibility and possibility with intentional practice: first knowing what inspires you and actively seeking it, looking to the engines to activate it, and building in habits along with support and accountability that help new behaviors last. Sustainable inspiration is a resource, something you can tap into and generate on command to yield extraordinary results.

So how can you sustain inspiration? There are a number of ways, listed below and offered in detail in Part III:

Resparking or remixing the engines of inspiration. The eighteen engines are sources of inspiration, so if you want to manifest it and retain it, refer back to what has made you feel inspired in the past. Also, consider new engines to try or ways to combine or mix engines.

Direct inspiration to desired outcomes. When a spark of inspiration is used to ignite successful action and results in the world, it begets more inspiration. Humans thrive on achievement, whatever they define that to be. One of the best ways to sustain inspiration is to take action in ways that are known to drive successful outcomes.

Use boosters to advance your inspiration. Progress and relationships are great motivators and can enhance your ability to sustain inspiration. Track, measure, and celebrate progress toward goals to keep yourself inspired. Also look for friends, family members, and coaches to partner with you to keep your inspiration high. Social support from people who care about you is invaluable, and coaches can help clear away obstacles that are interfering with you achieving your objectives.

Manage your energy to keep it positive and uplifted. This includes physical energy, emotional energy, and even cognitive energy (or mindset). Inspiration is a perspective and a positive emotion that is easier to experience when you're feeling energized, open, and joyful. When you have low energy or are feeling depleted in any of these domains, it is much harder to generate positive energy.

Again, intentional practice is about working inspiration like a muscle. The more you refer back to your inspiration engines and use them to generate positive emotions and creativity, the more easily you'll be able to evoke inspiration at will. Consistently putting yourself in the mindset and situation to spark inspiration will also make it possible to extend those bursts of inspiration until they last much longer. This is not easy or casual work; it takes commitment. This practice may feel a lot like focused work, or deep work, as Cal Newport[26] calls it in his book by the same name, where you set the stage for concentrating on what you need to accomplish.

Through each of these steps, you can develop the ability to call forth inspiration when you need it most, and then hang on to it for an extended period of time.

TRUTH 5: INSPIRATION IS CONTAGIOUS

Not only can inspiration become sustainable over time, it can also be shared with and spread to others. Like other emotions,[27] inspiration is contagious. And shared inspiration is powerful. Inspiration can be spread throughout teams, groups, and organizations and help them to thrive. It is exciting when it goes viral!

Inspiration is contagious.

Effective leaders know this and are thoughtful about how they share inspiration with those around them and throughout their organizations.

How and why is inspiration contagious? When a person feels inspired, he or she expresses these emotions through verbal or body language. People who are around an inspired person will pick up on the verbal and body language communication of inspiration and their *mirror neurons* will start to fire and replicate the same emotions of inspiration.[28]

This phenomenon occurs because humans have what is called an *open limbic system*: we pick up on one another's cues and are impacted emotionally by one another. From an adaptive point of view, the open limbic system and mirror neurons are what allow social bonding and trust to occur. A classic example of this is a mother whose open limbic system allows her to emotionally read the cues of her baby and understand her baby's needs.[29]

Within groups and teams, leaders have incredible opportunities to foster inspiration contagion. We have all had the experience of being around someone who is vocally negative or critical within a group or team; soon the entire group or team is feeling irritated, critical, and negative. Inspiration spreads similarly, though in a positive way.

We discovered these five key ideas about inspiration in our research. Knowing them helps us understand the roots of inspiration and why it's so important to us, fundamentally, as human beings. What we hear again and again is that people want to contribute in positive and meaningful ways in the world; they want to have a positive impact. Inspiration has guided Irving throughout his life. Similarly, inspiration can provide an important compass to guide individuals on the right path and to help them evolve over time and discover how they can contribute to the world in meaningful and positive ways.

WORK IT
What's Your Inspiration Fingerprint?

Think of something that inspired you from different decades of your life. For each, consider,

What was it?

What kind of emotion was associated with it?

What values were most important to you at that time, in that situation?

Who were you with?

What kind of positive impact did you have on the situation? Others? Society?

What similarities do you see between what inspired you then and what inspires you now?

Consider how memories of these times have influenced your life.

What choices have you made based on those inspired experiences?

Do you see connections or patterns over time?

Based on what you know now, how might you predict what will be most important to you in the future to help you stay inspired and inspire others?

PART II

SPARKING INSPIRATION

Often inspiration is thought of as an unexpected, sudden experience of transcendence—something that people long for and yet cannot create for themselves. In our conversations with clients and leaders, we heard again and again about individuals putting themselves in situations, mindsets, or conditions that made inspiration more likely to occur. We can, in fact, seek out inspiration and create it for ourselves and others.

In this section of the book we expand on this idea that *there are engines that reliably spark inspiration*. In the following three chapters, we describe and give examples of each of the eighteen engines we've discovered that you can use to proactively spark inspiration in yourself and in others. It's important to note that these engines of inspiration might generate various positive emotions, such as contentment, happiness, serenity, joy, or excitement.[1] These emotions are different from inspiration, and while they

"I get inspiration a lot of different ways. I get inspiration when I hear an exciting talk that challenges me to think differently about something or helps me think about the possibilities of something that I might be able to have an impact on that I never dreamt I could. I get inspiration when I see patients and doctors interacting and families grateful for what our physicians and providers have done for them and how that's impacted their lives. It's an inspiration to see when people overcome huge obstacles and many things that were put in their way, and they persevered and achieved their goals despite difficulties. When I'm inspired, I feel like I sit taller. I stand taller. I feel my body engaging more with people around me or whatever the situation is, as opposed to just sitting back and being passive."

—Cliff Bogue, MD, Chair of Pediatrics, Yale School of Medicine and Chief Medical Officer, Yale New Haven Children's Hospital

create a positive openness that is helpful, inspiration is distinct from each of these. As you work with the engines, remember that you are seeking that combination of greater possibility and invincibility that directs you to positive outcomes. How do you distinguish between happy and inspired? You are feeling inspired when you see your realm of what is possible expand and your confidence in your own invincibility increase.

Although all the engines are effective and readily available, there are differences among them and how they work. Some are more potent than others, some more idiosyncratic or situation dependent. Some are easier to generate than others, more accessible, feel more under our control. Some inspire toward very specific actions, while others generate a more abstract inspiration that can be directed in various ways. The way they inspire people will be different, depending on the person, the situation, and the experience.

These differences in how the engines activate are opportunities. As you read through them, pay attention to which resonate more or less for you. Recognize which have already played an important role in your life and work. For example, as authors, we learned the following during the process of researching and writing about the engines:

- Allison discovered how potent and important unstructured time and new environments are to sparking her inspiration, as they lead to new perspectives and ideas. She used to think of taking time away as self-indulgent. Now, knowing that these are important inspiration engines empowers her to prioritize and activate them when needed.

- Sandy recognized the special environments in her life, specifically California redwood groves and her classrooms in Kentucky where she teaches. She realized that they have always been her inspiration homes. Now, instead of just enjoying these places when she finds herself in them, she travels to them regularly, engineering time in the spaces with intention to find and cultivate inspiration.

- Through her master's program in applied positive psychology, Jen has reaffirmed that "the positive psychology of style" is important and lights her up. She used to think of everyday dressing as a strictly personal avenue of expression but has now integrated how people dress into her work with clients. She shares her research and methods to coach clients on how dressing enables powerful, positive mindsets that translates into a stronger presence and more influence.

Knowing the inspiration engines that are most potent for you allows you to utilize and activate them more often. The engines we don't use as naturally or as often are also potential opportunities to seek out.

The eighteen engines fall into three broad categories. We organize the following three chapters according to these categories of inspiration:

Chapter 3—Sparked by YOU:

Personal engines include sources such as hearing or reading information that leads to a new idea or perspective or giving voice to your values and purpose. This might have happened for you after hearing a news story on the radio or reading about a new business and having your curiosity piqued. That curiosity might lead to brainstorming and exploration that results in inspired ideas.

VALUES AND PURPOSE

ACTIVATING STRENGTHS

ACHIEVEMENTS

UNSTRUCTURED TIME

NEW PERSPECTIVES

BODY MOVEMENT & PRESENCE

Chapter 4—Sparked by OTHERS:

Relationships are another major category of inspiration engines and include other people in your life, such as mentors and heroes, or people you don't necessarily know but who you come across and discover are in need. People who push you to see things in a new light, or who fuel your confidence and your ability to be your best, can be inspiration engines, just as people who question your skills or who try and squelch your ambitions may fuel your fire.

BELONGING

MENTORS & HEROES

GETTING A LIFT

SERVING OTHERS

SHARED MISSION

VULNERABILITY

Chapter 5—Sparked by SITUATIONS:

Situations or circumstances that inspire include physical places or environments or shared collective experiences, such as a concert or rally. We all have places that are special to us, that take us to a different state of mind and transcend the everyday. Similarly, events, situations, or opportunities can also spark inspiration and reflection, whether it's participating in a protest, attending a wedding or funeral, or listening to a TED Talk.

ENVIRONMENTS THAT MOVE US

OVERCOMING CONSTRAINTS

WITNESSING EXCELLENCE

MAKING A DIFFERENCE

SHARED GROUP EXPERIENCES

GRIEF, LOSS OR FAILURE

As you read the three chapters in this section of the book, we encourage you to actively engage with each engine you discover: personalize it, take notes, put your own spin on one, and chart your list for which ones you want to pursue first.

CHAPTER THREE

SPARKED BY YOU

"The object isn't to create art, it's to be in that wonderful state which makes art inevitable."

—Robert Henri, artist

W hat can we learn about inspiration from the owner of a taco truck in Los Angeles? As this chapter unveils, he used personal engines of inspiration to revolutionize his industry.

Chef Wes Avila, the founder, in 2012, of Guerrilla Tacos, the L.A. food truck sensation, was a sous chef at Le Comptoir, a gourmet French restaurant. At that time, the restaurant only gave him work four days a week, and he needed more money to cover his bills. Prompted by sheer necessity for survival, he pulled out the last $167 in his bank account. With the help of his wife, Dr. Tanya Mueller, who was in graduate school at the time, he set up a simple food cart to sell tacos on the streets of L.A.[1]

Avila is part of a wave of L.A. chefs who blend gourmet flavors with everyday comfort food, sometimes leaving jobs at high-end restaurants to serve in food trucks.

AN INSPIRED IDEA

Avila, a child of one immigrant parent, grew up in Pico Rivera, east of Los Angeles. His mother, Judy, cooked for the family every day while he was growing up, shaping his appreciation for simple well-seasoned food. When he was fifteen, his mother passed away, and his father took over the cooking and taught Avila some new approaches to traditional dishes.[2] Although he was identified as a gifted child, he said in our interview with him that, after his mother's passing, he lost his way for a while and stopped pursuing his passions.[3] For seven years, he worked with his father, brother, and uncle in a box factory, driving a forklift. When he met his now wife, she asked him "What do you want to do?" and he replied, "I don't want to be a forklift driver. I love to cook." "Why don't you do that?" she asked. He decided to finally pursue something that had been a hidden passion of his for years, taking out loans to enroll in the California School of Culinary Arts.[4]

His first job out of culinary school was under Chef Walter Manzke at L'Auberge Carmel, inspiring his gourmet tastes; he later went to France to study further under Alain Ducasse at Le Centre de Le Formacion.[5] He relentlessly pursued his passion for culinary arts until he had his breakthrough idea of using tacos as a medium for blending the formative flavors of his parents' cooking with his newly honed craft in French cuisine and selling this unique food on the streets. The challenge of blending two different worlds and taking an entirely new perspective as a street food vendor was the spark of inspiration.

Featuring tacos as the "vessel" for his unconventional ingredients, Avila's high-quality food with its unusual flavors was a hit, and fans would line up around the block for the chance to witness his signature talent. However, without the proper equipment or permits, he found himself moving to different locations to sell his highly sought-after gourmet tacos, dodging the cops to avoid potential fines. "We were kind of bending the law, not necessarily breaking the law. We had to move around so we wouldn't get caught—you know, like guerrilla warfare. That's why we had that name because we'd be in random alleys, random streets, being kind of renegade like that."[6] Avila's wife came up with the name Guerrilla Tacos, which eventually moved from a cart to a fully legal taco truck.

Avila's willingness to rewrite the rules has paid off. In 2018, he opened up a brick-and-mortar restaurant in the downtown L.A. arts district,[7] and he has expanded his reach by coauthoring with Richard Parks III his first cookbook, *Guerrilla Tacos.*

Chef Wes returns to his original source of inspiration—blending his family cooking with his gourmet training—almost daily when he goes into his restaurant and gets ready for the day with his team. He describes what they bring in as new material—such as a fresh fish, a whole pig, or a unique vegetable from a farm that no other restaurant has access to. The challenge of figuring out how to use his talents to translate this material into extraordinary and novel cuisine is what creatively activates him.[8]

You can inspire yourself.

INSPIRATION STARTS WITH YOU

Avila's story showcases many different ways that he personally activates inspiration in his work. Similarly, you can deliberately increase the likelihood that inspiration will emerge by purposely igniting six engines of inspiration that come from your personal experiences, emotions, and mindsets.

The six engines of personal inspiration are

1. Connecting to and voicing your values and purpose
2. Using your strengths
3. Progressing toward and achieving success
4. Using your whole brain with unstructured time
5. Developing new perspectives
6. Activating body movement and presence

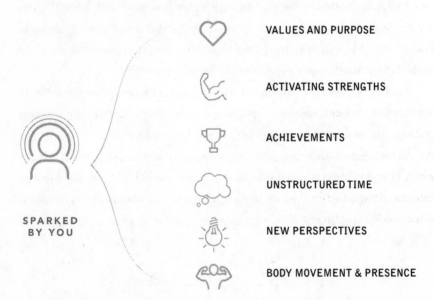

SPARKED
BY YOU

VALUES AND PURPOSE

ACTIVATING STRENGTHS

ACHIEVEMENTS

UNSTRUCTURED TIME

NEW PERSPECTIVES

BODY MOVEMENT & PRESENCE

While all engines are effective in sparking your inspiration, some have greater potency as they draw from the core of who you are, what you stand for, and what you have to offer. The top three on this list—which are about your purpose, strengths, and achievements—are different in nature from the rest of the list. Your passions and your calling are seeded in these engines, so they pack more punch in terms of inspiring you.

1. CONNECTING TO AND VOICING VALUES AND PURPOSE

Inspiration can be sparked by looking inward to your deeply held beliefs, which reflect your purpose, mission, meaning, values, or your faith—your inner why. Your why consists of the central motivating aims of your life, or, more simply, the reason you get up in the morning. You can actually have more than one why. In fact, you may have a different why for each different facet of your life. Your why influences your behavior, shapes your goals, and offers a sense of direction and meaning. For some people, their why is connected to their vocation—meaningful, satisfying work. For others, it lies in their responsibilities to their family or friends or to areas outside work, such as their faith, hobbies, or community.

Finding meaning and purpose in work has emerged as a top priority for many employees, the most prominent group being the millennial generation. Today's employees thirst for meaning and purpose in their jobs. As Aaron Hurst addresses in *The Purpose Economy*,[9] gone are the days when compensation alone motivated employees. Workers today want to feel that their contributions at work also serve the greater good, that their work is connected to their why.

> Workers today want to feel that their contributions at work also serve the greater good, that their work is connected to their why.

It turns out that employees who see their jobs as "integral to their lives and their identity"[10] are generally more satisfied with that work, reports Amy Wrzesniewski, PhD, professor of organizational behavior at Yale University's School of Management. Wrzesniewski and University of Michigan's Jane Dutton's research found that employees who were able to cast their job tasks in terms of their own values, including a hospital janitor who saw her why as about serving "her patients,"[11] are far more satisfied and fulfilled *and* more inspired to take action in new ways in their work. For example, the hospital janitor changed the artwork and plants in her patients' rooms each day to provide them with new stimulation. She even broke hospital protocol to walk patients' families to various parts of the hospital to ease the families' stress.

Our interview with Avila revealed how he activates his values and purpose in his work. First and foremost, he sees himself as a creative: "Inspiration is the drive to want to create, to reinterpret, reinvent, and to put forth something that is meaningful in my industry." He said everything in his restaurant is "there on purpose," from the graffiti art on the walls done by local artists to the raw ingredients and materials in the food. He emphasized his values around mental health and balance in an industry where self-sacrifice is a "badge of honor." He provides all employees with good benefits and insurance so they feel taken care of, remembering how his father took only one week and three sick days off during his entire work life—one week when he was seriously injured and one day each for the births of his three children. Avila values balance and makes it part of his purpose to promote this value within his industry.[12]

Looking inward and connecting to your own values, purpose, and personal why is a powerhouse source of inspiration—in fact, out of all the engines of inspiration, it may be the most potent of all. It can be daunting to try to winnow everything that's important to you down to a

> "Inspiration is the drive to want to create, to reinterpret, reinvent, and to put forth something that is meaningful in my industry."
>
> —Wes Avila, Chef/Owner, Guerrilla Tacos

single list of values or one purpose statement. Start by asking yourself: Where do I make my greatest contribution and why is it important to me? You can ask yourself this question across many different domains of your life: work, family, friends, and the like. Although your purpose may overlap across domains, there may also be distinctions between certain areas that are significant. Articulating your values and purposes is an important first step to connecting to opportunities that inspire you.

2. USING YOUR STRENGTHS

What makes you distinctly great can also be a source of inspiration. Both Dr. Chris Peterson and Dr. Martin Seligman, pioneering researchers in the field of positive psychology, have studied how people use their character strengths to make a positive impact in the world. In their research, they have found twenty-four distinct character strengths that are consistently valued across cultures as virtuous attributes, such as creativity, kindness, hope, love of learning, and fairness.[13] People who use one or more of their character strengths in their work regularly tend to be more engaged and have greater well-being at work.[14] In addition to elements of character, strengths can also be based on talents or skills.

Here is a thought experiment you can try to assess your own strengths, passions, and values. Think back on a time when you made a contribution that made you feel really proud. Maybe you had an innovative thought, maybe you helped someone, maybe you performed at a greater level than you usually do. What were you doing?

Recall the moment in detail—perhaps jot down a few notes to help you make it really vivid again in your mind. Now think about *why* you are proud of that moment. What does it mean to you? What makes it more important than other times when you've done well? What strengths were you using?

Your answers to these last questions likely reflect your personal and professional strengths and talents. Using these more often and more deliberately will be inspiring to you, whether you are already inspired or are seeking new inspiration.

As authors and entrepreneurs, each of us savors the opportunity to put our strengths into practice. Allison's creativity, perspective, and curiosity come to life through her leadership and executive coaching work, a great passion and source of inspiration for her.

Jen's appreciation for beauty, excellence, and creativity—a signature character strength of hers—is activated when she appraises physical presence and comportment, especially through dressing. A practitioner of embodied cognition, she takes delight in dressing deliberately for the energy and leadership styles required during her day. She also coaches others to organize their wardrobes to create the same. Exercising her strengths in this way brings her great inspiration.

For Sandy, teaching her students taps into her purpose, which is to help people become their best selves. When she reflects on her significant contributions, they almost always happen in the classroom, where she exercises her signature strengths of teamwork, justice, humor, and appreciation of beauty and excellence. Being in the classroom is inspirational for her.

Chef Wes crafted his current work around his strengths—his creativity, identified as a strength at a young age, combined with his gritty love of a challenge and his passion for cooking. Instigated by financial necessity, he crafted work that capitalizes on his greatest strengths.

Like Chef Wes, it can make sense to organize your work and home life to naturally activate your strengths more. Consider job crafting,[15] in which an employee customizes his or her job by actively changing tasks and relationships at work. It's sort of like taking your job to the spa to reshape it around your strengths—which involves mapping your time, attention, and energies according to your top values, strengths, and passions and adjusting your role at work to better fit these. What if your job itself could be a more reliable source of inspiration every day?[16]

🏆 3. PROGRESSING TOWARD AND ACHIEVING SUCCESS

When we set inspiring goals, make progress toward them, and accomplish something truly phenomenal, it inspires us. Inherent in this is the ability to choose our goals, drive our own actions, and create our own impact. In the wake of our striving, progress, and achievement, we recognize even more possibility and feel even more confident. Achievement is known to be an essential motivator in humans[17] as it taps into mastery and self-efficacy, basic psychological needs closely tied to well-being.[18]

During one of our very first workshops with clients, we asked one of the participants what inspired him, and he said: "I just want to do great work and be *awesome!*" Our interviews with leaders, such as Gary Garfield, retired CEO of Bridgestone, and Tom Kolditz, PhD, retired brigadier general, US Army, and founding director of the Doerr Institute for New Leaders at Rice University, echoed meaningful achievement as being a major driver of their inspiration.[19] Kolditz's organization is building one of the most comprehensive leader development programs ever launched at a university, impacting thousands of graduate and undergraduate students at Rice University. Imagine the cascading positive impact of hundreds of students given an executive-quality, evidence-based leader development experience, including one-on-one professional leadership coaching.[20] It's a pioneering endeavor and quite an accomplishment.

Interestingly, striving toward progress and achievement was mentioned by some as a source of inspiration, starting at a young age. Bill Jennings, CEO of Reading (Pennsylvania) Hospital, proudly hangs a framed picture of his Boy Scout badges in his office: "I'm very proud—that's my

> "Why I come rushing into the doors here every morning is because it's a purposeful enterprise and we're having success. Success is inspiring."
>
> —Tom Kolditz, PhD, retired Brigadier General, US Army, and Founding Director of the Doerr Institute for New Leaders, Rice University

totem pole. Scouting had a very significant influence on my childhood and probably has a lot of imprints on leadership development also—it was mostly about goal attainment for me. I never sat down and said, 'Gosh I'm just going to develop leadership skills.' I had no interest in that. I wanted to go camping and scuba diving and stuff like that. I was really motivated by advancement and learning and getting the token of the learning. The big prize was becoming an Eagle Scout, and there was never, ever any doubt that I was going to become an Eagle Scout." Today, he prides himself in furthering his goals of improving the hospital system. What inspires him most is when the system makes meaningful shifts in quality of service and patient safety metrics.[21]

What achievements are you most proud of in your life and work? Looking ahead, what are you striving to accomplish and what progress points can you celebrate along the way?

In Chapter 7, "Direct Inspiration to Desired Outcomes," we will dive deeper into positive impact and results. Striving for goals, making progress toward them, and achieving them can not only spark inspiration but also sustain it over time.

4. USING YOUR WHOLE BRAIN WITH UNSTRUCTURED TIME

Instead of trying to force new ideas through concentrated effort, you can allow inspiration to strike when your brain takes a sabbatical, or when you give yourself the time and space to do something relatively routine or mundane. This can allow ideas to emerge from outside consciousness. When you stop deliberately problem solving or actively thinking, new ideas or solutions are more likely to emerge. That's the value of unstructured time.

Inspiration often strikes when
your brain takes a sabbatical, or
when you give yourself the time
and space to do nothing, allowing
subconscious ideas to emerge.

Mentioned by many as a source of inspiration, this is not an unusual occurrence, and neuroscience backs this phenomenon up. Dartmouth College psychology professor, and one of our interviewees, Dr. Christian Jernstedt, an expert in the neuroscience of learning, explains that some of our best ideas emerge when our conscious minds are engaged in a task but not intently focused on solving a problem. For example, this often happens while taking a shower, taking a long drive in the car, or casually listening to a presentation. As the conscious mind passively focuses on a mundane task, the hidden mind—which may carry out nearly 95 percent of the brain's activity—can reveal results of our thinking outside conscious awareness to solve problems, synthesize ideas, and spark new ones.[22]

According to Jernstedt, multitasking decreases opportunities for inspiration; it is typically time sharing from a brain perspective and can get in the way of our recognizing our thinking outside conscious awareness. We need to plan time to incubate ideas, and we can put plans in place to create unstructured time. Then the time itself can allow more to surface than an active, forced, conscious effort to solve a problem or come up with an idea.[23]

When new concepts appear, they are related to subjects we have previously pondered. Nancy Andreasen, a neuroscientist and neuropsychiatrist who has studied creative geniuses for the last several decades, explained in a 2014 article in *The Atlantic*: "When eureka moments occur, they tend to be precipitated by long periods of preparation and incubation, and to strike when the mind is relaxed."[24] We need moments of this type of reverie to allow our minds to wander so that our unconscious minds can emerge.[25]

What types of situations give your brain a break? For some, the perfect cocktail for unstructured think time is a professional event, like a seminar or conference—something that takes people out of their typical work environment and puts them into new surroundings filled with novel ideas and inspiring people. New surroundings like these, even when they're work related, can provide ample time for mind-wandering reverie.

For Allison, the annual coaching conference at Harvard is one such opportunity. She says, "I find myself bombarded with unexpected ideas. In the middle of listening to a phenomenal speaker, my mind wanders off for a few seconds, and then *bam!*—a novel spark flies into my brain that infuses me with excitement, even euphoria. Some of my best writing and blog ideas, content ideas for clients, come to me at conferences."

Many have their best ideas in the shower or folding laundry or hiking up a mountain. One of our inspiration interviewees, Andrea Goulet, CEO of Corgibytes, says that driving in the car is when she feels sparks. Chef Wes in our interview said that the single most potent source of inspiration for him is traveling on vacation. He said that something about the new locations and unstructured time allows for inspiration to "fall into my lap." From there, in order for it to snowball, he needs to "jump on it and add fuel" by translating his ideas into action after he returns.[26]

Think back on the types of situations that give your brain a break from typical activities and that give you the space to think more freely. This is where sparks emerge. What are the brain sabbaticals that work best for you? Vacations? Long runs? Plane travel?

5. DEVELOPING NEW PERSPECTIVES

Learning new information—through reading, taking classes, or simply being exposed to new ideas in everyday conversation, events, or collaborations—is another pathway to inspiration. A spark can be ignited when you combine existing ideas in new ways, or combine new ideas with what you already know, providing an entirely new perspective.

University of Pennsylvania professor Adam Grant, author of *Originals: How Non-Conformists Move the World*, describes a phenomenon called "vuja de."[27] Where déjà vu is the familiar sensation that you have previously experienced your current situation, vuja de "is the reverse—we face something familiar, but we see it with a fresh perspective that enables us to gain new insight from old problems."

Take the Wright brothers, who are credited with pioneering flight. What isn't quite as widely known is that Orville and Wilbur Wright first ran a bicycle shop and were considered the local experts on the repair of bikes. It was that intimate knowledge of how a bicycle functions that sparked a new approach to flying. The Wrights applied a number of bicycle concepts to the design of a plane, confirms the Smithsonian National Air and Space Museum,[28] thereby finding a solution to many of the problems surrounding flight.

For Wes Avila, his exposure to the new flavors and cooking techniques of French cuisine, particularly when he studied in France, changed his approach to the traditional tacos from his childhood. Likewise, Steve Jobs, from Apple, made great strides in the field of computer typography thanks to a calligraphy class he audited at Reed College. The study of calligraphy opened Jobs's eyes to the importance and possibility of typefaces. Said Jobs,[29] "If I had never dropped out [of college], I would have never dropped in on this calligraphy class, and personal computers might not have the wonderful typography that they do. Of course it was impossible to connect the dots looking forward when I was in college. But it was very, very clear looking backward 10 years later."

Engineering opportunities to see things in a different way is a useful approach to igniting inspiration. Artists of all types do this often, but you don't have to be an artist to create opportunities to think in new ways. Consider an area where you feel stuck and uninspired. Imagine yourself looking down on it from a 30K-foot view. From way up high, what do you see that you didn't notice before? What moves you? Or think of a person who is the opposite of you in many ways: How might they see the situation where you feel stuck? In addition, consider shaking up your normal way of looking at things through exposure to new learning, ideas, culture—take a language class, talk to new people, travel somewhere interesting, go to a museum or concert, try a new restaurant.

6. ACTIVATING BODY MOVEMENT AND PRESENCE

Bodies are powerful vehicles for inspiration. How we move, how we dress, how we carry ourselves, our body language—all impact our energy. Our physical energy is inextricably linked to our emotional capacity, which is then linked to inspiration. Physical activity and presence enact chemical changes in endorphins, adrenaline, and other hormones that boost our emotions and spark our inspiration.

You may have experienced times when physical movement sparked new ideas. That mental jolt that comes with physical motion is why many people stop what they're doing and take a walk or go for a run to push past mental blocks they may be experiencing. Inspiration can work in the same way: physical activity can inspire, generating new ideas or solutions.

When you exercise, your brain releases endorphins, which reduce your perception of pain, as well as serotonin, which enhances your mood. These brain chemicals reenergize you. And since low energy can block or prevent inspiration, taking steps, literally, to generate endorphins and serotonin can have an immediate impact on your energy level and mental state.

Numerous studies confirm this energy-physical activity link. In one reported in the *British Journal of Sports Medicine*,[30] Hannah Steinberg, along with six other researchers, found that exercise improved creativity and levels of happiness. An article in *Scientific American*[31] explored the reasons for enhanced cognitive functioning after a walk, explaining that physical activity improves blood flow, which can activate the hippocampus, the part of the brain responsible for learning and memory.

Some companies, including Johnson & Johnson,[32] have accepted the importance of physical activity and encourage employees to refuel their energy through physical activity as a regular part of the workday, rather than squeezing in exercise during free time. Called corporate athletes at Johnson & Johnson, these workers see their activity routines as an integral part of their roles as leaders and necessary for them to perform at their best.

A number of high-profile businesspeople subscribe to the exercise-as-inspiration link.[33] According to *Business Insider,* billionaire entrepreneur Richard Branson believes he gets an additional four hours of productivity a day thanks to his regular workouts. *Vogue* editor Anna Wintour plays tennis many mornings before work to jump-start her brain and her energy level. Former president Barack Obama runs several miles a day. The majority of our senior-level coaching clients have a regular movement or exercise regime that benefits them similarly.

Companies are also conducting walking meetings as a way to spark inspiration and innovation in the moment.[34] LinkedIn, Facebook, and Twitter are just a few organizations that have embraced the power of physical activity when conversing and collaborating.[35] Rather than remaining sedentary around a conference table, employees now get up and walk for twenty to twenty-five minutes around headquarters while discussing the business at hand.

> Although pulling yourself away from a concentrated activity can be hard, getting up and moving around can be a reliable way to spark inspiration.

Together, these engines of inspiration are a road map to finding unleashed possibility and rational invincibility within ourselves. They show us that we can take responsibility for our own inspiration and activate it from within.

Thought Experiment: Activating Inspiration through Resets

How often have you sat down at your desk and committed to staying there to push through a tough task no matter how long it takes? Did you notice during those endurance tests that your productivity started to wane after a while? Humans have natural work rhythms that make extended periods of focused work challenging.

Knowing now that short mental and activity breaks actually boost your productivity rather than diminish it, what types of breaks would work best for you during your workday?

Here are some ideas used by our clients:

- Sitting or standing stretches
- Walking around the hallway or outside
- Holding a standing or walking meeting
- Listening to a high-energy song
- Meditating or listening to a guided visualization
- Briefly playing with a fidget tool
- Having a one-minute dance party

What can you commit to try the next time you are sitting at your desk for a few hours? We encourage you to look at your week ahead and strategically plan short breaks throughout your week, each day. Try out different things until you find a set of tools and a cadence that works best for you.

WORK IT
Sparked by YOU Inspiration Challenge

We all have the capacity to be inspired through all six of these inspiration engines. Yet, we likely naturally lean more on one or two than others. Use the tool below to take stock of the extent to which you are using each of the engines described in this chapter. Then, consider suggested ways and write in some of your own ways to tap into each of the engines more often.

ENGINE	HOW MUCH DO YOU USE IT? (SCALE OF 1–5)	WAYS TO TAP INTO THIS ENGINE MORE OFTEN (CIRCLE THE ONES YOU LIKE BEST AND ADD IN YOUR OWN)
Connecting to and Voicing Values and Purpose	———	**Some examples:** Consider accomplishments you are proud of and why they stand out for you. Think about the most important people in your life and why they matter. Ask yourself what would make your life successful: what kind of legacy do you want to leave behind? Ask yourself what your intention is for an upcoming situation (i.e., meeting, conversation, activity). **What would you add?**
Using Your Strengths	———	**Some examples:** What unique strengths do you have that can be used to have a positive impact on those around you? Examples might be character strengths like kindness, creativity, and wisdom or specific skills and competencies. Think of specific and new ways you can use these strengths to have a positive impact. **What would you add?**

(continues)

ENGINE	HOW MUCH DO YOU USE IT? (SCALE OF 1–5)	WAYS TO TAP INTO THIS ENGINE MORE OFTEN (CIRCLE THE ONES YOU LIKE BEST AND ADD IN YOUR OWN)
Progressing Toward and Achieving Success	————	**Some examples:** What types of accomplishments and achievements in your past give you the greatest sense of pride? Looking forward, what are some of your wildest, biggest goals you hope to accomplish? What kind of legacy do you wish to leave behind? **What would you add?**
Using Your Whole Brain with Unstructured Time	————	**Some examples:** Taking a long shower; taking a long drive; going to a conference; spending leisure time on the beach; using a percentage of your work week for open time and creative thinking; doing a mindless activity like knitting, folding laundry, drawing Zentangles, or washing the dishes; being still for a period of time. **What would you add?**
Developing New Perspectives	————	**Some examples:** Read a book or article on a different topic than usual. Take a course or lecture in a novel area. Travel to experience new people and cultures. Ask people questions to learn more about their ideas (get into their world). Challenge yourself to see something or someone in a different light. Solve a problem using an unexpected approach. **What would you add?**

ENGINE	HOW MUCH DO YOU USE IT? (SCALE OF 1–5)	WAYS TO TAP INTO THIS ENGINE MORE OFTEN (CIRCLE THE ONES YOU LIKE BEST AND ADD IN YOUR OWN)
Activating Body Movement and Presence	_____	**Some examples:** Stretching or shaking out your arms and legs; using fidget tools; dancing or going to a dance class; doing tabata; exercising, such as doing a set of push-ups or pull-ups; enjoying a long walk or run or swimming laps; gardening; house cleaning.

What would you add?

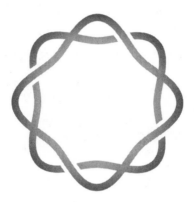

CHAPTER FOUR

SPARKED BY OTHERS

"My father always said, 'Malala will be free as a bird.'"

—Malala Yousafzai, *I Am Malala*

To the outside world, Malala Yousafzai was a very unlikely role model. She was born in 1997 in Pakistan's Swat Valley to parents Ziauddin and Toor Pekai Yousafzai in a culture that reveres boys. Fortunately, her family was different, and her parents were overjoyed at her arrival. They named their baby Malala, after a nineteenth-century

Pashtun heroine, Malalai Maiwund, who encouraged the Afghans not to give up their fight against the British.

Ziauddin, in particular, formed a special bond with his daughter. He was adamant that she would not become invisible like so many other girls in their culture. "Women are not known in public and their names are only known to family members," he explained in a BBC interview.[1] He did not want that fate for his daughter. "Malalai [the Pashtun heroine] had had a voice and I wanted my Malala to have the same—that she would have freedom and be brave and be known by her name," said Ziauddin to the BBC.

FINDING HER VOICE

Malala's father was a teacher and education activist, having started his own school for boys *and* girls. It was in that school that Malala would make appearances even as a toddler. Her father told stories about how Malala would wander into classes before she could even talk and pretend she was the teacher.[2] She shared her father's thirst for knowledge, and thanks to those appearances in class, she became well known in her community.

While her early years in the Swat Valley were idyllic, when the Taliban moved in to control the region in 2007, things changed dramatically for ten-year-old Malala. Under Taliban control, television and music were suddenly banned, cultural activities stopped, and, in 2008, girls were prohibited from attending school. To make clear their position, the Taliban began destroying schools; by the end of 2008, four hundred were lost.

But Malala would not be denied. Believing in her right to an education, Malala spoke out publicly on Pakistani TV against the Taliban. "How dare the Taliban take away my basic right to education?" she asked, with her father standing by her side.

A FATHER LEADS BY EXAMPLE

When supporters marvel at Malala's courage, passion, and poise, her father responded in an interview with the London *Telegraph*:[3] "Don't ask me what I did. Ask me what I did not do. I did not clip her wings, and that's all."

In Pakistani society at that time, however, many families did curtail their daughters' activities, he explained. Girls were required to stay home rather than attend school, and when they went out in public, they had to have an escort starting at age thirteen. If they did anything that called into question the honor of their family, they could be killed. Ziauddin did not want that kind of life for his daughter.

Ziauddin recounted in a *National Geographic* interview how he encouraged Malala to speak up in school. Not only did this hone her public speaking skills, it also helped Malala find her voice.

In 2009, Malala found additional outlets for her voice. She secretly began to blog about life in the Swat Valley under the Taliban rule on the BBC's Urdu language site, using the pen name Gul Makai to protect her identity. Her first post was titled "I am afraid" and described her fear of a coming war and the nightmares she was having about going to school in defiance of the Taliban. Had she actually gone to school, she and her parents would have risked public punishment and even death.

In May 2009, the Yousafzais, along with one million other residents, were forced to flee their home when the Pakistani army moved in to try and force the Taliban out.

BECOMING A PUBLIC FIGURE

Around this time, Malala's identity as the BBC blogger was revealed, and the *New York Times* featured Malala and her father in a documentary about their efforts to protect educational opportunities for girls in Swat.

Several weeks later, the Pakistani army successfully beat back the Taliban in Swat Valley, and the Yousafzais were able to return to Swat and Malala to her father's school. However, Malala recognized that the fight for girls' right to attend school was not over. She and her father used their new celebrity status to draw attention to the issue of education access for girls.

In the *National Geographic* interview,[4] Ziauddin spoke about his pride at being known primarily as "Malala's dad": "My friends in Swat, when they used to invite me to the podium, they used to say, 'Now we invite Malala's father.' So it was really something very inspiring. In a patriarchal society, men and women both, they are always known by their family, and I think I am one of those few—hardly any—who is known by his daughter. I'm very proud of it, and I'm thankful to God. I'm a blessed father to be known by my daughter."

For her efforts, Malala was nominated for the International Children's Peace Prize in 2011 and was awarded Pakistan's National Youth Peace Prize. Despite the positive recognition, there was also a drawback. Malala's newfound prominence and outspoken opposition to Taliban rule made her a target. Although her family never imagined anyone would actually try to kill her—a child—that's exactly what happened.

On October 9, 2012, while seated on a bus headed home from school, three members of the Taliban stopped the bus, and a gunman boarded it and called out for fifteen-year-old Malala. On finding her, he fired three shots at her, hitting her in the head, neck, and shoulder and injuring two of her friends. She was critically injured and flown to the United Kingdom for treatment. Fortunately, there was no brain damage, though Malala had to endure multiple surgeries, including several to repair a facial nerve on the left side of her face, which had been paralyzed.

In March 2013, Malala returned to school, this time in Birmingham, UK.

Despite the attack, Malala soon continued her campaign for girls' education with her father by her side. On her sixteenth birthday, Malala spoke in New York at the United Nations. Later that year she published her first book, *I Am Malala: The Girl Who Stood Up for Education and Was Shot by the Taliban*.

Since then, Malala has continued her campaign to make education for girls a reality everywhere. She has traveled extensively, met with world leaders, opened a school for Syrian refugee girls in Lebanon, and won the Nobel Peace Prize.

Although admired for his staunch support of his daughter, Ziauddin explained to *National Geographic* why Malala once stated that "he named me Malala, he did not make me Malala": "As a parent, you can only inspire your child. It's not like engineering. You can't construct somebody. I can simply inspire my sons and my daughters."[5]

THE IMPORTANCE OF OTHERS IN INSPIRATION

Clearly, Malala's father had a tremendous influence on her. He encouraged her, supported her, and even inspired her to stand up for what she believed was right, despite potential danger. He allowed her to be whatever she wanted to be, which turned out to be an education activist like himself.

She was also inspired by the girls around her, whose education was limited or prohibited simply due to their gender. The audiences she spoke to increased her inspiration. Even the Taliban's denial of her right to learn and have a voice inspired her. Overall, the people around her were great sources of inspiration for Malala.

Malala is not unusual. From both decades of research and common sense, we know that the people around us are critically important to our development. They impact every aspect of our lives, serving to inspire us and expand our opportunities.

That means that you, too, can draw on the power of other people as engines that ignite inspiration in your life. There are six engines of inspiration that come from those around you:

1. Belonging
2. Admiring our mentors and heroes

3. Getting a lift
4. Serving others
5. Sharing a group mission
6. Being vulnerable and transparent

These situations, relations, and interactions spark emotions, ideas, and opportunities that can lead to sustained inspiration, as Malala's father did, and continues to do, for her.

1. BELONGING

Recognizing what we share with others in our network, whether it's common beliefs, common interests, or common goals, forges a sense of community, of belonging. We share time with people, which reminds us of what we share and what we mean to them, much like what occurs within a tribe. It's self-affirming—the opposite of feeling isolated and alone. This sense of belonging, of feeling connected to others, can lay the groundwork for inspiration.

In relationships in which we feel supported, safe, seen, and appreciated, we can experience the courage to take risks, to be better versions of ourselves. Relationships can challenge and support us in positive ways—to stretch, to grow. When we have a shared history, they can also help us see how we've changed and evolved over time. We create meaning through telling our stories to others and hearing theirs; it's a way to share and express our identity and our sense of place within the group. When our relationships are positive ones, we can catch feelings of inspiration from others, experiencing emotion contagion.

In our interview with Dennis Driver, an inspiring human resources leader, he talked about how his sense of belonging to his alma mater, Stillman College, still enriches him as he serves on its board of trustees. In response to the question, What inspires you?, Driver talked about how listening to the student choir stirs his sense of belonging: "Whenever I have listened to this choir sing the song 'In This Very Room,' I am moved to tears. The reason is they are singing about the power of Christ in the room and the power of the people in the room, and the role that Christ has in their lives. It touches me deeply as I think about my role on the board, and the students who are singing and representing the body of the school, every voice mattering, every voice counting, and the lives being changed through this education."[6]

The Harvard Study of Adult Development found that positive relationships and the sense of belonging that results can even help us live longer.[7] This ongoing research project began in 1938 with the aim of finding out "the clues to leading happy and healthy lives." According to Robert Waldinger, director of the study, a psychiatrist at Massachusetts General Hospital, and a professor at Harvard Medical School: "The surprising finding is that our relationships and how happy we are in our relationships has a powerful influence on our health." In addition to delaying physical and mental decline, close relationships "are what keep people happy throughout their lives."[8]

The reverse is also true. People who lack close personal relationships and feel alone suffer health risks comparable to smoking, high blood pressure, and obesity. People with strong social ties are 50 percent less likely to die prematurely, concluded a review of 148 studies.[9] Likewise, Dan Buettner, National Geographic Fellow and author of *The Blue Zones: Lessons from Living Longer from the People Who've Lived the Longest*, has traveled all around the world and concluded that social connection and strong community bonds together are one of the most important factors that contribute to happiness and longevity.[10]

Think about groups where you have felt a strong sense of belonging and that inspired you. What stands out about these groups? What did others do and what did you do to create that sense of connection? In the groups where you feel less attached, what can you do to create stronger connections to increase your belonging? Look for similarities, for common interests and shared perspectives between you and the other members—even if they have nothing to do with what the group is about. Find the human connections.

2. ADMIRING OUR MENTORS AND HEROES

The people around us who show us how best to behave, how to achieve, and how to succeed are our mentors and heroes. Our research has shown that parents, teachers, role models, and people who believed in us and/or took a stand for us early in life or in our career and inspired us to take action in a new way can shape us over the long term.

Mentors and heroes don't have to be well-known figures or celebrities to be engines of inspiration, as long as they are mentors and heroes *to us*. They are people around us who love us or believe in us. They see our potential and want us to be successful. They help us recognize who we are and all that we can accomplish if we try, and they help us on our path. They are salient and formative to our evolving identities and lives. Recall Captain Irving meeting his hero Captain Gary Robinson in a bookstore, which changed the course of his life and career forever; to this day, Irving stays in close touch with Robinson who plays the role of a mentor.[11]

Heroes and mentors also
provide an identity link that
compels us to be better.

Recent research on hero worship shows how interaction with, and stories about, heroes provide us knowledge about how to be heroic, and at the same time, these stories energize and inspire us.[12] Stories of heroism lead to *elevated* emotions (a mix of awe, reverence, and admiration) that literally make us want to become better people. Heroes and mentors also provide an identity link that compels us to be better. If we can identify with those we look up to, if we can find a way we are similar to them, we are inspired to be more like them. For example, a 2017 study of undergraduate women pursuing degrees in science, technology, engineering, and mathematics found these students were more likely to continue their pursuit if they had a female mentor.[13]

But heroes can also be icons—people we don't know personally but who inspire us to be more like them or to share their values or mission. Yale School of Management professor Amy Wrzesniewski's experience with faculty mentors is an illustration of this. During her first year as an undergraduate at the University of Pennsylvania, Wrzesniewski took a job working within the psychology department for one of the professors.[14] One day, another faculty member, Paul Rozin, whose office was just a few doors down, asked if she wanted to help out with coding data. "It was fascinating!" she told us in our interview with her.

When she finished the coding work, Professor Rozin asked her, "You want to do research, don't you?"

"Yes!" said Wrzesniewski. "Why don't you come work with me next year then," he replied.

So she did, continuing to work with him during her sophomore, junior, and senior years at Penn. He became her "academic father," he proudly proclaims, and with which she agrees wholeheartedly.

Wrzesniewski admired Rozin's intellectual curiosity and his ability to follow his research to explore new subjects, to ask new questions. Where other professors built their careers on their study of a single subject, Rozin's interests were forever evolving. He started his career as a biological psychologist and had advanced from there, continuously exploring, and she appreciated his scholarly curiosity.

He included her in meetings with high level people and helped her develop advanced critical thinking skills. Observing his work was a great aha for Wrzesniewski.

She's the first woman tenured at Yale in the organizational behavior department in the School of Management. The impact of her research on meaning and purpose in work is groundbreaking. Her research is seminal in showing how important it is for our work to be meaningful.

> "People inspire me, and the people that I am inspired by are people that have achieved greatness against the odds. Whether things were stacked against them and they did it in spite of physical, mental, socioeconomic obstacles, whatever that might be."
>
> —Helen Russell, Chief People Officer, Atlassian

Rozin's belief in her has propelled her career. Long-term mentoring, such as Rozin's involvement in shaping Wrzesniewski's career, has the potential for providing continued inspiration and support, but even passing connections can make a difference.

Chance The Rapper remembers receiving a phone message out of the blue when he was a teenager from the rapper Common encouraging him to follow his dream. Those words of encouragement fueled his commitment to the music business.[15]

Common recalls: "Years ago, my grandmother asked me to call her friend's grandson. 'I want you to give him some words of encouragement,' she said. 'He wants to be a rapper.' She gave me his number, and I left him a message." So, Common says, "I told him to keep following his dreams. Then I forgot all about it."

Years later, Common's teen daughter played a mixtape by a new artist that sounded vaguely familiar. "I could tell he really knew hip-hop," he said. When the two finally met in person, Chance told him, "You won't remember this, but you called me when I was a kid." It was a call that helped launch his career.

So many of the leaders we interviewed talked about mentors and heroes who inspired them. These examples reflect what we know about the encouragement heroes and mentors give us, which is an emotional lift, leading to our next engine of inspiration.

Thought Experiment: Activating Inspiration in Your Relationships

- Make a list of five to ten of the most significant relationships in your life right now.
- Which ones are most inspiring to you and why?
- For those that are less inspiring (but still positive) to you right now, consult the list of engines in this chapter and identify three new ways to spark inspiration in them.
- What are the relationships in your life that provide no inspiration or are dragging you down? What do you want to do about these? Can you flip them to be more inspiring?
- To whom are you an inspiration and why?
- How can you bring more inspiration to others through relationships?

3. GETTING A LIFT

As human beings, we are by nature social creatures, thriving on connection and support from others, so much so that we can get a positive emotion lift simply from being around people. When people around us are actively supporting us, cheerleading us, the positive emotion lift can lead to feelings of inspiration. Many of the leaders we interviewed mentioned being *lifted up* by someone else who believed in them and actively cheered them on. Different than mentoring, the person doing the cheering could be a friend, a stranger, or even a celebrity who notices a need to help and steps in to encourage. Famous for this, Oprah champions people she loves to the point where the term the *Oprah Effect* refers to the boost in sales, traffic, or attention someone receives after being on the show.[16]

> Many of the leaders we interviewed mentioned being *lifted up* by someone else who believed in them and actively cheered them on.

Another kind of lift comes through personal connections. Your champion doesn't have to have Oprah's fame or platform. Within business, leaders often get inspired by others giving them a boost, sometimes when they need it the most. Examples abound. Help in business has even been institutionalized in the form of executive groups like the Entrepreneurs' Organization,[17] a global network of entrepreneurs designed to lift one another up. Other examples are tech incubators, such as the organization Plug and Play Tech Center,[18] which offers opportunities for businesses to get boosted through accelerators that are designed to spark inspiration around new business approaches, products, and ways to grow revenue.

"Our goal is to connect entrepreneurs with all of the resources they need, no matter what stage, so they can focus on building their company. Time is the most important resource they have, so we aim to lift and accelerate their business and save them time by connecting them with money, customers, and expertise," says Michael Olmstead, Plug and Play's chief revenue officer.[19]

Take a look at your personal network. Of the people you know, how many can give you a meaningful lift? Who are the people who expand your view of what's possible? Who makes you feel more confident? What would it be like to ask one of those people for a leg up? Also consider, to whom have you offered a lift recently?

4. SERVING OTHERS

Seeing a need or opportunity to serve others is also an engine of inspiration, pushing us to take action and help. As humans, we have an innate drive to affiliate with and support one another. For many people, this translates into a sense of responsibility to help those in need. While most people naturally react with sadness and pity over others' difficult situations, some become inspired to take action in a helpful way—to do something that will improve the lives of those who are less fortunate.

Usually, the closer to home or the more personal the connection to the person in need, the stronger the inspiration to help. It could be a child in your daughter's class at school, a dad at your company, a family at your church or temple or other house of worship—typically the more connected you are to them, the greater the likelihood you'll feel inspired to get involved in helping them.

Many leaders have been inspired to take action in big ways as a result of seeing people they care about in need. Maggie Doyne saw a chance to make a difference for orphans in Nepal. The eighteen-year-old had just graduated from high school and decided to travel around the world before committing herself to more schooling. She eventually found herself in some of Nepal's most poverty-stricken communities. In one, she came across a young girl, called Hima, selling rocks to help provide food for her family. Touched by Hima's resourcefulness and resolve, Doyne spent some of her money to buy the girl food and clothes and paid for her school tuition, so she wouldn't have to continue splitting rocks every day.[20]

She changed one child's life, and then another and another, until she decided she needed to do something bigger, that would have a larger impact on the community. So she took her five thousand dollars in life savings from babysitting money and used it to buy land in Surkhet, with the goal of building a home for children of families who couldn't afford to feed them. She then reached out to her hometown of Mendham, New Jersey, to ask for help to build the home and fill it with needed supplies.[21]

The Kopila Valley Children's Home opened in 2008 and is now home to more than forty youngsters, all of whom are cared for by Doyne and a team of "aunties and uncles." Two years later, in 2010, the Kopila Valley School was built and serves more than 350 students in Surkhet. Doyne cofounded the BlinkNow Foundation to continue to fund work in Surkhet and to change the lives of children in the area.[22]

Inspiration to help can also follow tragedy. Following the 2012 shooting of twenty six- and seven-year-old students and six teachers and administrators at Sandy Hook Elementary School in Newtown, Connecticut, plastic surgeon Dr. Michael Baroody was spurred to action to try to make a difference. He founded the 12.14 Foundation to provide Newtown-area students with a positive, creative outlet to help them overcome the feelings of grief, anger, fear, and sadness that had gripped the town and the country for months.

As he was forming the 12.14 Foundation, he researched expertise in leadership and sought a meeting with retired brigadier general Tom Kolditz, who was at the Yale School of Management at that time. As our firm, InspireCorps, was part of Kolditz's leadership coaching team, he asked that we join. During the meeting Baroody explained why he felt compelled to take action: "I couldn't let these kids grow up in the shadow of this event, in the darkness. We had to bring light back to the community."[23]

One way he felt he could help do this was through the performing arts. He was not the typical performing arts leader, but he recognized that he had an opportunity to shape children's lives. He wanted to help children challenge themselves in new and creative ways and work together in a community to make something beautiful. As part of the 12.14 Foundation, he established a summer theater program during which students from Newtown work together to write, practice, and then perform a musical in collaboration with Broadway performers and under the leadership of New York–based theater director Michael Unger. Baroody partnered with the Yale School of Management and InspireCorps to incorporate content on leadership development into the summer theater program so students could internalize how they were growing as human beings and leaders during this process. In our interview with Baroody, he talked about his spark of inspiration being the opportunity to serve and empower children to "rise above, go beyond" (the 12.14 Foundation tag line) what they thought possible for themselves.[24]

Recent survey-based research by Roy Baumeister in the *Journal of Positive Psychology* shows that helping others contributes a sense of meaning in life.[25] It was Aristotle who said that we find fulfillment by loving others rather than by being loved.[26] Why does this happen? Netta Weinstein and Richard Ryan have researched this, giving subjects the option to give money to someone else, or not, and then compared them to a control group whose members were mandated to give and also told how much to give. They found that the group that chose to give money experienced a higher sense of well-being because some of their psychological needs, such as feeling competent and connected, were being met.[27]

Research has shown that individuals feel better about themselves and their support of people and organizations in need when they know how the money will be used. The donor donates more, the fund-raiser raises more, and the donor feels wealthier after having donated, Yale School of Management's Zoë Chance discovered. Though giving away money should, logically, have made donors feel less wealthy, the opposite was the case.[28] This is likely why Charles Best's organization DonorsChoose .org is so successful—because donors know exactly whom their money is benefiting and how.

This research was confirmed in a study done by Adam Grant and a team at the University of Pennsylvania. Grant arranged for a group of call center workers to meet with scholarship students who benefit from money the call center workers produce. That five-minute meeting was enough to inspire callers to greater performance. A month later, callers who had interacted with the scholarship students spent more than twice as many minutes on the phone and brought in vastly more money: a weekly average of $503.22, up from $185.94. "Even minimal, brief contact with beneficiaries can enable employees to maintain their motivation," the researchers reported.[29]

Think about how great it feels to have others help you. Who in your life could benefit from your help? What opportunities do you have for helping others in need, through your work or outside it, such as involvement with a charity or community organization? You'll serve your own inspiration by helping others, and you'll do some good.

5. SHARING A GROUP MISSION

Another inspiration engine that hinges on others is having a shared mission. Just as Malala and her father unified over their shared mission related to education, groups that bond over a common goal or mission are able to achieve performance levels well above what was expected or has been obtained before. The act of working together toward a unifying objective sparks inspired thinking, ideas, and actions. It can also create a great sense of meaning and connection. Sebastian Junger, author of *Tribe: On Homecoming and Belonging*,[30] in his TED Talk speaks to the deep bond of brotherhood soldiers feel and miss when back in civilian life.

That was certainly the case in a study that found common mindsets improve a sense of team and team performance. John E. Mathieu, along with four other researchers, formed fifty-six undergraduate teams who "flew" missions on a flight-combat simulator and found that teams who shared team- and task-based mental models had better processes and performance. This finding has important ramifications for teams in the workplace.[31]

> In today's organizations, where
> individuals are increasingly
> motivated by finding meaning in
> their work, a shared sense of what
> binds the team and what the team
> values are particularly inspiring.

In today's organizations, where individuals are increasingly motivated by finding meaning in their work, reports Wrzesniewski,[32] a shared sense of what binds the team and what the team values are particularly inspiring. Marissa Thalberg, global chief brand officer of Taco Bell, speaks to us about the power of a shared group mission when working on a team and crafting communication to bring the team and external audience together and elicit positive emotional connection.[33]

Shared mission is an engine of inspiration because it is a celebration of a common purpose. Although individuals may have different roles and objectives, the group itself has a goal that everyone is working toward. That mission strengthens individuals' connections to one another and to the core objective, whether it's world peace, banning cosmetic testing on animals, or allowing skateboarding on sidewalks.

A recent example of the inspiring power of a shared mission involved Tom Kolditz, mentioned earlier. When Hurricane Harvey was bearing down on Houston, Texas, in August 2017, most of Rice University shut down and sent its personnel home for their safety. But Kolditz, the founding director of The Doerr Institute for New Leaders at Rice and former US army brigadier general, decided that the institute would remain open through the hurricane. Kolditz said: "Lillie [institute cofounder] and I had just finished teaching a class virtually on Zoom, because we didn't want to cancel it because of the hurricane. And at the end . . . we were supposed to have a group photo. Lillie got all their images on the screen and took a screenshot and emailed it to me as our group photo. That act alone started to inspire me . . . I thought, we're not gonna let a hurricane get in our way." Kolditz e-mailed the photo to the Provost, saying that The Doerr Institute would remain open during the hurricane and would be happy to help if needed.[34]

Three hours later, the provost called him back, asking, "Rice students want to help people trapped all over Houston. Do you think you can help mobilize students around a relief effort?" Classes were canceled, so the students were available to help. Kolditz mobilized his team like a tactical operation in the military. Within twenty-four hours, with the help of a volunteer computer science professor and other volunteers, he devised a system for deploying groups of students and tracking where they were going and when they returned safely. He helped secure 130 vehicles and more than two thousand students who were passionate about serving their community, making a difference for thousands in need and keeping all of them safe and accounted for as the cleanup began.[35]

Although most organizations have a written mission statement, the "mission" we appeal to here is when we feel truly connected to and inspired by shared values and goals. In the case of Lin-Manuel Miranda's composition of the musical *Hamilton*, he created a powerful mission to bring to life a historic story that could shed light on modern issues, like the immigrant experience. This mission was embedded in the fabric of the musical, not just in the content of the songs but in the entire production process: the cast was diverse and profits were shared, for example.[36] The result of this powerful and embedded mission was an incredibly inspired cast and crew that brought forward new possibilities in theater.

The connection that happens as a result of a shared mission or belief can be inspirational. When individuals express their own feelings and perspectives on an issue, they generate the opportunity for like-minded others to connect with them. Then together, the group can work to accomplish a collective result that everyone in the group feels aligned to and part of—and inspired by.

Think of the groups you're a part of—at work, at home, in your community. Which have a mission that inspires you? If it's most, terrific. If it's only a few, consider launching or joining a group with a shared mission that is inspiring to you.

6. BEING VULNERABLE AND TRANSPARENT

Inspiration can also appear when you finally admit that you need help. Being willing to be vulnerable and to ask for the help or guidance that you need can get you past perceived obstacles. Rather than pretending that everything is under control, admitting that you're stuck builds trust and allows progress to occur. You could be stuck in not being able to see a solution to a work problem, you might be facing an impossible project deadline or lack of resources, or maybe you're stuck in a relationship; whatever your personal situation, being open and honest with those around you opens up inspired new opportunities. Taking action, by asking for help, leads to progress and new ideas, and inspiration becomes more likely.

Social scientists have been studying the impact of transparency and vulnerability for a long time. Prochaska's stages of change readiness, for example, posits that being transparent and showing vulnerability are critical steps on the path to change readiness.[37] Indicating a willingness to change then triggers a shift from complacency to feeling inspired to take action. Leaders who are vulnerable with their teams establish the trust, respect, and safety to be open to new ideas.[38] Furthermore, transparent decision-making and sharing of emotions has been noted as a key aspect of authentic leadership.[39]

> Admitting that you're struggling, or that you've encountered a problem you can't solve on your own, opens the door to support and inspiration.

Admitting that you're struggling, or that you've encountered a problem you can't solve on your own, opens the door to support and inspiration. That's exactly what happened when Archana Patchirajan, founder of the Indian startup company Hubbl, told her employees that the company was shutting down and that they'd all have to find new jobs. Rather than turning on her in the face of bad news, the staff refused to give up, offering to take half pay until the company got back on its feet again. Their commitment to Hubbl inspired Patchirajan to find a way to make the company successful, later selling it for $14 million.[40] In an *Inc.* article about Hubbl, Emma Seppälä, the associate director of Stanford University's Center for Compassion and Altruism Research and Education, is quoted as explaining, "vulnerability is not about being weak. It's about being courageous enough to be yourself." She says that "leaders can be vulnerable by replacing the professional distance you're used to with honesty about yourself and care for your employees' lives."[41]

Margaret Greenberg, executive coach and author of *Profit from the Positive*, told us in her interview with us how her unexpected vulnerability and transparency at a keynote presentation inspired her and others. She was invited to give a talk to over three thousand attendees of a Happiness Forum on the topic of positive psychology and resilience sponsored by a university. The night before her talk, she learned that the university had lost one of its students, along with her mother and brother, in a tragic car crash. She knew the community was grieving, and the way she typically addressed resilience might not resonate with the audience that day. Instead of canceling her talk or staying with her original talking points, she dared to share a very personal story of resilience about her own mother's suicide. Although she had never hidden her mother's suicide from others, she had

> "I've noticed that really inspiring people tend to be very accessible—it's part of who they are."
>
> —Christine Carter, PhD, sociologist, Senior Fellow at UC Berkeley's Greater Good Science Center, and author of *The Sweet Spot: How to Achieve More by Doing Less* and *Raising Happiness*

never before this time spoken about it in such a public forum. She knew that it was the right thing to talk about; it was the story these students needed to hear in this moment of tragedy. Her openness in this public forum was received warmly; people came up to her after her talk to tell her how she moved them. This inspired Greenberg to continue to be more open in different contexts about this very personal story, making it easier for others to talk openly about suicide and other tragedies. People became more comfortable about bringing the topic up themselves, giving them new ways to deal with their grief.[42]

Being vulnerable and transparent can be difficult for some as it requires opening up and letting people see what's inside. How do you muster up your courage? You can start small: What's one thing you can share with others that will let them know the real you more? You may be surprised to discover that by sharing in this way, you feel a greater sense of possibility and confidence in yourself, while also inspiring those around you.

As human beings we are social creatures who thrive on contact with and support from others. Not surprisingly, the people around us can be important sparks of inspiration for us.

WORK IT
Sparked by OTHERS Inspiration Challenge

We all have the capacity to be inspired through all six of these inspiration engines. Yet, we likely lean on one or two more naturally than others. Use the tool below to take stock of the extent to which you are using each of the engines described in this chapter. Then write in some of your own ways to tap into each of the engines more often.

ENGINE	HOW MUCH DO YOU USE IT? (SCALE OF 1–5)	WAYS TO TAP INTO THIS ENGINE MORE OFTEN (CIRCLE THE ONES YOU LIKE BEST AND ADD IN YOUR OWN)
Belonging	_____	**Some examples:** Common values, interests, beliefs, and experiences can lead to a sense of belonging. In what groups and with which people in your life and work do you feel the greatest sense of belonging? Contrast this to situations where you feel different, outcast, or isolated. **What would you add?**
Admiring Our Mentors and Heroes	_____	**Some examples:** Who makes you want to be a better person? Who challenges you to dig deeper within yourself? Whose life do you want to emulate? These mentors and heroes fuel our inspiration. **What would you add?**

ENGINE	HOW MUCH DO YOU USE IT? (SCALE OF 1–5)	WAYS TO TAP INTO THIS ENGINE MORE OFTEN (CIRCLE THE ONES YOU LIKE BEST AND ADD IN YOUR OWN)
Getting a Lift	_____	**Some examples:** Who are your biggest supporters and cheerleaders? When can you benefit from an assist from others? Consider ways to be a part of groups that naturally lift one another up, such as support groups, performance groups, book clubs, and so on. **What would you add?**
Serving Others	_____	**Some examples:** There are likely many ways that you already help and serve others: What are they? What types of helping activities inspire you the most? Consider ways you can do more of these or think outside the box for new opportunities to serve others in big or small ways. Challenge yourself to help someone in a small way every single day. **What would you add?**

(continues)

ENGINE	HOW MUCH DO YOU USE IT? (SCALE OF 1–5)	WAYS TO TAP INTO THIS ENGINE MORE OFTEN (CIRCLE THE ONES YOU LIKE BEST AND ADD IN YOUR OWN)
Sharing a Group Mission	———	**Some examples:** Which mission-based groups are you a part of that have the potential to inspire you? Perhaps you are part of a group that has a mission, but you don't feel connected to it. Think about your own personal values and purpose: how can you align them with your group's mission? **What would you add?**
Being Vulnerable and Transparent	———	**Some examples:** Ask yourself if there are areas in your life where you feel less inspired. Communicate something you are not proud of to someone you trust; own up to balls dropped or mistakes. At InspireCorps, we celebrate "the beautiful oops" as soon as they happen. Look for opportunities to ask others for help (when you may be more inclined to try to solve a problem on your own). **What would you add?**

CHAPTER FIVE

SPARKED BY SITUATIONS

Charles Best had no idea how privileged his educational experience had been until he took a position as a high school teacher at Wings Academy in Bronx, New York, in 2000. During his own high school years, Best and his fellow students took field trips, read numerous books, interacted with guest speakers who came to their school, and had access to virtually any technology they needed.

Those resources didn't exist in his new history classroom. "I saw first-hand that schools were not treated equally," he said.[1]

So as a teacher, Best paid for classroom supplies like books, writing implements, and even photocopies from his own wallet. It turns out, he is in the majority. Public school teachers spent $1.6 billion of their own money on classroom supplies during the 2012–2013 school year, reported the Education Marketing Association.

In fact, it was while making photocopies of *Little House on the Prairie* at the twenty-four-hour Staples copy center off Manhattan's Union Square that Best's mind wandered. He was photocopying parts of the book because he didn't have the classroom budget to get the actual books for his students. "I started thinking about all the other resources that my colleagues wanted for their students and figured that there were people out there who would help teachers like us, if they could see where their money was going," he says.[2]

His challenge was connecting teachers who had resource needs with donors interested in supporting educational programs. One afternoon he sketched the design for a rudimentary website that would allow teachers to describe their projects and donors could search for projects they wanted to support. Then he paid a recent immigrant from Poland two thousand dollars to create a simple website for that purpose under the URL DonorsChoose.org.[3]

Once the basic site was operational, Best turned to fellow teachers at the school and baited them with some of his mom's delicious roasted pears in exchange for posting requests for support for their projects at the new DonorsChoose website. Ten teachers posted requests that ranged from a Baby Think It Over infant simulator for a new pregnancy prevention program to test prep books to help students study for the SAT, and fabric, needles, and thread for a big quilt another teacher wanted to teach the students how to make.

To demonstrate public support for the concept, Best himself funded all ten of the projects anonymously, unbeknownst to his colleagues. Surprised by the idea that people outside the school wanted to support their work, the teachers got excited. Really excited. They began posting hundreds of requests for support.

Immediately realizing there was no way he could fund all of the projects, Best's students offered to help initiate a letter-writing campaign to two thousand potential donors. Those letters, sent nationwide, generated $30,000 in support. Best was shocked and excited.

Wanting to continue fueling this growth, Best turned to the media to ask for support. Then September 11, 2001, happened and few media outlets were interested in stories that didn't have a 9/11 angle. So he came up with stories about projects on DonorsChoose from teachers and classrooms that were impacted by the attack and secured coverage in *Newsweek* and the *New York Times*.

The reporters proclaimed DonorsChoose as "the future of philanthropy"—a microphilanthropy initiative that pioneered the crowd-funding industry. From there emerged organizations such as Kiva, Indiegogo, Kickstarter, Fundly, and Crowdrise, to name a few later entrants. By 2019, Best's concept had connected 3.5 million donors with more than 1.3 million teacher project requests at eighty thousand schools to the tune of more than $785,000,000. *Fast Company* magazine named DonorsChoose one of the fifty most innovative companies in the world in 2014.[4]

CIRCUMSTANCE AS AN INSPIRATION SOURCE

The third and final set of engines driving sparks of inspiration are related to specific situations: when conditions surrounding an individual or group or event are the trigger that spark inspiration.

While previous chapters focused on the self and others as sources of inspiration, we turn our attention here to what frequently comes to mind when people think about inspiration: what's in their immediate environment. This might include common settings, like a beautiful sunset or a wedding, or hearing a great orator speak. But sources of inspiration are not limited to the beautiful and eloquent. Negative experiences or circumstances can also inspire us, largely from the opportunities they bring to light. Witnessing an injustice or someone being treated unfairly can spur people to take action to prevent similar situations in the future.

Being sparked by these sources of inspiration entails a mix of engineering circumstances you know will inspire you, like stepping outside to witness that beautiful sunrise, combined with maintaining an openness and presence so you notice inspiring circumstances that unexpectedly come your way.

There are six engines of inspiration that come from specific circumstances or situations including

1. Seeking out environments that move us
2. Overcoming constraints
3. Witnessing excellence
4. Using your unique passions or qualifications to make a difference
5. Sharing experiences with large groups of people
6. Experiencing grief, loss, or failure

SPARKED
BY SITUATIONS

ENVIRONMENTS THAT MOVE US

OVERCOMING CONSTRAINTS

WITNESSING EXCELLENCE

MAKING A DIFFERENCE

SHARED GROUP EXPERIENCES

GRIEF, LOSS, OR FAILURE

1. SEEKING OUT ENVIRONMENTS THAT MOVE US

An intentional or unintentional change to make the environment around you more emotionally moving can be a source of inspiration. Imagine that this can happen through something specific about a new milieu, such as a different culture that piques curiosity or admiration, inspiring music or art that fuels creativity, awe-producing nature that encourages being in the moment and appreciating beauty, or a school or museum that is particularly meaningful.

A common theme from our interviews is that particular environments frequently spark inspiration—and the more novel and the more outside one's comfort zone, often the bigger the impact. Part of this may be due to the novelty, part of it may be due to the environment itself, especially in nature, and part of it may be due to the specific experience within that environment. Recent controlled experiments that examined walking in nature versus walking in urban settings showed that walks in nature increase well-being, positive affect, and cognition and decrease negative rumination.[5] And yet novel environments, whether they are in nature or not, seem to increase openness and creative thinking. Inspiration can be sparked unintentionally, such as by moving to a different location, or it can be brought forth purposely, by heading to a place that has proven inspirational in the past.

In our interview with Margaret Greenberg, she talks about snowshoeing, spirituality, and writing, explaining that experiencing new environments, especially in nature, is a consistent engine of inspiration for her.

> "I was putting on snowshoes, walking around the property, enjoying the beauty of the blue skies, the trees, and out of nowhere popped a title for a LinkedIn blog post, and I thought, 'Where did this come from?'"
>
> —Margaret Greenberg, Executive Coach and coauthor of *Profit from the Positive*

Being in nature is inspirational for Greenberg. "Nature for me . . . I feel spiritual, close to God, more so than church; nature is where I find inspiration to write and take photos." Even when she isn't necessarily on the hunt for inspiration, it can appear, she says. "[I'm] not necessarily thinking about something and it just comes out of nowhere."[6]

The benefit of spending time in nature has been found to have a number of health-improving properties. From reduced blood pressure to reduced stress levels and increased white blood cell activity, forest bathing[7]—the practice of spending time in the woods, immersing yourself in the environment, and focusing on the nature around you—is another way to reset your brain and clear the way for inspiration. Stanford researcher Vinod Menon reports that even a few minutes spent in nature can encourage mind wandering, which is conducive to creativity and inspiration.[8]

Researcher Adam Galinsky studies connections between international travel and culture and creativity and has found that foreign travel increases cognitive flexibility. In his 2014 study in the *Academy of Management Journal,* he and three other researchers studied 270 creative directors in fashion. The more often they lived abroad, the more creative the fashion lines they produced. Maybe people love to travel because it typically inspires them; being in new cultures and environments encourages us to pay more attention to our surroundings, and through the resulting cognitive flexibility, we open ourselves up to new possibilities.

In fact, a trip to Milan is what sparked Howard Schultz's idea for Starbucks. He wasn't there looking for inspiration, but he found it nonetheless. One day in 1982 he walked into a coffee shop and was treated to an experience unlike anything he had ever had before. He describes the process of the preparation of his cup of coffee in great detail, characterizing the barista's act of pouring the drink "with precision," and the group of customers in the shop as more like a "community." Watching the employee prepare the coffee, Schultz thought to himself that "this is not his job, it's his passion." He was inspired.

"For a tall guy who grew up playing football in the schoolyards of Brooklyn, being handed a tiny white porcelain demitasse filled with dark coffee crafted just for me by a gracious Italian gentleman called a barista was nothing less than transcendent," he says.[9]

Schultz was so taken by this experience that he was inspired to try to replicate it in the United States, returning home and pursuing local investors to start his own retail coffee company, Il Giornale, and later purchasing Starbucks.

While Schultz inadvertently stumbled on inspiration in his travels, it is possible to pursue inspiration, to take targeted, purposeful steps to tap into environments that are emotionally moving. That is what Pixar filmmakers do when they go on research trips to locations where movies are set. During the production of the animated film *Ratatouille*, for example, filmmakers traveled to France and ate in Michelin-starred restaurants to get a true feel for the environment and the experience of fine dining that they could then incorporate into the movie about a chef in an upscale restaurant. They also went to San Francisco to investigate whether it was possible for a fish to survive traveling down a drain and out to sea as part of their research for *Finding Nemo*.[10]

Professional artists in need of a steady stream of inspiration often take steps to create environments that will be conducive to creativity and new ideas. Designating or even building a space they consider a sanctuary,[11] where art is formed, is a proactive approach to generating inspiration when needed.

Environments don't need to be physical spaces. We can create an environment of sound just by putting on headphones or turning on a sound system. Those who appreciate music can escape to a new world by listening to recorded or live performances of favorite pieces or new works. Similarly, one can create a "space" by diving into a book of visual arts and immersing oneself in the beauty within it. In fact, this is where new trends in virtual reality and augmented reality are going, as they

"With my art I get really inspired by things around me, the energy, passion around what I do when I'm outside painting landscapes. It's the people I observe, the nature, the colors I'm trying to mix, birds playing in a pond, kids running up and down the stairway, through that energy I feel awe."

—Madeline Adams, MFA, fine artist and art educator

> "If I have to inspire myself . . . music is the quickest path to that. The music that works best for me when I need inspiration to face a challenge is probably electronic music . . . this is the music I listened to coming up in high school. So there's a bunch of tracks that I will play that can click me into that gear if I need to. And I will do that sometimes when I'm coming into work. I put headphones on, get my playlist together, and just use that to try and blast myself into the right head space."
>
> —Didier Elzinga, Chief Executive Officer, Culture Amp

attempt to produce compelling and emotionally moving environments through technology.

Certainly, some people are more attuned and sensitive to their environments than others. What we learned in our research is that we often underestimate the power of our environment to influence our emotions.

Close your eyes and transport yourself to your favorite place, one where you feel a heightened sense of possibilities and emotions. Where are you? Look around and notice the qualities that make it inspiring to you. How can you bring the critical aspects that distinguish this place into your everyday environment? What new places you have not yet visited might also have these same characteristics?

2. OVERCOMING CONSTRAINTS

Psychologists Angela Duckworth[12] and Karen Reivich,[13] at the University of Pennsylvania, study grit, perseverance, and resilience: the ability to stick with challenging goals and bounce back in the face of adversity. A major obstacle, challenge, or constraint—whether at a micro level (someone else's expectations of you) or at a macro level (involving cultural mores or social oppression)—that requires grit or resilience to overcome can actually ignite inspiration. When someone says, "You can't do that!" that person has a fixed and limited mindset about you. For example, acceptance of women in combat roles within the military is still a struggle for some, as is recognizing the legitimate role of stay-at-home dads. Cultural and social barriers can confine us within certain roles and set expectations that constrain us.

For some people, this external challenge ignites intrinsic motivation and inspiration to drive their own destiny.[14] It seems counterintuitive that a negative, limiting comment can inspire. And yet this phenomenon is what prompted Malcolm Gladwell to write the book *David and Goliath*[15] about the power of underdogs and researcher Dan McAdams (Northwestern University) to study redemption stories,[16] how facing our greatest fears and overcoming difficulties leads to increased well-being. Fighting these societal constraints or disproving underdog status is a true inspiration engine.

For example, Steve Squinto, original founder of Alexion Pharmaceuticals, gets fired up when he's told no. He told us, "I get inspired when I see a problem that requires a call-to-action. The one thing that inspires me the most, and motivated me throughout my career, is the two-letter word *no*."[17]

Being told that "no, something is not solvable" excites Squinto and gets the gears in his brain moving. "I've been told no a lot," he says, so it's not a rare occurrence. But while 90 percent of the people who are told no back down, Squinto takes that as a challenge and becomes determined to find a way past the no he's just heard. It's as if he wants to prove the other person wrong as he proceeds to brainstorm all the ways to work around the challenge in front of him.

Squinto isn't the only person to step up when everyone else backs down. Somewhat surprisingly, again and again in our interviews, we heard stories of leaders inspired by obstacles and constraints, sometimes seemingly insurmountable. While no one likes being told some variation of no, for some people, that response is a rallying cry that fuels new thinking and action—a combination of invincibility and possibility. It inspires them.

Consider an obstacle or constraint you are facing now. Can you turn it on its head, into an opportunity? A challenge? A way to stretch yourself or learn something new? Rewrite your story for how you are thinking about this constraint and what overcoming it can look like.

3. WITNESSING EXCELLENCE

Interestingly, simply witnessing the excellence of others can move us to feel more confident and see greater possibilities for ourselves. This can happen while watching elite athletes perform (i.e., the Olympics), attending a performing arts concert, or taking in a fine art show; it can also occur when witnessing moral excellence. In areas where you want to feel more inspired, such as a work project, a productive step can be seeking out examples of excellence of others in that specific area. If you're prepping to deliver a talk, search for and watch the best TED Talks of all time. If you're looking to enter a new market or launch a new product, observe those who set the mark for excellence in that area.

Psychologists Sara Algoe and Jonathan Haidt have studied this and explain the rush we get from seeing others exceed our expectations. We feel elevation, gratitude, and admiration.[18] Unlike other positive emotions, such as happiness or amusement, these "other-praising" emotions make us want to be better ourselves, motivating us to want to do more good in the world and to connect with others more. When our appreciation of excellence turns to awe, we experience both psychological and even physical health benefits. We are motivated in the same way to do good in the world. Recent research shows that experiencing awe is related to increased life satisfaction and lower risk for heart disease.[19] While these studies did not look specifically at inspiration, positive emotions like these are often correlated and experienced together.[20] In our interviews, we found that many leaders experienced feelings of inspiration when they witnessed excellence or activated feelings of awe and admiration.

Irish poet and philosopher John O'Donohue was interviewed by Krista Tippett for the podcast *On Being* about his experience at a concert at Lincoln Center and expressed this sense of wonder and appreciation for the skills of the musicians onstage:

When I came in to New York last Thursday evening and checked into the hotel, I found out that there was a Tchaikovsky concert on in the

Lincoln Center. And I went over there, and I got a ticket, one of the last tickets, which was two rows in the front. And I've never been so near an orchestra, and I said, 'My God, I'm too near.' . . .

But I knew why I was given the ticket then, at the end, because it was Tchaikovsky's Violin Concerto in D, and Lorin Maazel came out to conduct it. And then this beautiful violinist, Janine Jansen, a Dutch violinist, it was her debut in New York, and she played this. It was just unbelievable. I cried. After the first movement, people spontaneously stood up and wanted to give her a standing ovation, and she just held it, and we all went back again into our seats.[21]

And then, at the end, people were just blown away, because an event, an ecstatic event had happened. This is a complicated piece of music. Everywhere—she was playing a Stradivarius from 1727—everywhere she went on this violin, she got exactly what she was looking for. She held it. And Maazel was so sovereign and so—like a huge patriarch. And three or four times—I was up close enough to see them—he looked at her with the wistful, proud gentleness of a grandfather. And there was this woman, this beautiful, slim body, and you could almost see the music hurting her, even when she wasn't playing. So it was a huge—everybody, and there were hardened New York critics there, but everybody was so touched.

Janine Jansen's transcendent violin performance was riveting, bordering on spiritual for O'Donohue and reminded him of what beauty really is.

That appreciation for the years of practice and dedication to excellence is why we love watching the Olympics, cheering on competitors from all countries who demonstrate commitment to their sport. We are enthralled by witnessing excellence in action, marveling at what others achieve when they push themselves to their limits. The experience of watching the Olympics on TV alongside others who are cheering for their favorite athletes is another opportunity for emotional contagion—for personal emotions to be shared and transferred to those who are witnessing excellence with us. Emotions can actually shift in positive ways when we see others' success.

When was the last time your jaw dropped witnessing what someone could do? What types of excellence move you: Is it in the arts? Athletics? Excel spreadsheets? Parenting? Giving a presentation? Look for—meaning *actively seek out*—opportunities to witness and savor the kind of excellence that matters most to you more often.

4. USING YOUR UNIQUE PASSIONS OR QUALIFICATIONS TO MAKE A DIFFERENCE

There are times when a situation calls out for what you uniquely bring to the table. We have found in our interviews that when people see situations where they can use their distinct passions or qualifications to have a positive impact, they feel an inspired motivation to take action.

A great example of this is Temple Grandin, professor of animal science at Colorado State University, who has a unique ability to empathize with animals. Diagnosed as autistic with Asperger's at a young age, Grandin uses her unique neuropathology to advise slaughterhouses on how to make their environment more humane.[22] In her book *Thinking in Pictures,* she talks about how her unique neurology helps her see things other people don't and experience an environment more closely to how animals would experience it.[23] She goes into slaughterhouses and lies down on the floor, puts herself into cages, and crawls through metal chutes to understand the animals' experiences and then makes recommendations to reduce stress.[24] "I think we can eat meat ethically, but we've got to give animals a good life," she said in a *National Geographic* feature. As the article highlights, "you would think slaughterhouses were primed for someone like her to come along."[25] However, it hasn't been an easy battle to fight for thirty years; what has inspired Grandin all along is the possibility for improvement. What gives her the confidence to make these changes is knowing that her unique way of thinking and feeling could make a difference.

"Lost Boy" Salva Dut, who walked for months from his former home in Sudan, leading 1,500 other young boys away from civil war and to a refugee camp in Kenya, was eventually resettled in the United States in 1996.[26] After earning a college education, Dut wanted to do something to improve conditions in his homeland. He knew access to water would alleviate many of the tensions between tribes and provide opportunities for education and income earning. He formed the nonprofit Water for South Sudan and began raising money to buy well-drilling equipment to install wells. His unique knowledge and ability to network with local leaders, negotiate with tribal elders, and navigate the sometimes dangerous terrain are the reason the organization has successfully drilled 304 wells in South Sudan as of 2018 and is in the process of repairing existing wells, digging new ones, and shifting its educational emphasis to hygiene in order to continue to improve lives in the region.

Many know the story of Steve Jobs's departure from and then return to Apple. But we don't often view the story in terms of what inspired Jobs to return to Apple over ten years after he first left. When Jobs was asked to leave Apple in 1985, his passion for his own ideas (to the exclusion of others) was noted as his downfall.[27] In Jobs's absence, the company, under John Sculley, experienced multiple failed products and strategies. The company was operating at a loss by the late '90s, in need of creative direction to bring it back to its former glory.[28]

So Jobs returned in 1997, now celebrated for his "zealotry" in pursuit of great products, in part because Jobs had managed to focus his passion toward commercially viable endeavors and in part because he'd smoothed down some of the hard edges of his management style.[29] But the most significant factor in his return was his unique strengths—his passion for product innovation and his unwavering pursuit of things thought to be impossible—made him a perfect match for Apple's needs at the time. That fit of distinctive strengths and talents to a specific need or opportunity lights a compelling spark of inspiration.

We've already discussed finding more opportunities to use your strengths through personal engines of inspiration. Here, our focus is on situations that call for your distinctive passions, abilities, and capacities.

What situations are calling for you? Nothing coming to mind? Think hard and start asking around. Your contributions are needed.

5. SHARING EXPERIENCES WITH LARGE GROUPS OF PEOPLE

Attending events with others can have an impact on our perspective and emotions—how we feel and how we view our lives and the opportunities around us. Going to concerts, performances, movies, shows, special events, or political rallies are all examples of what psychology scholars call the *amplification hypothesis*. Research shows that having a common experience with another, whether or not there is any interaction between you, enriches the experience; the experience is amplified.[30]

We often reflect on significant experiences from the viewpoint of who we were with at the time. That was certainly the case for generations of diehard Chicago Cubs fans who had dreamt of a World Series win for their beloved Cubbies. The last championship win was in 1908. Every new baseball season would begin with hope and promise, only to be dashed by a loss somewhere down the line, ending that year's playoffs chances. Finally, in 2016, the Cubs were victorious, bringing their fan base of an estimated 9.9 million people[31]—more than any other MLB team—the World Series Championship trophy. That win brought their fans joy, euphoria, pride, bliss, and gratitude—feelings often associated with inspiration.

Similar emotions were felt by fans of the Philadelphia Eagles football team, which had never won a Super Bowl. Sure, the team had played in two previous championship games—in 1980 and 2004—but had never succeeded in winning until 2017.[32] Legions of Eagles fans took to the streets, as is their custom in Philly, to celebrate the long-awaited victory.

In businesses, shared group experiences can take the form of town halls, all-hands meetings, even department gatherings and retreats. Meaningful experiences that are shared with others can be potent drivers of inspiration.

What meaningful shared experiences are coming up in your calendar? It's worth seeking them out and even consider organizing ones if you'd like to find more.

6. EXPERIENCING GRIEF, LOSS, OR FAILURE

When channeled properly, loss or failure can be a source of inspiration. In some ways, it is counterintuitive, even off-putting, to think of grief, loss, or failure as being inspiring. Yet, in many of our interviews people mentioned these as sources of inspiration to them when the difficult emotions that ensued were channeled properly and held close—but not too close. When people make constructive meaning out of their grief or loss, it can then inspire them to take action in meaningful ways.[33]

A number of organizations and professional endeavors are rooted in loss. Dr. Leah Osowiecki of Holistic Home Veterinary Services feels passionate about supporting families in helping their pets go through their final stages, offering deep care and partnership through the process. Although the work itself is emotionally difficult because of the loss she witnesses every day, she said that she is inspired by the work. It enables her to bring peace to families and meaning to the final stages with their beloved pets.[34] Facebook's Sheryl Sandberg was transparent about her grief when she lost her husband, using that as a catalyst for authoring the book *Plan B*.[35] Additionally, Joe Kasper, an MD who also has a master's in applied positive psychology, created a model called Co-Destiny, which helps people create legacy in loss by doing good in the names of people they have lost.[36] Kasper was inspired by the loss of his nineteen-year-old son Ryan.

There is a body of research on post-traumatic growth (PTG),[37] the phenomenon that occurs when people are able to create powerful narratives and experience positive personal and social outcomes in the face of serious illness, trauma, loss, or grief. It is currently unclear why some people experience post-traumatic stress (PTS) and struggle to recover, while others can move from PTS to PTG. Although we would never propose seeking out grief or loss as an engine of inspiration, our interviews and the research on PTG shows that when it occurs, if we are mindful about it, we can use these difficult experiences to gain meaning and move forward stronger and in inspiring ways.

Jenna Bell, a keynote speaker and heart disease survivor, is a great example of this. She received an incredibly difficult diagnosis of cardiomyopathy at the young age of twenty-three. When told that she required a heart transplant to stay alive or would face a premature death and that she would be unable to have children, she grieved the loss of a normal life.[38] Bell shared that because of her size and weight, the odds were against her as she competed with younger patients who would be higher on an eligibility list, but she received a transplant on February 16, 2016. In her interview with us, she shared that rather than letting the trauma of her situation get her down, she learned from it. She learned how to say no without having to justify it. She learned how to use her voice—both in advocating for herself medically and telling her story. She learned how to express gratitude, writing thank-you notes to everyone who came across her path ("cafeteria staff, x-ray staff, custodial staff, nurses, doctors, everybody") because she wanted them to feel valued and do their best as part of her team, and she learned to look out for her true tribe, the people who would help her and support her when she really needed it. She now gives keynote presentations on how she has grown and what she has learned as a result of her trauma.[39]

Finally, the experience of failure, when accepted and viewed from a growth mindset lens, can lead to inspiration. One example of this is Stacy London, TV fashion guru and bestselling author who was fired from *Mademoiselle* magazine. Being fired from the magazine devastated her, but it also opened a door for her and inspired her to audition for the TV show *What Not to Wear*. In an interview with Whitney Johnson, Stacy London said this situation "made me realize that I had been unhappy in that job for two years and I had stayed two years too long out of pure laziness. Knowing that I had a 401(k), knowing that I had insurance." Rather than letting this public, professional failure define her and discourage her, she felt inspired to take action and eventually thrived on the TV show.[40]

It's critical with loss to let yourself feel it, to process and acknowledge it. Seeking inspiration is not a way to avoid trauma. But, when you are ready, you can allow yourself to create meaning in what you've experienced and create new possibilities and newfound confidence. Think about a time in your past when you've experienced a hardship and from which you've grown. Going forward, as you confront losses and failures—small or large—allow yourself the opportunity to write an inspiring story from what you lost or how you overcame it.

Like all the other engines, these engines of circumstance drive the initial spark of inspiration that combine feelings of invincibility and possibility. There is a leadership opportunity inherent in these engines. Leaders can work to create circumstances that will inspire those who work for them. Warren Bennis, a highly respected scholar on leadership, describes the opportunity to set the stage as follows: "One can sing and dance. Or one can create an environment in which singers and dancers flourish."[41]

WORK IT
Sparked by SITUATIONS Inspiration Challenge

ENGINE	HOW MUCH DO YOU USE IT? (SCALE OF 1–5)	WAYS TO TAP INTO THIS ENGINE MORE OFTEN (CIRCLE THE ONES YOU LIKE BEST AND ADD IN YOUR OWN)
Seeking Environments That Move Us	_____	**Some examples:** Do an assessment of your current environment (i.e., office, house). Do you feel inspired in that environment every day? If not, what can you change to make it more interesting and inspiring? Consider ways you can strategically alter your environment when you need a boost: for example, walking in nature or going to a museum before brainstorming for an important project. When your energy is low and you are feeling uninspired, change your environment in some way, big or small. **What would you add?**
Overcoming Constraints	_____	**Some examples:** Have there been times in your life when you were told "no, you can't do something" and it made you feel even more determined to accomplish something? What can you learn from that situation? Looking forward, the next time you experience a block, rather than focusing on the obstacle or discouraging emotions, ask yourself how you can shift your mindset and reach out for support from others to tackle the obstacle—to bring your feelings of possibility and invincibility to it. **What would you add?**

ENGINE	HOW MUCH DO YOU USE IT? (SCALE OF 1–5)	WAYS TO TAP INTO THIS ENGINE MORE OFTEN (CIRCLE THE ONES YOU LIKE BEST AND ADD IN YOUR OWN)
Witnessing Excellence	_____	**Some examples:** What types of excellence inspire you the most? For some people, they love watching professional sports events or theater; for other people, they get fired up when they see colleagues being excellent in their work. It's likely that the type of excellence that inspires you closely aligns to some of your most closely held values and priorities. Actively seek out opportunities to see this talent and excellence in action. **What would you add?**
Using Your Unique Passons or Qualifications to Make a Difference	_____	**Some examples:** Do an audit of your top talents and skills (unique qualifications) and passions. When you look at these together, do you notice any themes you could use to have a positive impact? Reflect on times in your life when you have been able to impact a situation using talents that were unique to you. Looking ahead, what's the type of impact you hope to have in the future? Imagine yourself giving a TED Talk or being featured on TV talking about this impact and how your passions and qualifications made it happen. **What would you add?**

(continues)

ENGINE	HOW MUCH DO YOU USE IT? (SCALE OF 1–5)	WAYS TO TAP INTO THIS ENGINE MORE OFTEN (CIRCLE THE ONES YOU LIKE BEST AND ADD IN YOUR OWN)
Sharing Experiences with Large Groups of People	_____	**Some examples:** Remember the last time you shared an experience with a large group of people (i.e., conference, concert, social gathering) that inspired you. The types of collective experiences that inspire you the most are unique to you. Knowing that sharing important experiences can inspire, how could you bring these experiences more into your work (i.e., shared team experiences) or your personal life? **What would you add?**
Experiencing Grief, Loss, or Failure	_____	**Some examples:** You don't usually have control over experiences that lead to grief, loss, or failure. It is important to have self-compassion and give yourself the time and support you need to process these difficult situations. Sometimes these situations can ignite feelings of inspiration in us to move forward with new meaning or understanding. Is there a past loss or failure that you could look at with new understanding? What has that situation taught you about yourself and how might you use that knowledge to make a positive difference? **What would you add?**

PART III

SUSTAINING INSPIRATION

We know inspiration can be created using the engines of inspiration, but the problem with sparks is that they are hot, exciting, and intense and can burn out as quickly as they are created. When faced with the day-to-day grind and mundane challenges, inspiration cannot just be sparked; it must also be intentionally sustained over time.

The prospect of sustaining inspiration is one of the key and unique insights of this book. In this part of the book, we explore the analogy from the introduction that inspiration is like a muscle that needs to be exercised through intentional practice and focus. Although the initial spark of inspiration is characterized by feelings of invincibility and possibility, sustaining inspiration requires intentional practice and focus over time. Intentional practice is more than mindless repetitions. It's a special type of behavior that is designed, purposeful, and systematic, requires focused attention, and is conducted with the specific goal of improving performance. We need systems, tools, resources, and ongoing, regular practice to keep our feelings of inspiration growing, salient, and strong.

You'll learn how to sustain inspiration in four distinct ways:

1. **Respark the engines.** We think of this as keeping the spark alive by going back to the sparks again and again, sometimes combining engines in new ways to make the sparks even more potent.
2. **Direct inspiration toward desired outcomes.** Inspiration as an emotion feels good, but when it's translated into great performance that leads to meaningful and desired outcomes, the result is a feedback loop of more inspiration.
3. **Give your inspiration a boost.** Most fires need the flames fanned. Critical to keeping inspiration alive is to build into your day positive rituals, accountability, and social support.
4. **Manage your energy.** Inspiration is energy; therefore, if your energy is suffering over time, it will get in the way of sustained inspiration. Managing energy through your body, emotions, and mindset are critical so you can bounce back quickly from setbacks and keep your inspiration flowing.

The four chapters in this part go into detail about how to intentionally *sustain* inspiration over time using these methods of intentional practice. These chapters focus more on the "how to" and provide specific tools for bringing inspiration more often and for longer periods of time.

CHAPTER SIX

RESPARK THE ENGINES

"You can't wait for inspiration. You have to go after it with a club."

—Jack London

nspiration doesn't have to be a fleeting state. It is possible to extend its presence, to sustain it and practice it so it becomes enduring. One of the ways to maintain inspiration over time is by intentionally going back to the inspiration engines and sparking them more often and in different ways, with a deliberate focus on keeping the sparks alive. Inspiration is a muscle that needs to be exercised and trained; without regular use it will atrophy. But

> "Inspiration: it's a muscle. It can atrophy, it can be worked out, it can be flexible, it can be rigid, it can be strength giving. It can be all of those things."
>
> —Paul Bennett, Chief Creative Officer, IDEO

over time, with the help of systems, tools, and ongoing, regular practice, you can make inspiration a near-constant presence in your everyday work and life.

At this point, you've likely identified some of the engines that inspire you. Now it's time to learn how to manifest inspiration when it wanes, when you feel its absence, or when you want more of it—when you want more of it, specifically by tapping into, or mixing engines of inspiration in new ways. An engine that was a spark of inspiration at first may still hold energy for you and can be an ongoing spark. But often times, it is useful to draw from another engine, either on its own or in combination with the original. Engines in combination with one another can be more powerful, driving more frequent and more lasting sparks that endure over time.

Lin-Manuel Miranda's initial spark for creating the revolutionary musical *Hamilton* came from reading on the beach while on vacation[1] ("unstructured time" engine), but over time he found other sources of inspiration to sustain him. He took his initial idea for a mixtape about Alexander Hamilton and fleshed it out, refined it, and eventually created the musical that reinvented musical theater. One way he did that was by visiting the Morris-Jumel Mansion in Manhattan,[2] once owned by Aaron Burr, the man who killed Hamilton, and spending time in Burr's bedroom, channeling that time in history and that energy. He supercharged his unstructured think time by changing his environment in an intentional and meaningful way ("seeking environments that move us" engine). When he needed ongoing inspiration, he returned to that house to compose songs, including "Wait for It" and "The Room Where It Happens."

Being in the space where Burr had been—and so closely connected to Hamilton—was a source of inspiration for Miranda. That ritual became a reliable spark for him. You, too, can find reliable sparks for yourself. It all starts with paying attention to how your energy level varies in certain scenarios and then knowing what inspires you.

KNOWING WHEN YOU'RE NOT INSPIRED

The first step in maintaining inspiration is taking a pulse on your own level of it. You need the self-awareness to be able to tell the difference between when you are or are not inspired. When you're inspired, you may feel superproductive, your thinking may seem clearer, new ideas may come to you quickly, and you likely feel optimistic, even fearless. When you're not inspired, you may feel deflated, discouraged, or even resigned.

> The first step in maintaining
> inspiration is recognizing
> your own levels of it.

To spot the difference, pay attention to your body and how it's performing. What is normal or typical for you? What is your energy level? How do your muscles or your body as a whole feel? Are you level-headed emotionally? How about cognitively—how easy or difficult is it for you to complete typical tasks at work and at home?

When you can recognize what is normal, or baseline, you can start to recognize when your inspiration is on as well as when it's off. Feeling unstoppable, elated, or confident are signs that you are inspired. On the other hand, a tight stomach or lack of energy—exhaustion—may be your body's way of telling you that your inspiration levels are down.

Emotions are data points for you. Your emotional state can indicate that you aren't inspired and need to do something to turn the situation around. Sometimes other people notice it first, asking you what's wrong or commenting that "you look tired." These can be signals, data, that you need to increase inspiration.

Self-awareness can help you notice when your inspiration is waning and in need of rejuvenation. You might realize that you typically experience a sense of letdown after you complete a big project or achieve a goal and that it's difficult to motivate yourself for the next big thing. Maybe you feel lost in direction or purpose. Or maybe you feel like you're out of sync with someone you work with regularly, or just not plugged into what's going on at work. It's not the same for everyone, so you need to learn what your individual indicators are that alert you when your inspiration is dipping.

Thought Experiment: Take the Inspiration Inventory

Take a minute to tune in, reflect, and rate yourself on a scale of 1–10 on the questions below. How strong (1 lowest to 10 highest) do you feel in each of the following areas:

○ Openness to new ideas and possibilities?
○ Level of confidence, even invincibility, to undertake or accomplish your goals?
○ Ability to focus and engage on the person or topic (versus being distracted, restless)?
○ Productivity or ability to take action in the ways you want?
○ Feelings of optimism, excitement, or hope?
○ Desire to connect with and interact with others?

Although you can't expect to feel inspired *all* the time, take note if your score dips below 5 on any of these areas, especially more than one. The good news is that once you recognize when you're feeling less than inspired, you can take action to address the situation proactively before your inspiration dips down too low. You can turn to your inspiration engines to recharge yourself.

RENEWING AND SUSTAINING YOUR INSPIRATION

In this chapter, we explore two different ways to renew and rejuvenate feelings of inspiration through the engines: (1) drawing from engines you know work for you, and/or (2) curating new sources of inspiration from different engines or different combinations of engines. Depending on your situation, you may wish to respark inspiration by going back to familiar engines you know work for you, or you may be in need of a new approach.

DRAWING AGAIN FROM ENGINES THAT TYPICALLY INSPIRE YOU

What inspires each of us is individual and personal. You may find inspiration at the beach or in the mountains while others may seek out conversation and art museums for his or her inspirational fix. We're all different. However, by reflecting on where ideas have come from in the past, we can start to zero in on what sparks new ideas and renews passion for each of us.

When world-class skier Lindsey Vonn looks back on her career to try to spot what set her on the path to Olympic greatness, she points to a couple of memories as being pivotal. A key one was having a role model, she says in an interview:

> I met [ski racer] Picabo Street when I was nine at an autograph session at a local ski shop in Minnesota. She really inspired me to want to be an Olympic skier. When I met her, I was like, *this is what I really want to do. I just want to be her.* I waited in line for three hours to see her, and I met her for two minutes. It was like meeting a superhero. She's who inspired me.[3]

She was inspired by someone who was doing what she aspired to do ("heroes and mentors" engine). She followed Street's career and races, continually being inspired by her performance. News of Street's successes served as an inspiration engine for Vonn.

But she also was inspired by the possibility of excellence. She admired great performances in others ("witnessing excellence" engine) and was inspired to set lofty goals for herself ("progressing toward and achieving success" engine), allowing their successes to broaden her sense of what is possible. "My mom said that I would draw pictures when I was six or seven of me winning races and writing 'The Greatest Skier of All Time,' and signing my name to it. I don't know where that came from because no one ever told me that."[4]

This formula isn't limited to athletes. All of us can be reinspired by returning to our inspiration engines. Bill Bornschein, who teaches religion in a Catholic high school in Kentucky, told us when we interviewed him that he reminds himself of his purpose daily when he wonders if he's making a difference ("connecting to and voicing your values and purpose" engine). He does this by reflecting on the teachings of the Buddha. He shared with us a story, in his own words, that when the Buddha achieved enlightenment, he was tempted like Jesus. In this last temptation, a "demon" said to him that no one would understand his teachings, that his teachings would be distorted and misunderstood. The Buddha touched the ground, claiming the earth as his witness, and responded that some would understand.[5]

In seeing an image of the Buddha every day, Bornschein reminds himself that with roughly twenty-five students in one class and several classes a day, he's not going to reach everyone. He said that sometimes teachers, himself included, can have high expectations, wanting to positively impact all students, and this can put them at risk for burnout. "I'm there for those who have ears," he says—those willing to listen. "I will get nonverbal feedback from students that they get it. There might be fifteen in here, and if three or four run with it further, that's great."

The possibility that even a few students will resonate with ideas discussed in class and be inspired to think in new ways is an inspiration engine for him[6] ("values and purpose"). Furthermore, Bornschein acknowledged being part of a larger team that is tasked with reaching students. He draws hope from the realization that students will be inspired by other teachers and mentors—that together, educators are part of a village.

Bornschein is realistic but not daunted. He's inspired by the possibility of reaching all of his students, realizing that he personally may only get through to a few. And that's OK. Knowing there is a larger village of educators to reach the students and knowing he can get through to some is the opportunity that sparks inspiration for him. One of the ways he sustains his inspiration for teaching is going back to this story that reminds him of what is possible.

IGNITING NEW SPARKS FROM DIFFERENT ENGINES OR COMBINATIONS OF ENGINES

When returning to engines that have sparked inspiration for you doesn't work, or isn't possible, another strategy is to look to new sources or combinations of engines. Using inspiration engines you haven't drawn on before, or combining them with other engines, can serve as a new source of sustained inspiration.

Jadav Payeng of India found his life's purpose as a teenager and has sustained it for decades. Payeng was called to protect animals in need of shade in his native Indian village, Aruna Sapori, a river island.[7]

After going away for schooling as a young child, Payeng returned to the island in 1978 as a teenager and was horrified to find dozens of dead snakes on a deserted sandbar. Without shade, they were washed up and killed by the sun. He was struck by their plight and inspired to help them. Payeng turned to the Deori community village for guidance on how to help the animals. They explained that there was nothing he could do alone[8] because without a hospitable habitat they were doomed. The only way to change the situation was to bring back the forest, they explained—a task they said he could not do by himself.

That advice shaped Payeng's life in ways no one could have imagined. Payeng felt a duty to do something, anything, to help the animals survive, despite others telling him it was an impossible task. In fact, being told no may have served as another inspiration engine for him ("overcoming constraints" engine). Undeterred, he became invincible in his quest to forest the dry lands. He sought bamboo seeds and saplings to place on the sandbar. He planted the bamboo and continued replanting regularly, gathering seeds and saplings throughout the year and then planting them between April and June annually. At first, he struggled, as few plants would grow in the sand. So he switched to silk cotton and other varieties, to try and find what would survive. The green began to spread. Inspired by progress and achievement, Payeng continued on his quest to reforest the barren island.

Payeng says, "I measure success in terms of the greenery I spread till the day I [die]."[9] His personal mission has become providing a safe habitat for animals, made possible only through more plantings. He is inspired by the progress he has made so far but knows there is always more work to be done. There are always more animals to protect.

In five years, he covered one kilometer with trees. Today, forty years later, the lifeless sandbar has become 1,360 acres of dense forest, home to five Bengal tigers, 115 elephants who visit each year, deer, wild boar, and countless species of birds. Known as "the Forest Man of India," Payeng is now making plans to plant a new forest in another village. He is finalizing plans to raise another forest on nearly five thousand acres near India's Kaziranga National Park.

Although Payeng's singular commitment to animals has sustained his inspired actions, sometimes what inspires us evolves or shifts over time. At first for Payeng, being told "no, it's impossible" stirred him to action. Then it was his own progress, his great achievement, that complemented his commitment to the animals ("progressing toward and achieving success" engine). As the Forest Man of India, it is his unique strengths of compassion, perseverance, and hope that inspire him to continue ("using your strengths" engine).

Janet Patti, EdD, professor of educational leadership at Hunter College and one of our interviewees, was inspired by Dr. Robert Muller ("admiring our mentors and heroes" engine), a French underground soldier in World War II who was captured by and escaped the gestapo[10] and went on to spend more than forty years working with the United Nations to sow peace.[11] After seeing the brutalities of war, Muller chose "a profession of peace,"[12] a lifelong pursuit similar to that of Albert Schweitzer, whom he met as a young child.

Years ago, Patti spent a day with Muller in the mountains where he lived outside the University of Peace in Costa Rica. She was moved by his question: "Why don't we teach the history of peace rather than the history of war?" Muller himself and his question became a guiding force in her life and her career.[13]

She had been a teacher, counselor, and school administrator for many years and decided to go back to school in her forties to earn a doctoral degree in education ("developing new perspectives" engine) so that she could play a larger role in teaching peace. She now teaches at Hunter College in addition to running a consulting firm, Star Factor Coaching, which focuses on building empathy and emotional intelligence skills in educational leaders. Her firm was built on her personal mission of leadership development for a better world ("connecting to and voicing your values and purpose" engine). The emotional intelligence and empathy training and coaching she has provided in the last ten years in collaboration with the Yale Center for Emotional Intelligence has positively impacted the New York Department of Education, deputy chancellors, superintendents, and principals across more than forty school districts in all New York City boroughs, which has then indirectly impacted thousands of teachers and students.[14]

While Patti's initial spark may have been the new possibilities opened up by the moving introduction to Muller's own mission of world peace, through the years she has returned to that original connection for inspiration and also built on it, exploring other engines as a way to sustain her own personal mission, from relationship building to new perspectives, to values and purpose, to name a few.[15]

Sources of inspiration can evolve for individuals as well as for organizations, as was the case with Dutch Bros. Coffee.[16] Dutch Bros. (pronounced "brose") was founded in 1992 by Dane and Travis Boersma, brothers of Dutch descent, as an alternate source of income after their family's three-generation dairy farm was forced to shut down due to restrictive government regulations ("overcoming constraints" engine). Travis had been captivated by the delicious mochas sold at a pushcart at Southern Oregon University, where he was a student ("witnessing excellence" engine). Although Dane was more of a plain coffee drinker, he was hooked after tasting a vanilla latte.

They set up shop on their own pushcart, having invested $12,000 in the cart and an espresso machine. Within six months, the cart was generating $200 a day in income, and the brothers were enjoying hanging out with customers and listening to music, while earning a living. By comparison to farm life, "this didn't feel like work," said Travis.[17]

On the heels of the growing cultural obsession with quality coffees and espressos, the Boersmas added a drive-through to their coffee operation. Then they started sourcing their own beans from El Salvador, rather than buying them through a broker. The next step was to open a physical storefront, which they did briefly with a partner (who was later bought out). Culture was important from the start to the Boersmas ("connecting to and voicing your values and purpose" engine), and they trusted their employees explicitly, relying on them to provide the same personal attention and care that the brothers had from the beginning. That combination of personal care ("serving others" and "belonging" engines) and quality coffee attracted coffee lovers.

Today, Dutch Bros. is America's largest privately held drive-through coffee retailer. It has more than 290 locations and more than 7,500 employees.[18] What has made Dutch Bros. an unconventional business success is its values, which stress relationships over product. Employees interested in opening their own franchise need only spend a few thousand dollars and can receive financing from the company for its property and equipment. And customers become part of the family—employees are expected to get to know every one of their coffee drinkers. Dutch Bros. makes a mean cup of coffee, but it is inspiring culture that is fueling the company's success. The Dutch Bros. company has tapped into many different engines, as the story illustrates.

The key to sustaining inspiration is to curate your own elixir of inspiration engines over time based on what works for you. It's part of the process of actively claiming inspiration as a focal point and opting in to practice it regularly. You can choose, through your actions, to return to the inspiration engines you've previously tapped into for insights and ideas. Or you can explore new sources of inspiration from a comprehensive list of inspiration engines we have identified—new engines that may prove even more fruitful or reliable than engines you've long relied on. What's critical is finding out what sparks inspiration for you now and exploring what else may be inspirational for you.

WORK IT
Road Map to Sustain Inspiration around a
Particular Area of Focus

Identify an area of focus (work, life, relationship, project, etc.) where you want more inspiration or you want to renew your inspiration:

- First, identify the engine(s) that originally inspired you and circle them in the Road Map to Sustaining Inspiration below.
- Next, consider additional engines you currently use that lead to inspiration and how they inspire you (in the same aspect of your life); write notes in the second column below.
- Review the list of engines again to find new possibilities—either engines you have never tried in this area of your life and/or current engines you can use in a new way. We've learned from our interviews that people tend to find an "inspiration home" in one of the categories of engines (personal, relationships, situations) or specific engines they use regularly. We encourage you to stretch to new categories. Look for a sense of connection or resonance with one or two engines that are new and consider the question prompts below.
- In the last column, write ideas for how to fold these new engines into your current approach to staying inspired.

ROAD MAP TO SUSTAINING INSPIRATION THROUGH THE ENGINES

PERSONAL ENGINES (SPARKED BY YOU)

ENGINE	CURRENTLY USING? (Y/N) AND HOW?	QUESTION PROMPT TO CONSIDER HOW TO USE THIS ENGINE	HOW WILL I USE THIS ENGINE IN A NEW OR DIFFERENT WAY?
Connecting to and Voicing Your Values and Purpose	⸺	*What are my most cherished values? How do they relate to this area? What is most important to me about this area?*	
Using Your Strengths	⸺	*How am I currently using my strengths in this area? Where could I bring more of my strengths into the picture (and how)?*	
Striving Toward and Achieving Goals	⸺	*What would I ideally like to accomplish in this area in the next year? Three years? What would make me feel successful?*	
Using Your Whole Brain with Unstructured Time	⸺	*Looking at the calendar, when can I find a chunk of time to just breathe, decompress, play?*	
Developing New Perspectives	⸺	*What's a new way of thinking about this area, a view I haven't considered before? Consider asking a friend or colleague for a new perspective.*	
Activating Body Movement and Presence	⸺	*When and how can I build in a physical activity, movement, or a reset into my day?*	

(continues)

RELATIONSHIPS ENGINES (SPARKED BY OTHERS)

ENGINE	CURRENTLY USING? (Y/N) AND HOW?	QUESTION PROMPT TO CONSIDER HOW TO USE THIS ENGINE	HOW WILL I USE THIS ENGINE IN A NEW OR DIFFERENT WAY?
Belonging	——	*Where can I find common ground in this area with others? In what ways do I truly belong?*	
Admiring Our Mentors and Heroes	——	*What mentors or heroes in this area can I reach out to for inspiration? Consider scheduling time to talk or simply reminding yourself of their wisdom and character.*	
Getting a Lift	——	*Who gives me an emotional lift and how can I spend more time with this person or these people to boost inspiration?*	
Serving Others	——	*How can I be generous and be of service to others in this area?*	
Sharing a Group Mission	——	*Who shares the values that underlie this inspiration with me and how can I connect with them?*	
Being Vulnerable and Transparent	——	*Who can I let in and share some of my concerns about this area?*	

SITUATIONS ENGINES (SPARKED BY SITUATIONS)

ENGINE	CURRENTLY USING? (Y/N) AND HOW?	QUESTION PROMPT TO CONSIDER HOW TO USE THIS ENGINE	HOW WILL I USE THIS ENGINE IN A NEW OR DIFFERENT WAY?
Seeking Environments That Move Us	——	*What types of environments inspire me? Consider places, colors, smells, textures, images, and so on. How can I either change my current environment or go to a new one that will inspire me more?*	
Overcoming Constraints	——	*What barriers or obstacles are getting in the way in this area? What can I do to overcome them?*	
Witnessing Excellence	——	*Who about their excellence in their life, work, or other domains inspires me? How can I see models of excellence in this area where I want more inspiration?*	
Using Your Unique Passions or Qualifications to Make a Difference	——	*What are my unique passions and qualifications that I can bring to this area of my life/ work? What can I do that no one else can do to make a difference?*	
Sharing Experiences with Large Groups of People	——	*Is there a meaningful shared experience—doing an activity, learning something new, seeing a performance—I can organize and create to bring more inspiration to this area?*	
Experiencing Grief, Loss, or Failure	——	*If I have experienced a significant loss or a recent failure, especially in this area, what can I learn from it? What do I want to carry forward with me?*	

CHAPTER SEVEN

DIRECT INSPIRATION TO DESIRED OUTCOMES

"The best time to plant a tree is twenty years ago. The second-best time is now."

—Ancient Chinese proverb

The spark of inspiration represents potential—the potential for an idea to go from concept to reality through action. But a spark is really just a starting point. Without purposeful, volitional attention or action, it dies out; the idea goes nowhere.

For example, what if roommates Joe Gebbia and Brian Chesky were content simply to rent out their loft to make some extra rent money rather than rolling out their idea worldwide as Airbnb? Or if Blake Mycoskie of TOMS, on witnessing Argentinian children without shoes, had simply written a check to buy shoes for the village rather than designing a business model that would provide an ongoing supply of shoes? What if Maggie Doyne of BlinkNow had been inspired to pay for one child's school tuition and continued on her trek through Nepal rather than staying and building an orphanage and adopting dozens of children? What if Malala Yousafzai had focused on obtaining her own education rather than fighting for the right for all girls to receive an education?

Thankfully, the leaders in these stories did not stop once they felt a flicker of inspiration. Instead, they autonomously and intentionally put their inspiration into practice. They set their sights on the success they envisioned, drove forward, and were strategic and tenacious in their pursuit of goals.

Still, in all these cases, if the spark of inspiration had been allowed to fade rather than fed with encouragement and action, we would never have seen new business models emerge, or these social initiatives take hold. That's the difference between feeding a spark to reach a desired outcome and merely allowing it to fade and die out.

That initial spark of inspiration feels good, it's uplifting, but again, it can be fleeting. Another pathway to sustaining inspiration comes from directing your attention and effort toward a particular outcome, which converts that spark into a steady flame. Taking action is what transforms an idea into an outcome.

> To sustain inspiration you
> need to direct your attention
> and effort toward a particular
> outcome, which converts that
> spark into a steady flame.

The process of applying meaningful action to a spark to achieve a positive impact is, in and of itself, inspiring. It's the translation of the emotion of inspiration into successful performance, of taking a spark and making it last over time by translating it into behaviors that will result in desired outcomes.

SUSTAINING INSPIRATION THROUGH DIRECTED ACTION: FOUR CATEGORIES OF BEHAVIOR THAT LEAD TO DESIRED OUTCOMES

We have identified four specific categories of behavior—driving to results, intentional alignment, connection and trust, vision and innovation—that are most useful when directing inspiration to positive outcomes. These four categories of behavior are consistent with what we know from working with our clients and from existing research. For example, the CEO Genome study[1] of seventeen thousand executives discovered that high-performing executives exhibit four behaviors consistently, setting them apart from average or subpar C-suite execs. These behaviors were

- **Deciding with speed and conviction.** Even with incomplete information, successful leaders "make decisions earlier, faster, and with greater conviction," reported *Harvard Business Review*.[2]
- **Delivering reliably.** Consistently delivering results was perhaps the most important behavior of all four, the researchers found. "Boards and investors love a steady hand, and employees trust predictable leaders" was the summary.
- **Engaging for impact.** They work hard to get buy-in from employees and important stakeholders.
- **Adapting proactively.** Most CEOs juggle thinking about the short-, medium-, and long-term implications and adapt as needed, though the study found that more successful CEOs spent at least 50 percent of their time pondering long-term implications.

Inspired executives successfully exhibit behaviors that correspond to these four categories.[3]

Additional support is found in *The Leadership Code*. David Ulrich and his team report that successful leaders display four behaviors, namely human capital developer, strategist, executor, and talent manager.[4]

The four categories of behavior we advance here are informed by the research above and emerged from two critical continuums of behavior that pose interesting paradoxes to be wrestled with to achieve success. One continuum spans from openness (to ideas and people) to determination (think task driven). The other continuum goes from grounded stability to dynamic flexibility. These two dimensions encompass behaviors shown to be most effective at driving success. When we cross these two dimensions, they create four key categories of behavior: flexible/determined, determined/stable, stable/open, and open/flexible.

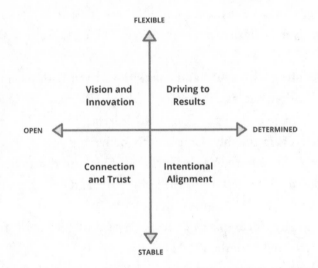

These four categories of behavior have been shown to, together, yield success through agility and balance across all four. We've named them to reflect the central organizing principle that comes from the blend of the two dimensions represented. They are driving to results, intentional alignment, connection and trust, and vision and innovation.

Driving to results (flexible/determined). Key to successful outcomes are ambitious goals and the drive to achieve them. Directing inspiration toward *driving to results* includes goal setting, defining desired outcomes, and identifying the actions to reach success (think Mycoskie creating TOMS Shoes or Avila with his taco trucks). What strengths of yours will be useful in achieving your goals? How will you know if you've reached them? Flexibility can afford asking the question, Is there a better, faster way to proceed?

Intentional alignment (determined/stable). A results focus is useful but can be detrimental if it is rash or reckless (think of big banks in 2008). This is where intentional alignment comes in to ensure that goals being achieved and decisions being made are rooted in your values. Integrity is a big part of intentional alignment. It protects reputation, accountability, and reliability. As you are working toward your ambitious goals, ask yourself: Are you *really* defining success in alignment with your values? What risk can you tolerate and how do you mitigate higher levels of risk? What standards or regulations will you uphold to succeed?

Building connection and trust (stable/open). Success rarely happens in isolation—we are wired to be connected to one another. Building connection and trust is key to forging relationships with others who can support you and your efforts (think Gebbia and Chesky focusing on how to build enough trust between strangers so that both guests and hosts feel safe—critical to cracking the Airbnb code).[5] What can you do to garner support from those around you who matter? How will you share the joys of winning together? What can you do to better support others as they work toward your common goals?

Vision and innovation (open/flexible). The ability to visualize and create a desired future for yourself is key to achieving it. Using vision and innovation, you brainstorm and envision new ways of progressing toward your desired result or even new desired results (think Captain Irving developing the Flying Classroom curriculum for children around the world to learn about aviation). Achieving your goal will likely require zigging and zagging rather than proceeding on a straight line. What unconventional steps can you take to move forward? What new approach might work even better than what you originally planned?

Imagine a result you aspire to achieve. That might be increasing revenue in your business unit by 10 percent this quarter, reducing overtime pay, coming up with a revolutionary new product idea, or developing a new way to increase visibility within your target market. Whatever your desired outcome, investing time and attention across the four categories described previously will generate the best results.

WHY IT'S IMPORTANT TO DIRECT INSPIRATION TO PERFORMANCE AND POSITIVE IMPACT

Part of the reason that Airbnb and TOMS shoes now exist is that humans have an innate desire to express their capabilities and to succeed, according to humanistic psychology.[6] That drive toward self-actualization is why sparks of inspiration are often sustained. Humanistic psychology, which became prominent in the mid-twentieth century, states that expressing one's own capabilities and creativity is human nature. That is, reaching our full potential and being successful is our ultimate goal.

> "When at a top level of inspiration, it feels incredibly productive—there is a sense of accomplishment; you feel like you're making the right moves. It's like an athlete when they are locked in and keep hitting their shots; it's coming a little easier. It's all that practice that they have been putting in, and sometimes it works better than other times, so when it all falls into place a little bit easier, that's an incredible feeling."
>
> —James Grady, Assistant Professor of Fine Arts and Design, Boston University

Striving toward a particular outcome we have envisioned is inspiring to us. The act of working toward a particular goal feeds that spark of inspiration. According to humanistic psychology, human beings set goals and strive to achieve them, seeking meaning, value, and creativity in the process.

Success also breeds success.[7] The more we work toward a goal and achieve it, the more we are inspired to continue striving. This process of goal accomplishment or achievement is essential to our own well-being, according to research by Martin Seligman.[8] Because as we strive toward achievement, we stretch our knowledge base and learn new skills. By attempting new experiences and succeeding, we boost self-efficacy. Our capacity for self-efficacy develops over time the more we try new things, try new experiences, and witness achievement.[9]

Self-efficacy results from realizing success from possibility and invincibility. The more we strive, the more we attempt to achieve, the more we are capable of achieving and the more we are willing to try. Teresa Amabile's and Steven Kramer's[10] progress principle supports this positive spiral. They show, in their book *The Progress Principle,* that progress toward achieving meaningful goals is hugely motivational. Again, the more we achieve, the more we want to keep going.

People who sustain their inspiration put it into practice in specific ways—not just taking random action but instead translating their spark of inspiration into action across the four categories that, together, lead to heightened positive results.

PUTTING THE FOUR BEHAVIOR CATEGORIES OF INTO PRACTICE

The idea of enacting behaviors in these four categories is simple and attractive. But what does it actually look like to do it?

USING INSPIRATION TO **DRIVE TO RESULTS**

KEY BEHAVIORS

- Set ambitious goals
- Gather and utilize resources

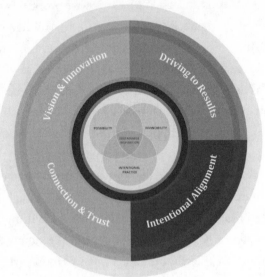

- Activate strengths
- Create a plan
- Clear obstacles to action
- Mobilize commitment

You are probably familiar with the story of the Jamaican bobsled team thanks to the movie *Cool Runnings*. Although the movie is a fictionalized version of the tale, what is less known is the behind-the-scenes work that it took to make the team a reality. Those efforts illustrate the drive to results.

The Jamaican Olympic bobsled team that competed at the 1988 Calgary Winter Olympics—the first time *any* Jamaican team had competed at a Winter Olympics—was actually inspired by a friendly challenge given to former US government official George Fitch. During a conversation with his tennis partner while on the island of Jamaica, Fitch commented that there was no reason Jamaican athletes couldn't be competitive at the summer *and* the Winter Olympics. After all, many of the skills and talents required for success carried over, he asserted. This idea inspired Fitch, who felt the notion of sending a team to the Winter Olympics might actually have merit.[11]

While contemplating what Olympic sport might be a fit for athletes used to tropical weather, Fitch heard about the annual pushcart derby being held the next day on the island. He realized the similarities between the pushcart race and bobsledding, which might make an Olympic appearance possible.

"Half the race is how quickly you can push a 600-pound object before you jump, and then the driver just lets the sled steer itself,"[12] he explained to ESPN. His was an ambitious goal, but he was confident the local athletes had the innate talent to make a strong showing.

That was the spark that led Fitch to begin a six-month effort to get a Jamaican team to compete in the Winter Olympics. But rather than let the idea fade, Fitch took steps to make a Jamaican bobsled team a reality. He first approached the Jamaica Olympic Association with the idea to form a bobsled team. They approved, so he began researching coaches and available training facilities, landing on Austria and Lake Placid, New York. Then he found his athletes.[13]

Legend has it that he recruited local track stars, but one of the Jamaican Olympians disputes that tale, explaining that Fitch turned to the Jamaican army and found his competitors there, according to Dudley "Tai" Stokes. Stokes and teammate Devon Harris were two members of the Jamaican Olympic team.

Fitch's goal was clear from the outset: get a Jamaican team to the 1988 Winter Olympics, which were less than six months away. Stokes confirms that the first time he laid eyes on a bobsled was in September 1987. In February 1988, he was competing at the Olympics. In between was intensive training.

As obstacles arose, Fitch found ways around them, because he was inspired by the goal of giving the team the best odds of success. He was truly driven.

Consider the following questions to develop behaviors that translate your spark of inspiration within the category of "drive to results":

- *What ambitious goals should we be focused on?*
- *Which of our individual strengths can each of us use to achieve them?*
- *What obstacles do we need to overcome to clear a pathway to success?*

USING INSPIRATION TO **CREATE INTENTIONAL ALIGNMENT**

KEY BEHAVIORS

- Know your values
- Protect your values
- Align your goals to your values
- Work with integrity and credibility

On December 1, 1955, Rosa Parks was arrested for her failure to give up her seat on a public bus to a white passenger. She was properly seated in the "colored" section, but since the "white" section was full, the bus driver asked her to give up her seat so that a Caucasian passenger could sit. She said no, not because she was tired, as has been widely reported, but because she had reached her own personal limits of mistreatment due to the color of her skin.

Her refusal triggered a series of events that ultimately led to the repeal of segregation on buses. But that action was not the result of a well-thought-out plan to raise awareness of segregation or to signal anything other than the fact that, as Parks says, she was just tired of giving in. She was inspired to take a stand and was arrested.

"I had not planned to get arrested. I had plenty to do without having to end up in jail. But when I had to face that decision, I didn't hesitate because I felt that we had endured that too long. The more we gave in, the more we complied with that kind of treatment, the more oppressive it became," she explained in an NPR interview in 1992, cited in an article on the website The Undefeated.[14]

Parks said no because it was in alignment with her own personal beliefs about fairness. She was sparked to take a stand against injustice, in the hopes that she might inspire others to do the same. That spark was then sustained by the actions she had to take to defend herself and to inspire others to take a similar stand in the name of civil rights.

This single act of defiance is now credited as one of the defining moments in the birth of the civil rights movement. Inspiration is contagious.

Consider the following questions to develop behaviors that translate your spark of inspiration in this category of "intentional alignment":

- *In order to achieve our goals, what do we need to learn or know?*
- *How do our goals align to a larger context, our team values, or our higher purpose?*
- *How will we persevere in achieving our goals, even when we have setbacks?*

USING INSPIRATION TO **BUILD CONNECTION AND TRUST**

KEY BEHAVIORS

- Connect and collaborate with others
- Find common ground and common goals
- Give trust to build trust
- Consider a broad array of others' perspectives
- Attend to others' emotions

One advantage the cofounders of the Bill & Melinda Gates Foundation have is their marriage of more than two decades, during which they've built deep connection and trust with one another. That bond allows them to work collaboratively on many issues the foundation is concerned with, but especially combating poverty and health issues in developing countries and reforming the US education system. Yet while the Gateses are of like mind when it comes to what needs to be done, they often approach the problems and the solutions from different angles, explains Melinda Gates. A *Fast Company* article describes this dynamic in the following way: "Bill looks at the statistics surrounding various issues, while Melinda operates with more intuition, looking at the human stories that data doesn't always reveal."[15]

Their complementary approaches to assessing situations and developing potential philanthropic solutions sustains their inspiration. Part of the reason for their success as partners appears to be their sincere interest in the other's perspective. Recognizing that they see things through different lenses, they appreciate hearing what the other has noticed. That appreciation for the other's view has strengthened their relationship and the work they've been able to do together through the foundation. It's a reflection of their connection and trust.

Said Melinda at a 2014 TED Talk: "I know when I come home, Bill is going to be interested in what I learned. And he knows when he comes home, I'll be interested. We have a collaborative relationship."[16]

Melinda Gates explains that their shared vision for the work to be done keeps the couple grounded and in alignment and this "grist" in their conversations helps them grow and deepen their understanding of each other. Despite differing opinions from time to time, their discussions and mutual goals help sustain their productive collaboration. That back and forth, information sharing, data analysis, and reflection on their priorities keeps them excited about making a positive difference in the world. Granted, they don't always succeed, but they keep striving.

Bill Gates describes one of their failures: "So we spent, you could say wasted, five years and $60 million on a path that had a very modest benefit" to treat leishmaniasis, a rare tropical parasitic disease. They lean on each other during such failures, to chart a course forward and build on what was learned. Staying connected to what matters to them, as a couple, keeps them inspired.

Consider the following questions to develop behaviors that translate your spark of inspiration in this category of "connection and trust":

- *What binds us as a team?*
- *How can we share success?*
- *How can we show care and trust for one another?*

USING INSPIRATION TO ADVANCE VISION AND INNOVATION

KEY BEHAVIORS

- Challenge status quo
- Create and communicate bold vision
- Develop a strategy
- Embrace innovation and change
- Activate positive emotions in self and others

A photograph on the front page of the *New York Times* of a Yazidi refugee and her children walking toward mountains in Iraq caught Hamdi Ulukaya off guard.[17] The CEO of Chobani says the image reminded him of his native Turkey, and the haunting, empty look in the woman's eyes inspired him to do something to help. He didn't know what he could do, but his own experience drove him to try and do something positive.

He started by calling the United Nations Refugee Agency and the International Rescue Committee the next day. He couldn't sit back and do nothing, he felt. Next, he created an organization, the Tent Foundation, to meet the humanitarian needs of refugees, which he believes is one of the biggest crises the world has faced since World War II.

As previously described, he also took steps to hire more refugees at Chobani, to create new opportunities for them. Today, 30 percent of the

Chobani staff are refugees, and twenty different languages are spoken inside the company's facilities. Says Ulukaya,

> If you want to build a company that truly welcomes people—including refugees—one thing you have to do is throw out this notion of 'cheap labor.' That's really awful. They're not a different group of people, they're not Africans or Asians or Nepalis. They're each just another team member. Let people be themselves, and if you have a cultural environment that welcomes everyone for who they are, it just works.[18]

Rather than ignoring the issue of refugees, Ulukaya was moved to consider what he could do to help people who were a lot like him—people who had left or been forced out of their homes, with nowhere to go and an uncertain future. He approached the issue from a macro- and a microperspective, helping care for refugees abroad and helping to settle and provide for refugees who had arrived in the Upstate New York community where Chobani was based.

Ulukaya was sparked to find a new way of helping refugees in need. Instead of providing a safe haven for vulnerable immigrants, he had the vision to provide a means for them to find their own success in the United States, all while advancing his own business.

Consider the following questions to develop behaviors that translate your spark of inspiration in this category of "vision and innovation":

- *If there were no constraints, what could we achieve?*
- *In what ways can we iterate, experiment, and learn from the process?*
- *In what ways can we activate positive emotions in ourselves?*

A FINAL NOTE ON AGILITY IN PERFORMANCE

Altogether, these four categories are essential to performance. Being able to move in and out of them, combine them, blend them, and monitor levels of each is critical to putting them into successful practice. We call this blending and movement across all four *agility*.

By focusing time and attention in all four of these categories, you can coax a spark of inspiration into a sustainable flame that leads to unexpected results and accomplishment. Focusing solely on one area won't be sufficient to sustain inspiration: attention needs to be paid to all four. The four categories are interdependent, interconnected; focusing too much on one category leads to lack of activation in another, which can stunt overall performance.

Effective agility, including recognizing and engaging in one category when it is particularly useful, requires self-awareness and swift adjustments from one category to another. In other words, you have to know which categories you are focusing on and how to shift your focus so you are balancing all four. Sometimes shifting across categories can feel jarring or unnatural, and yet in this discomfort lies the opportunity for stretch and growth.

For example, Ulukaya at Chobani was clearly innovative as we highlighted above. But he also showed a **drive to results** by building a successful company; **intentional alignment** by taking action to protect refugees and affect policy at the highest level, despite many obstacles and even death threats; and **connection and trust** by providing a good life for refugees, including employment, benefits, paid leave, and even equity in the company.[19]

Sustaining inspiration comes from achieving desired outcomes. Achieving desired outcomes comes from directing activity across the four categories described above. Take what inspires you into these four categories to create outcomes that feel good, that fulfill you, and that have lasting positive impact.

WORK IT
Create an Inspiration Action Plan

1. Identify a spark of inspiration you'd like to cultivate, expand, bring to fruition, and sustain.
2. Consider each of the four performance domains:

DOMAIN	ACTIONS: WHAT WILL YOU DO?	TIMING: WHEN WILL YOU DO IT?
Driving to results *What ambitious goals should we be focused on?* *Which of our individual strengths can each of us use to achieve them?* *What obstacles do we need to overcome to clear a pathway to success?*		
Intentional alignment *In order to achieve our goals, what do we need to learn or know?* *How do our goals align to a larger context, our team values, or our higher purpose?* *How will we persevere in achieving our goals, even when we have setbacks?* *What systems and infrastructure support do I need to be successful?*		
Connection and trust *What binds us as a team?* *How can we share success?* *How can we show care and trust for one another?*		
Strategy and innovation *If there were no constraints, what could we achieve?* *In what ways can we iterate, experiment, and learn from the process?* *In what ways can we activate positive emotions in ourselves?*		

CHAPTER EIGHT

GIVE YOUR INSPIRATION A BOOST

B y now you know what inspires you and what you can do to set the stage for more inspiration. Fortunately, inspiration isn't either present or absent; it's more like a spectrum or continuum. And there are things you can do, systems you can put in place, to kick inspiration up a notch once you're already feeling inspired. You can boost it. This is a third way you can intentionally practice and sustain inspiration in concert with resparking the engines and directing inspiration to positive actions.

Inspiration isn't either present or absent; it's more like a spectrum or continuum.

By boosting feelings of inspiration, you can effectively turbocharge that experience. When you take inspiration up a level, you become even more engaged; you see results faster, and those results have an even greater impact.

Boosting your inspiration is a lot like fanning a campfire. To get the fire started, you strike a match and light the kindling. When you add some sticks, you're giving the fire energy to sustain it long enough to cook marshmallows for s'mores. The fire will burn for a while and then eventually burn out if you leave it alone. But if you add more pieces of wood, the fire becomes hot enough to cook hotdogs and hamburgers. That accelerant is your inspiration boost.

So what kinds of inspiration boosts are out there? We've identified three: positive rituals, accountability, and social support.

POSITIVE RITUALS

Positive rituals are actions you take to prepare yourself for a task, a process you go through that lifts you emotionally and gets you primed to perform. These rituals keep success uppermost in your mind.

In 1726, at the young age of twenty, Benjamin Franklin decided it was time to take control of his life; he wanted to be a better person. He had determined that his life wasn't going the way he wanted it to and that he needed to make some changes. Self-improvement was his goal.[1]

So he identified thirteen values and characteristics to which he aspired, calling them his thirteen virtues. They included temperance, silence, order, resolution, frugality, industry, sincerity, justice, moderation, cleanliness, tranquility, and chastity. At the urging of a friend, he added humility (since he had little, apparently).[2]

To encourage himself to pay more attention to each virtue, Franklin created a grid containing the seven days of the week across the top and then listed each virtue down the side. He then tracked his performance on each virtue daily as a tool for self-improvement. Each day when he failed to display the designated virtue required a tick mark in his journal; his goal was never having to mark a failure.

Franklin recognized that attempting to address all thirteen virtues simultaneously would only lead to failure, so, instead, he focused on one virtue each week, cycling through all of them four times in a year. Such repetition was designed to improve overall performance across all virtues.

Franklin succeeded in creating a ritual for himself that helped remind him of his bigger goals. Rituals of positive behaviors and habits help build positivity and focus into our days. They can be as mundane as making your bed first thing in the morning to start the day off with a simple accomplished task,[3] or they can be higher level, like Franklin's virtue tracking or a modern equivalent of writing in a gratitude journal every day.

Positive rituals help sustain inspiration.

Decorated Olympic swimmer Michael Phelps exhibits a number of positive rituals at the pool before a race. His process usually begins about two and a half hours before he competes with a high-calorie meal, followed by stretching, a warm-up lap, getting into his bodysuit (which is so tight it takes twenty minutes to squeeze into), and about thirty minutes of listening to hip-hop music on his headphones. These positive rituals prepare him, and when he hits the water, he is physically, mentally, and emotionally focused on the task at hand.[4]

Other athletes find confidence in rituals rooted in superstition, choosing to wear the same pair of socks or not shave for fear of doing something to jinx their track record of success. Their rituals often include doing the exact same thing in preparation for a big game as they did the last time the team won. Sports teams often huddle and repeat a rousing mantra before a game. Like other rituals, these are actions for honing and directing your energy toward the desired result. While such behavior may seem silly to some of us, the sense of control we gain from following these recipes for success makes us more confident and optimistic about our prospects for greatness, which can actually lead to greater success.

We can learn from elite athletes' performance rituals and translate them to our work. Many of us have routines, even informal ones, we go through prior to an important event, such as a major presentation or negotiation. Business teams are increasingly using early morning huddles—brief standing meetings held in a circle—to kick off the day and get everyone on the team aligned before beginning work.[5] Some teachers have developed special handshakes or greetings to welcome their students into the classroom each morning so they start the day off feeling positive and connected. These are just a few examples to offer ideas. As you can imagine, rituals are highly personal; a meaningful ritual to one of us wouldn't have the same impact for you. Building in daily positive rituals that can become habitual and give you a little boost every day is a way to sustain inspiration toward your larger goals over time.

But rituals aren't the only tool for boosting inspiration. Adding accountability is another way.

ACCOUNTABILITY

We can all benefit from some support in implementing our intentional practice of inspiration. One way to do that is to build in accountability to another person for what you are planning to do. If you want to impress your manager, tell a coworker you plan to get the draft report on your manager's desk a day early. Ask your coworkers to check with you to confirm you did it. Want to speak up more in meetings? Tell your team or promise your coach or mentor that you'll make the effort and then check in with them on it. Declaring your commitment to taking a certain action significantly increases the odds that you'll do it.[6] Being accountable to someone else for a particular behavior change helps set up a structure to support you. Individuals naturally strive to act in ways that are consistent with what they say they will do. You can lean on this desire for integrity to prop up your plans.

It works the same way for inspiration.

When you want to sustain your practice of inspiration around a particular goal or area in your work or life, you can use tools to set up checkpoints on your path to success, such as interim due dates for big projects or deadlines.

It is on this premise that entrepreneur Angela Jia Kim leads her employees at Savor Beauty, a New York–based natural skincare and spa brand inspired by Korean beauty rituals.

Every Wednesday, her HQ team gathers for a meet-and-work day where they share successes, brainstorm solutions to challenges that arise, share new goals and initiatives, and leverage individual skills to support one another. They work as partners, in teams, with Kim to course-correct, and they push one another to achieve their best. The Wednesday meetings provide a "themed day" when everyone knows they will be held accountable for their weekly goals in a supportive environment. There's also a healthy dose of competition: if you know your colleague shows up week after week meeting her goals, it inspires you to do the same. The team increases their collective sense of possibility and invincibility through these conversations, and they count on one another for accountability to enact these.[7]

SOCIAL SUPPORT

The support of other people can be an incredible lift factor that boosts your inspiration, either on its own or in combination with positive rituals and accountability.

Thousands of different social organizations exist with missions around connecting members to support one another in meaningful ways. The Entrepreneurs' Organization (EO),[8] one of our clients, leverages positive rituals, accountability, and social support to provide EO members with inspiration boosts. The

> "I really think it just comes down to the fact that we're social creatures and that we're incredibly empathetic, more so than we even realize, with each other. There needs to be that feedback loop of energy or inspiration, going in and out."
>
> —Leslie Kruempel, Mission Executive, Organic Valley

organization's paying members support one another through EO's established network of thousands of entrepreneurs, receive and participate in peer-to-peer learning and live events, and benefit from connections to mentors and experts. Another such organization is IVY: The Social University, which has built a network designed to inspire new knowledge and connection through curated events. The stated mission of IVY is "to trigger transformative ideas and collaborations that lead to unprecedented human unity, progress, and fulfillment."[9]

Boosting inspiration can be easier when you're part of a group, surrounded by people who want to see you succeed—conspirators in your success. These like-minded people fuel your positive feelings and confidence, giving your emotions a lift that enhances inspiration. In addition to your own personal cheerleading squad, surrounding yourself with people who genuinely care about you and your well-being can also boost inspiration. People who are there to encourage you, listen when you're struggling, and offer hugs of support and who don't judge you for your weaknesses can also lift your mood and accelerate inspiration.

Thought Experiment: What to Do When Relationships Aren't Inspiring—Sustaining the Positive Emotions in a Relationship

- Work extra hard to see positives and create opportunities for positive experiences and connections.
- Remember that we tend to give negative emotions more attention and weight than we give positive ones. Intentionally practice downplaying or forgiving weaknesses or things that you find frustrating.
- Work within realistic expectations: relationships don't have to be entirely or constantly inspiring. There are likely to be sparks of inspiration and sources of sustained inspiration and everything else in between.
- Always be looking for spark opportunities in your relationships: find them, engineer them, celebrate them!

COMBINING WAYS TO BOOST INSPIRATION

COACHING

We have found coaching provides this inspiration power punch by combining all three ways to boost social support, accountability, and positive rituals. Having a partner to hold you accountable for deadlines, set challenges, and stay true to the inspiration that drives you can be helpful for sustaining it over time. Companies now frequently invest in coaching as a way to help develop or accelerate the development of employee performance. In fact, between 25 and 40 percent of Fortune 500 companies hire executive coaches.[10] Part of that coaching process often involves discovering or clarifying what inspires the coachee at work. Most people are doing work that inspires them in some way or another, and coaches help them fan the flames of inspiration, set meaningful goals, and design positive practices—or rituals—that support their growth. A big part of the coaching process is helping employees get or stay connected to what matters most to them, rising above the day-to-day tedium. Research in coaching shows benefits like increased performance, especially related to goal achievement, and better work-related attitudes, well-being, and coping skills.[11] Our coaching clients and interviewees frequently mention inspiration—either resparking or sustaining—as being a key outcome of coaching.

If you are looking for a way to boost your inspiration, coaching is worth exploring. If your company or organization does not typically offer it, try looking for other opportunities like asking a mentor or friend for some coaching or participating in a peer-coaching group. For example, one client of ours mentioned starting a peer-coaching group over fifteen years ago that continues to meet biweekly via video conference for conversations. She said it has been a driving force in her life and career. Remember, it is critical to first inspire yourself if you are looking to inspire others.

PULSE MEETINGS

At InspireCorps we developed and use a tool for one-on-one meetings that activates inspiration through an everyday lens of work and includes positive rituals, accountability, and social support. We call these 4-3-2-1 meetings, as a reminder that there are four steps, with the first step addressing four agenda items, the second step three, and so on. Counting down:

The first step is to share four pieces of good news. What are you working on that you love or is particularly challenging and rewarding, something you want to acknowledge or thank others for? What huge advance or progress do you want to report?

The next step is to share three top priorities and key updates. Is your project on track, delayed, or ahead? Discuss and clarify pathways that are unclear. What is needed to progress? Solicit requests for collaboration.

Next is to share two aspects of your work that you are really enjoying or are learning from. It could be a project you like so much that you lost track of time while working on it or one that has presented an enjoyable challenge. Or it could be something that didn't go as planned and that you might do differently next time.

Finally, you close the meeting with one piece of positive and constructive feedback. Note something you particularly appreciate or witnessed that you thought was extraordinary or well executed and that inspired you—along with some constructive feedback and a suggestion for how to have more impact in the future.

ENEMIES OF INSPIRATION

Despite what we may do to sustain inspiration over time, the regular challenges, frustrations, and difficulties of life can get in the way. There are three types of energy we manage (physical, mindset, emotional) to sustain inspiration—and we will explore these in further detail in the following chapter. These three areas of energy can also be what we call "enemies of inspiration" if they dip too low. To reduce the impact of such enemies, we need to train ourselves to be more self-aware—to recognize when they exist and what we can do about it. Next, we explore three common "enemies of inspiration"—emotional, cognitive, and physical—and how to address each of them.

EMOTIONAL ENEMIES OF INSPIRATION

Emotional enemies are unpleasant feelings that interfere with or block inspiration. It becomes harder to be inspired or sustain inspiration when we're weighed down by these emotionally draining factors.

Negative moods. When left unchecked negative moods can lead to obsessive worrying or rumination that gets in the way of inspiration. Negative emotions might include jealousy, envy, apathy, insecurity, anger, fear, or anxiety. While these emotions provide us with important information to process and pay attention to, when left to fester over time, they can turn into moods (longer-term states) that get in the way of sustained inspiration.[12]

Amygdala hijack. When we're grabbed unexpectedly by a high-intensity emotion signaling a threat, we react with fight, flight, or freeze. We let our emotions take control, we go on the attack, we run from the situation, or we are paralyzed. But we certainly don't feel inspired or uplifted.[13]

Combativeness or defensiveness. Sometimes we look for conflict when it doesn't exist or we feel unnecessarily threatened. Spoiling for a fight or digging in our heels when getting useful feedback can distract us from potential learning or inspiration.

Abusive or corrosive relationships. The impact that others have on us can't be discounted. Relationships that damage us mentally, physically, or emotionally can also damage our ability to create sustainable inspiration.

Ambivalence in relationships. Not knowing how people feel about us, or not knowing how we feel about them, creates ambivalence that can lead to feelings of uncertainty and insecurity, and blocking inspiration.

Loss. When something that is inspiring is taken from you (losing a job, losing a relationship), in that moment you can experience extreme distress, confusion, or disappointment. As you process that grief and loss, those experiences can eventually lead to inspiration, but in the moment, they can be hard to overcome.

Isolation. Negative emotions can make us want to dissociate from others, to just be alone. A need for solitude is often accompanied by the rumination discussed above and can be helpful to some extent. However, if it turns into dysfunctional withdrawal or escapism, this shuts out many of the possible engines of inspiration.

Numbing. Avoiding or escaping difficult emotions to dull them is a barrier to feeling a full spectrum of emotions including inspiration.

What to Do about Emotional Enemies of Inspiration

Fortunately, you can constructively manage and process unpleasant or negative emotions so that you can continue to support your ongoing practice of inspiration.

Feel them. It's important to feel unpleasant or difficult emotions when they are appropriate, such as grief, sadness, and anxiety, rather than pushing them away and denying them. Give yourself permission to fully process them in the moment, to move through the anger, fear, or loss.

Experiencing them and naming them, perhaps with a friend or therapist, can help you move through them in a healthy way.

Explore them. If you don't know why negativity has become pervasive in your life, work to find out why these emotions are so prevalent. Has something changed? Is there a theme? What information are the emotions telling you? For example, perhaps some of your core values are being denied, causing you pain—the negative emotions can help you understand this and change it.

Identify the cause. Recognize when we're feeling negative emotions and what is causing them (such as anger caused by injustice, sadness caused by a loss, fear caused by danger). Trace back to find the source of the emotion. If you're feeling anger, what's the injustice? If you're feeling sadness, what's the loss? If you're feeling anxiety, what's the danger?[14]

Shift away from them. Developing methods to manage feelings of negativity so you can release yourself from them to allow other emotions in is called *emotional agility*. Susan David's work on emotional agility suggests four steps to "unhooking" negative emotions from your evaluations and values, so you can move past them.[15] They include recognizing your patterns, labeling those thoughts and emotions, accepting them, and acting on your values once you have the distance to see what's going on. Separating your emotions from the situation is key to finding new strategies for dealing with them.

A very important note about emotions. It's normal for everyone, adults and children alike, to experience a wide range of emotions—from joy and contentment to frustration, anxiety, and sadness.[16] Sometimes individuals struggle with managing their emotions to a point where they need professional support or clinical intervention (i.e., therapy, medication). Previous suggestions, as well as approaches like social and emotional learning (SEL) programs[17] and tools like Yale's Mood Meter App,[18] are helpful for people of all ages to learn strategies for being more self-aware and managing their emotions. These types of strategies and knowledge complement professional support like therapy but don't replace it when individuals need it.

COGNITIVE ENEMIES OF INSPIRATION

There are appropriate times and places for different types of mindsets. There are times when it can be productive or helpful to think critically, for example, while in other instances being critical can stall progress. None of these is inherently dysfunctional or bad. Our point here is that some mindsets can interfere with sustaining inspiration:

Constraint mindset. A constraint mindset focuses on limitations or challenges rather than opportunity and abundance. This type of thinking is more oriented to evaluating than seeing possibilities; it focuses on what can't be done rather than what can. It is an inability to dream big, to visualize success. Cynicism is an example. Part of the challenge in overcoming a constraint mindset is the story you're telling yourself. If you create a negative story about yourself, such as that you're bad at math or you have no money, you'll begin to believe it, others will believe it, and it can shape your emotions, decision-making, and thinking going forward.

Closed mindset. A closed mindset has a lack of openness to new and different ways of thinking or seeing things. It has a dislike of or inability to listen to and consider opposing views. A closed mind judges the self and others, going beyond observation to form opinions and having a lack of respect for the difference in values.

Fixed mindset. A fixed mindset perceives abilities and capacity as unchangeable or unchanging. There is no opportunity or capability for growth or learning beyond the current reality.[19]

Negative thinking. Negative thinking occurs when your thoughts are predominantly pessimistic; such thinking often accompanies bad moods. Negative thinking can originate from different sources, including

- *Negative self-talk.* What you tell yourself about the situation. This sets up an expectation that the outcome will not be what you wanted, that the news will be bad.
- *Negativity bias.* The human inclination to weight negative experiences and emotions more heavily than positive ones. It's an adaptive function that has helped humans survive over centuries but doesn't always serve us in modern situations.[20]

Values or behavioral conflict. When things we believe in are in conflict with one another or when our behavior is in conflict with our beliefs, we experience unrest in the form of cognitive dissonance. There is pressure to resolve the conflict, which pushes out opportunities for inspiration to take hold because we are so focused on resolving the conflict.

Upward social comparison. Constantly comparing ourselves unfavorably to others can lead to insecurity and negative emotions or feeling like we're less worthy or successful than others.

Lack of direction. Diffuse or unclear objectives or purpose equates to a lack of direction or an absence of purpose and plan.

What to Do about Cognitive Enemies of Inspiration
As with emotional enemies of inspiration, there are remedies to address cognitive enemies of inspiration:

Recognize the mindset. First, recognize the mindset that is getting in the way. Name it, using the previous terms or come up with your own terminology.

Assess the impact of your mindset. How are these thoughts impacting you right now (emotions, behaviors, energy)? What is the impact on how you think about yourself? What evidence do you have for these thoughts? Are they true? Can you be sure they are true?

Interrupt your pattern of thinking. Disrupt your current pattern of thinking by questioning it. Ask a friend for evidence that your current thinking is true (or not). Take a break from what you're doing and do something positive (use your strengths). Speak out loud, or to a friend, what you're thinking or the alternatives you are considering.

Go to your purpose, your values. Once you have disrupted your current mindset, with a clear head, go back to your purpose and values. What means the world to you? Are you being the person you want to be? Your best self? Are you thinking and acting in ways that align with your values and your purpose?

Write a new story. The field of narrative psychology has discovered that your stories "can shape your future"[21] and can unknowingly support or hamper your own growth and success. However, the concept of prospection suggests that we can conceive of multiple possible futures for ourselves, different potential outcomes, from a hopeful perspective.[22] Narrative is powerful in shaping our beliefs. Examine the story you're telling yourself in your current mindset and then rewrite the story using your purpose and values-based mindset. When we craft stories for the future that are hopeful and forward thinking, they can lead to different actions toward this future.

Self-compassion. We are our own worst critics; no one else is harder on us than ourselves. To combat this tendency, we need to embrace self-compassion, says Dr. Kristin Neff.[23] Self-compassion involves extending kindness and understanding to yourself rather than harsh criticism, seeing your experiences as part of the larger human experience rather than as separate and isolating, and holding those painful thoughts and feelings in balanced awareness rather than ruminating and overidentifying with them. Pose questions to yourself such as

- *What kindness can I extend to myself right now? If I were my best friend listening to this, what would I say?*
- *Look at this situation from the grand scheme of things (30K-foot level). What do I see now?*
- *Yes, I have faults—and what are some of my strengths? Unique attributes? Positive qualities and talents? What am I grateful for?*

PHYSICAL ENEMIES OF INSPIRATION

Even when your mind is clear and positive, and you have access to positive emotions, inspiration can still be thwarted by a variety of different physical factors, such as

Overreaching commitments. Being in a comfortable secure state is the best place for learning. But when too many obligations overhelm us, we can quickly move from comfort into a panic zone, which makes it impossible to learn because we're too busy retreating or controlling our fight, flight, or freeze instincts.

Fatigue. Poor energy management due to lack of sleep, movement, or proper nutrition can lead to fatigue. A lack of ability to change physical and emotional fatigue results in shutdown. We also make the situation worse by relying so heavily on our smartphone, resulting in too much screen time. Where physical activity can be an engine of inspiration, the reverse can hamper it.

Limited environment. A lack of exposure to new, stimulating, or interesting milieus can stifle inspiration. It can be self-imposed, by choosing to never go anywhere, or situation-imposed, such as a lack of financial resources or a physical restriction, such as an injury or incarceration.

Hedonic treadmill. The hedonic treadmill is a concept that explains how an activity that once brought lift no longer generates those positive emotions at the same levels. People become habituated to stimuli, and things we once found pleasurable become less so through overexposure. As a result, we have to work harder and diversify our experience to create the same level of positive emotions again. Our mind and body adapt to a standard and then that has to be exceeded.[24]

What to Do about Physical Enemies of Inspiration

Of the three inspiration enemies, physical may actually be the easiest to address. There are a number of things you can do to refuel and shift gears with respect to your body.

Attend to your physical energy. Get more sleep, if that's what you've been lacking. Or get some exercise to lift your mood. Or eat something healthy to fuel your body. (See Chapter 9 on energy management.)

Attend to your stamina. Since people experience stamina in different ways, there may be different approaches that will work for you. Knowing what your individual physical energy boosters are is step one, as well as what will have the biggest impact. Will taking a nap do more than taking a walk when you're in need of a mood boost? Or will a nap only make you more tired and lethargic? Does the length of the nap or pace of the walk matter? You need to crack that code for yourself.

Unplug. Research suggests that screen time—computers, tablets, smartphones—interferes with sleep cycles and can distract us, making us feel more stressed and socially isolated.[25] So cut the cord and read a book or reconnect face-to-face with the people in your life to lift your spirits.

Reclaim your calendar. Don't allow your schedule to be controlled by others. Instead, choose how you spend your time. Look at your to-do list and identify which tasks are important and which are urgent—there's a big difference. Urgent activities, such as meeting a deadline for buying concert tickets, can sometimes hijack what's important, such as watching your child's basketball game. Let your values guide your commitments (who and what gets your attention).

Block off untouchable time.[26] This is time that you carve out for yourself that no one else can intrude on for things that are important but not urgent. This is your time for creative output or strategic thinking (and is consistent with the inspiration engine of unstructured time).

Create patterns in your schedule. Rather than approaching every day as a blank slate, establish patterns or rituals to help you get more done. For example, only read your e-mail from 8:00 to 9:00 a.m. and 4:00 to 5:00 p.m. Or if you know that emergencies generally erupt around lunchtime, keep that time open to attend to what typically comes up.

Let go of unimportant tasks. There is a physical cost to an overcrowded mind, so what can you let go of to enable yourself to better focus your thoughts and energy on results? What tasks or activities can be delegated to others?

Sometimes before you can boost your level of inspiration, you need to first reduce negativity and get your mood to at least a neutral place. That requires pivoting away from enemies of inspiration. At the same time, you can be thoughtful about designing opportunities to *boost* your inspiration regularly through connection to other people, accountability structures or partners, and positive rituals that help you stay on track.

Thought Experiment: Inspired Thinking

- How can you help others maintain their inspiration? Do you know someone who would benefit from an accountability partner? Or some peer coaching?
- Thinking about others can help you get clearer about what inspires you and what helps you sustain your inspiration.
- Consider reaching out to that person for coffee or a chat; have a conversation about ways you can be a social support or accountability partner for that person's inspiration lift.
- Take note about what resonates for you. Which of these would be useful to you and in which ways do you differ from your friend in how you are impacted by each lift opportunity?

WORK IT
Inspiration Boost Plan

Typically, inspiration boosts and enemies of inspiration coexist, adding to and detracting from your level of inspiration simultaneously. By knowing this and being attuned to them, you can deliberately cultivate the lift factors and reduce the negative impact of the enemies. This process will guide you:

What are the lift factors and enemies of inspiration that are active for you right now?

First, catalog the lift factors available to you:

Positive rituals

Accountability

Social support

Take a minute be grateful for these forces in your life. To whom do you want to convey that gratitude?

Second, identify an enemy of inspiration that is active in your life right now, emotional, mental, or physical. Follow the steps previously identified for overcoming that enemy.

Note what works well to reduce the influence that enemy has on your inspiration.

What will you do the next time it surfaces?

CHAPTER NINE

MANAGE YOUR ENERGY: BODY, MINDSET, AND EMOTIONS

"Fatigue makes cowards of us all."

—Vince Lombardi

nspiration requires a reservoir of aliveness and openness, so energy management plays a large role in sustaining it over time. Left unattended, energy can wane, so it needs to be monitored and replenished regularly.

Energy is the "currency of
high performance."

Researchers Jim Loehr and Tony Schwartz argue that energy is the "currency of high performance," and effective energy management enables great performance, health, and happiness. "The number of hours in a day is fixed, but the quantity and quality of energy available to us is not.

It is our most precious resource. The more we take responsibility for the energy we bring to the world, the more empowered and productive we become."[1] Often when people talk about energy, they think of it in physical terms—the energy in your body. But energy is not just a physical state. Instead, Loehr and Schwartz say it consists of four dimensions: physical, mental, emotional, spiritual. Not only that, but they argue that these different types of energies impact one another: for example, lower physical energy takes a toll on emotional energy. It makes sense; we are more likely to be irritable when tired. Informed by Loehr and Schwartz and our own research and work with clients, we focus on three distinct forms of energy that need to be managed to sustain inspiration over time: body, mindset, and emotions. In our framework, spiritual energy falls within these three.

To be clear, energy and inspiration are not the same thing. Rather, being energized is a necessary (though not sufficient) condition for sustaining inspiration. Physical, mental, and emotional energy fuel inspiration-related states in the following ways:

- **Possibility.** As a positive, optimistic high-energy state, possibility requires energy to achieve and to sustain when depleted.
- **Invincibility.** Passion and confidence underscore feelings of invincibility; both are harder to sustain when depleted and require energy to maintain.
- **Intentional practice.** Intentional practice of inspiration takes focus, attention, and self-discipline, much like a violinist practicing day after day requires both brain power and physical energy. As energy wanes, intentional practice becomes more difficult.

In this chapter, we explore all three dimensions of energy and how to create resets that help sustain inspiration through energy management.

MANAGING ENERGY THROUGH THE BODY: NUTRITION, SLEEP, ACTIVITY

It can be very difficult to maintain inspiration over time when you are feeling physically depleted, sleep deprived, or hungry. Providing your body with the fuel and opportunity to rejuvenate regularly lays the necessary groundwork for being able to spark inspiration at will and to sustain it. In an example from parole board judges in Israel, researchers Shai Danzigera, Jonathan Levav, and Liora Avnaim-Pessoa show[2] how depleted physical energy can impact performance. The *New York Times* reported that prisoners who came before the parole board early in the morning or right after the lunch break had a 65 percent chance of being granted parole. That percentage dropped steadily as the morning wore on, hitting 0 percent, or close to it, right before lunch. Rejuvenated following their midday meal, however, the judges then started the afternoon session granting prisoners freedom 65 percent of the time, with those odds then dropping again throughout the afternoon.[3]

The judges revived their physical and mental energy by refueling at lunch, showing it's important to eat! But, of course, what you eat also matters for keeping your energy (and thus your openness to inspiration) up.

NUTRITION

Nutrition and vitamins also impact energy levels, making inspiration more or less likely. The type of food you eat and the time of day you consume it affects how energized you feel and for how long. Experts recommend eating every four to six hours, relying on complex carbs and omega-3 fatty acids more than processed foods and caffeine, which boost your blood sugar in the short term but subside quickly. Iron, folic acid, and thiamine are also essential for proper brain functioning and mood management.[4] Vitamin D, and the lack thereof, also affects mood and energy levels. Research on sunlight found that depression can occur when vitamin D is depleted, especially during winter months.[5]

Everyone's nutritional needs are different, and yours may need to be determined in consultation with a nutritionist or medical professional. What is true for all, though, is that ensuring your body receives sufficient nutrients helps manage energy over time. Still, sustenance isn't the only thing your body needs to perform optimally. Sleep is also essential for your body to restore its energy reserves.

SLEEP

Media mogul Arianna Huffington has recently become a sleep evangelist, extolling the importance of a good night's sleep to everyone who will listen. Sleep is essential if we want to perform effectively, she believes. The benefits of sufficient sleep are many, and according to her: "Empathy increases, our decision-making improves . . . As a result, every aspect of our lives improves."[6]

Huffington was once sleep deprived. She was also much like the majority of Americans—very few adults in the United States are getting enough sleep, reports Gallup.[7] The average American gets 6.8 hours of sleep a night, when at least 7 hours is really necessary to be fully functional. Unfortunately, 40 percent of Americans routinely get less than 6 hours of sleep and are, essentially, sleep deprived. It's ironic to think that many of us could be more poised for inspiration just by sleeping another hour every night.

ACTIVITY

Physical movement is another source of energy. Research has shown that exercise releases endorphins, which enhance our mood. That elevated mood then makes sparks of inspiration more likely or, once sparked, helps sustain them. Movement can include individual activity, such as swimming laps, or group exercise, such as yoga or Zumba. In the workplace, activity can be integrated into the day by taking the stairs rather than the elevator or implementing walking meetings. Dance, or moving in community, can be especially powerful, perhaps harkening back to ancient times when tribes danced around fires in preparation for a hunt or in celebration of success. (Note that dancing in unison activates three inspiration engines at one time—"sharing a group mission," "activating body movement and presence," and "belonging.")

> Physical energy management through nutrition, activity, and sleep is essential to high-quality and inspired performance in the workplace.

Elite athletes understand the importance of managing their physical energy through good nutrition, sleep, and taking care of their bodies: they have to so that they can physically perform at their best. And yet we have found that many of our clients compartmentalize physical energy from their jobs. They think of exercise and eating healthy as desirable but not necessary, meaning they get pushed off the to-do list by higher priority items. We argue that paying attention to our bodies, including eating well and getting necessary rest and movement, helps us monitor our overall physical energy levels and keep them at a high level, which optimizes our ability to become and stay inspired.

MANAGING ENERGY THROUGH YOUR MINDSET

Mindset can also impact energy, which in turn can impact our ability to sustain inspiration. Our mindset reflects how we approach our current reality—the stories we create and tell about ourselves or others or the stories we hear from others. When in a negative or judgmental mindset about ourselves, others, or a situation, energy is likely to drop: you will likely see faults more easily than positive qualities. Likewise, when in a more positive, learning-oriented mindset, energy is higher. Therefore, the ability to both identify what kind of mindset we're in and shift the story as needed is a powerful approach to sustaining energy and inspiration.

Although your mindset is shaped by your circumstances and influences, it is not cast in stone. You can shift your mindset to be more aligned to your purpose, values, and what drives you. The "connecting to and voicing values and purpose" engine energizes us to continue striving toward our life's purpose. In fact, in doing so, you can expand your capacity for inspiration.

> "If I think about the biggest super-power or almost only skill that I've had to lean on, it's storytelling, over and over, whether it's with my co-founders and we are questioning the right thing to do at the right time, or in recruiting, whether it's convincing investors that this is inevitable and possible. It's all story-telling. What is the story that you're telling yourself that's different than the other cofounder, or the engineer, or the designer, or the salesperson? And tailoring the overall message, and trying out thousands of different stories, and helping people actually rewire the story, in their mind, of what they're doing and why they're doing it."
>
> —Alex White, Vice President of Content and Programming, Pandora

Stanford researcher Carol Dweck and her team demonstrated this when they discovered that there are two types of mindsets: fixed and growth.[8] Dweck found that when students believed they had the capacity to improve, they put in the effort and succeeded. They had a growth mindset. However, students who believed that their capabilities and control were fixed or limited did not invest the extra effort and did not progress. They had a fixed mindset. They gave up trying to change their circumstances while those with a growth mindset continued to strive for improvement and change—and achieved it.

Nelson Mandela is a prime example. Most people, when sentenced to life in prison, might succumb to the environment and accept their fate.

Not Mandela. Soon after being sentenced to life in prison in 1964, he arrived at the place that he would call home for decades and almost immediately began encouraging small acts of rebellion among the prisoners. Although he was behind bars, his anti-apartheid work and rebellion continued unabated. For example, instead of rushing to the quarry to crush gravel each day, the prisoners slowed their walk to the point that they would barely reach the quarry before it was time to return. The prison guards eventually had to negotiate with Mandela to get the prisoners to quicken their pace. He refused to be a prisoner and instead became a leader; he shifted his mindset to look for opportunities to make the lives of his fellow captives better.[9] Despite being in prison for twenty-seven years, Mandela kept his mind and spirit alive by focusing on what he could accomplish behind bars: "I am fundamentally an optimist. Whether that comes from nature or nurture, I cannot say. Part of being optimistic is keeping one's head pointed toward the sun, one's feet moving forward."[10]

But mindset shifts like Mandela's don't have to involve traumatic life events, such as imprisonment. They can also occur in the moment, based on the situation. As we discussed in Chapter 8 ("enemies of inspiration"), when you notice negative or self-defeating messages you are telling yourself, you have an opportunity to recraft the story by remembering what matters to you the most.

MANAGING ENERGY THROUGH YOUR EMOTIONS

Stories and mindsets affect not just your cognitive energy but also your emotions, the third source of energy. While positive emotions tend to generate energy, negative emotions deplete it, making inspiration a more challenging state to reach. Researchers at the Yale Center for Emotional Intelligence found that positive, high-energy emotions are more effective for brainstorming and inductive reasoning—considering *possibilities*, an important part of inspiration. On the flip side, negative, low-energy emotions, while adaptive and helpful for critical thinking, can get in the way of cultivating inspiration.[11]

The ability to take charge of our own emotions, to effectively process ones that are difficult, and to generate positive emotions when needed is a skill called *emotion management*.[12] Managing emotions does not mean trying to be happy or positive all the time. In fact, difficult emotions, which are a natural part of the human experience, can provide us with information about what is most important to us. As psychologist Susan David says: "Discomfort is the price of admission to a meaningful life."[13] However, we need to be emotionally agile, to process daily stresses and frustrations swiftly, generate upbeat emotions when needed, and sustain them when faced with challenges.

Music is one of the quickest ways to shift emotions and generate sparks of inspiration. A company called 001[14] (pronounced "double-oh-one") has made a business out of engineering positive emotional experiences through music. It brings together groups and teams of employees and partners them with musicians in a recording studio, where they witness and make music together. The experience is designed to inspire, by making people part of the creative process as a collective—working together to create music and listen to music (engines of "shared experiences" and "new perspectives").

Retreats are another type of experience that can stir up positive emotions or memories that can refill your energy reserves and help sustain inspiration. People often use personal retreats and meditations as a way to manage their emotions over time or recharge. Attending a retreat is an intentional practice of placing yourself in environments designed to create positive emotions. In fact, twice a year Jen goes on retreat to recurring events in October and June. One is a rich stimulating reunion and conference at the University of Pennsylvania and the other a quiet meditative escape at Tydeman farm in the Hudson Valley with friends. She knows that she needs this time to reboot and reset deeply. Participating in these retreats has become an intentional practice to get away from the daily grind of work, so that her emotions stay high and she's in a good place to create inspiration.

While there are many types of experiences that can generate positive emotions, you know best what types of situations do this for you.

The important skill to develop is noticing when your emotional energy is low—noticing when you feel irritated, bored, apathetic, discouraged, or pessimistic—and, when ready, doing something to shift your emotional energy back up to a higher quality.

THE IMPORTANCE OF SELF-AWARENESS

Just as monitoring your inspiration levels is critical to sustaining them, part of the ability to sustain your inspiration comes from monitoring your energy levels so inspiration doesn't wane. Being aware of your energy levels and when changes occur—either when you receive a boost of additional energy that fuels you or when you're feeling unmotivated or tired—it is essential to recognize when you need to respark your inspiration and/or engage it by directing it to positive outcomes.

There are numerous tools and technologies that have been developed to aid in self-awareness. Many wristwatches, for example, report on physical activity, heart rate, and other physical characteristics. The FitBit monitors footsteps. The Mood Meter App[15] helps you track your mood and assess whether how you are feeling is ideal for the situation at hand or if you need to shift. You can use these types of tools to improve self-awareness or develop your own systems and processes to monitor your own energy levels. When we're able to monitor the energy that comes from our bodies, mindsets, and emotions to keep ourselves energized, upbeat, and open, we can sustain inspiration more easily.

INTENTIONAL PRACTICE OF ENERGY MANAGEMENT: RESETS

We know that our emotions, mindset, and body are important for keeping inspiration high, but how, exactly, do we boost or renew our energy—especially when life gets busy and stressed? The key is to focus on intentional practice, or consciously choosing to refuel our body, mind, and energy levels. That's how we sustain inspiration over time.

A common approach is to focus on one specific area at a time, such as committing to getting more sleep or drinking more water. However, a more holistic approach is to reboot your body, mindset, and emotions simultaneously, since they are all interrelated, using something we call a reset. Although a reset that just uses one of the three—body, mindset, emotions—can be effective, a reset that uses all three at the same time has more potency to shift our energy. We call a reset activating all three areas 3-D, or three dimensional. For example, an example of a 3-D reset that Allison uses regularly to manage her energy is listening to a particularly energizing song (emotions) while doing a series of kickboxing punches (body) and thinking of the strengths she will activate in an upcoming situation (mindset). Any one of these three activities would boost her energy, but all three together carry a power punch.

Resets are practices we recommend using throughout the day. You can shift your energy through a *general energy reset*, get back on track quickly when things go awry with a *pivotal reset*, or prepare yourself for an upcoming situation with a *pregame reset*. Resets are personal and quite varied; they can be anything from a thirty-second quick mental shift to a two-minute breathing exercise to a two-week sabbatical.

Resets work by essentially creating a firewall to prevent previous feelings, memories, or physical symptoms from the past from staying with you. They are a way to break away from a negative mindset, jettison baggage from earlier in the day or the week, and move forward with a positive attitude and an invitation to inspiration. Resets often overlap with inspiration engines and are a short-term intervention strategy, not long term. However, when resets are practiced regularly and you develop an improved ability to monitor and manage your energy using resets, you are in a much stronger position to sustain inspiration over time.

THREE TYPES OF RESETS

As noted earlier, there are three types of resets: general energy, pivotal, and pregame. *General energy resets* clear your mental slate and refresh your focus and energy when you feel stuck, tired, negative, or distracted. Some of the most effective general resets include breaking away from the situation to clear your head, taking a walk, engaging in measured breathing, listening to music, or holding a yoga pose. To clean the slate and refresh your focus when you're feeling tired, stuck, or negative, try box breathing, a technique used by the US Navy SEALs to stay calm and focused before combat.[16] Inhale to the count of four while moving your hand along one side of an invisible box, hold for four while sliding your hand across the top of the box, exhale for four while you move your hand along the third side, and hold for four while your hand goes across the bottom. Do this at least three times. Listening to music is another way to reset, or you can try one of many meditation apps like the Smiling Mind[17] or Calm, which can help you ground and calm yourself.[18]

Pivotal resets are effective when you're caught off guard emotionally by something in the moment and need to recover from it quickly. For example, imagine you are offering a solution in a business meeting that the CEO publicly shoots down in front of all your colleagues—in a moment like this, you might become emotionally grabbed by frustration or anger or feel discouraged. At the same time, it may be *pivotal* for you to take a quick reset to stay engaged in the meeting and communicate effectively. Some great examples of pivotal resets include taking a series of deep breaths, relaxing your arms and shoulders, putting both feet on the ground and thinking of a positive result you want, cracking a joke to inject some humor and dissipate tension, or asking a question of someone nearby. You can also use a rubber band on your wrist that you snap when you recognize negative thoughts that you need to break free from; snap the rubber band to distract yourself and focus on something new.

Pregame resets are intentional energy shifts to feel inspired for something coming up. They are purposeful preparation that activates your mind, body, and emotions at the same time. A perfect example of a pregame reset is the haka, a war dance of the Maori tribe of New Zealand, originally performed in unison as a group to psych out the other warring faction. It is rhythmic, with stomping feet and loud chanting. Today, the haka is used as a unifying battle cry before sporting events or special events. The New Zealand rugby team the All Blacks is known for performing a haka before every match.[19] Performing a haka is a way to unify the thoughts and actions of a group. Haka is not just for sports. After hearing the history of the haka during an engagement with us, one of our clients, Peach, decided to create their own. Each member of the team contributed to the battle dance, which they use to focus everyone's minds on the task at hand. At Peach, the haka is a call to inspiration—a shared experience to focus the team's energy on the task in front of them.

The most effective pregame resets are experiential, like the tribal haka ritual; although the major emphasis of the haka is on the body (through dance), it aims to shift the emotions and mindsets of the players to be more in tune with one another, focused on the game, and confident. Pregame resets can also involve other types of physical activity, such as a long walk in the woods before a major presentation or listening to an upbeat song before making a sales pitch. When you need to prepare for an upcoming situation that may be challenging or stressful, try a pregame reset, like doing something nice for someone around you to put yourself in a positive mood, taking a walk around your building, or listening to your favorite song while thinking of your strengths. These resets act as vaccines against negativity.

Your energy level, influenced by your physical state, emotions, and mindset, has an enormous impact on your capacity to become and remain inspired. Taking steps to manage your body, mind, and emotions can positively impact the degree to which you can spark inspiration and sustain it over time personally and professionally.

Thought Experiment: Pivotal Resets

You are in a difficult situation—a tough conversation, a tense meeting—and need to reset in order to be your best. Try one of these pivotal resets:

- When grabbed or knocked off course by difficult emotions, engage in some physical activity: stand up, stretch, or start writing on the notepad in front of you.
- Practice incognito box breathing by inhaling and exhaling while tracing the outside edges of the box with your finger on the palm of your other hand under a table or behind your back (where no one can see you doing it).
- Privately think to yourself: *Why am I here? What do I want to accomplish? What strengths do I want to use right now, in this moment, to regroup and be my best?*
- When you're feeling agitated and need to calm down, focus on your breathing and slow your mind.
- Reenter the conversation and connect with those around you by making eye contact, asking open-ended questions, and engaging.

WORK IT
Manage Your Energy

STEP 1: ASSESS YOUR ENERGY

On a scale of 1–10, rate the level of your energy in the following three
areas:

Body (sleep, nutrition, activity)

Mindset

Emotions

STEP 2: ENVISION THE FUTURE

Think of an upcoming situation:

A situation in the future where you know you need to be your best

A situation in the future that you know will be stressful or likely to
trigger stress (i.e., preparing for a big presentation, going into a
meeting with a difficult colleague, etc.)

Imagine yourself at your best: Who do you want to be? Visualize and
describe how you show up at your best in this situation:

What are the positive outcomes that result from you being your best?

How will you positively influence those around you?

If something goes wrong in the moment, what type of pivotal reset (see sidebar for examples) will you use to get back on track?

In that situation, in order to prepare, will you need an energy lift or will you need to calm your mind and emotions?

Based on your answer, design a pregame reset that either boosts your energy or calms you and activates all three types of energies:

Body

Emotions

Mindset

EXAMPLES

A senior leader who starts the day by walking up eight flights of stairs (body) to his office while listening to his favorite song (emotions) and thinking about what he wants to accomplish that day (mindset) gets to the top of the stairs feeling energized and empowered, with clarity of focus.

A woman who prepares for a difficult conversation with her partner by breathing deeply (body) while sitting with both feet on the ground and eyes closed, thinking about the values her argument is grounded in and why this conversation, though challenging, is so important (mindset) and visualizing success (emotions).

An author who prepares for writing sessions by taking a walk in nature (body) and thinking about her higher purpose, which activates her feelings of peace, joy, and connection (mindset and emotions).

PART IV

SCALING INSPIRATION

nspired individuals achieve extraordinary, even superhuman, accomplishments. Their ideas and ability to capitalize on opportunities is an amazing resource. Now imagine an entire team fueled by the possibility and invincibility of inspiration. Imagine your whole organization collectively enjoying the same. Therein lies the path to massive success.

In recent decades, the world of work has changed dramatically. Leadership today is less about authority and directing people than it is about helping people find meaning and purpose in their work. Individuals want to *choose* to work, or at least they want to have a sense of meaning and purpose in what they do. In short, they are demanding inspiration from their work. This tremendous opportunity to scale inspiration from individuals to teams to organizational culture is exactly what today's world of work calls for. By modeling it, inviting others into intentional practice, coordinating inspiring activities within teams, and cultivating a culture of inspiration, you can scale inspiration across your whole organization. We know this approach is needed since research indicates that today fewer than one out of eight employees is inspired at work.[1]

Up to this point, we've focused mainly on how we can inspire ourselves, which is important for achieving individual peak performance. Indeed, we all have an opportunity to lead from where we stand, and a leader's first job is to inspire self. However, in organizations, leaders have the opportunity—and the responsibility—to inspire those around them. Teams have a responsibility to generate and harvest inspiration to produce better results. Organizations have a responsibility to put systems and processes in place that cultivate a culture of inspiration throughout. When organizations tap into inspiration at the individual, leader, team, and organization levels, they can scale it as a resource to produce extraordinary performance and results at all levels.

> A leader's first job is to
> inspire self.

In this last part of the book, we begin to explore how to scale inspiration across leaders, teams, and organizational cultures. We explore how to direct inspiration toward desired outcomes using the four categories introduced in Chapter 7. In addition, we talk about characteristics specific to leadership, teams, and organizations and opportunities inherent in each to cultivate and optimize the way that inspiration is directed.

Leaders, teams, and organizations each introduce new and more complex ways to scale inspiration as a resource. As we explore scaling inspiration across these three organizational contexts, the engines of inspiration and the practices for sustaining them still apply. To optimize how inspiration is scaled within these contexts, we overlay opportunities and responsibilities specific to the roles at each level.

Whether you lead as an individual contributor, as a team leader or member, or by overseeing whole parts of an organization, you'll gain insights into how to encourage, direct, and apply inspiration in your world of work.

CHAPTER TEN

INSPIRING LEADERS

eadership is a critical ingredient in sparking, sustaining, and scaling inspiration across individuals in organizations. Inspiring leaders bring out more in you than you may have realized you were capable of, or activate behaviors in you that you couldn't manifest on your own. Such leaders recognize what different members of their team need and find ways to give it to them. Jack Zenger and Joseph Folkman, authors of *The Inspiring Leader*,[1] reported in a *Harvard Business Review* article titled "What Inspiring Leaders Do":

> Of the 16 leadership competencies we most frequently measure, inspiration is clearly the one that stands out . . . the ability to inspire creates the highest levels of employee engagement and commitment. It is what most powerfully separates the most effective leaders from the average and least-effective leaders. And it is the factor most subordinates identify when asked what they would most like to have in their leader.[2]

We challenge our clients to think about leadership more broadly than having a managerial role. We define leadership in a way that is outside formal authority over a team. Our definition of leadership is

Actions and choices that inspire commitment by activating possibility and invincibility toward a shared mission. It's about mobilizing efforts through intentional practice and systems to both achieve results and build capability in the process.

> "I work very, very hard at being inspiring. And to be inspired. I'm not a policeman; I'm a coach. So it's very important for me. I don't control other people's creativity, I unlock other people's creativity, and in order to do that, I have to be highly performing."
>
> —Paul Bennett, Chief Creative Officer, IDEO

From this perspective, any individual can step into leadership at any time without having a formal leadership role on an organizational chart. In fact, from this definition, people can lead outside work environments, such as in parenting or personal relationships.

WHY INSPIRING LEADERSHIP IS ESSENTIAL IN TODAY'S MODERN WORK

Bain and Company research has shown that "inspired employees are more than twice as productive as satisfied employees."[3] This is especially true for up-and-coming leaders in the workplace today, where inspirational leadership is essential to success. Traditional authority-based leadership won't cut it anymore. "Because I said so" doesn't work with millennial workers, who are demotivated by hierarchy and bureaucracy. They want managers to work alongside them, not above them, and to coach and mentor them, not bark orders.

Bain's research found that "inspired
employees are more than twice as
productive as satisfied employees."

Millennials are focused on purpose and intrinsic motivation as reasons to come to work. They are driven by what they care about more than by money or external rewards, as previous generations have been. They want accelerated learning, skills, and capabilities in order to have impact in the world. And they respond best to leaders who speak to that sense of purpose and values.[4] That means leading up-and-coming workers requires new leadership skills. Good leaders need the ability to inspire and to nurture an inspiring workplace.

Regardless of who they are leading, inspiring leaders want to make things better for themselves and others. They lead their own growth and thriving. They seek out more challenges and responsibilities and want to build new things, better. They strive for achievement and progress. They embrace the responsibility and the opportunity that leadership presents. Leadership can happen—and is called for—from wherever they stand in the organization. They inspire others to inspire others, and in doing so, they help to build a culture of inspiration.

> "Inspiration, to me, is caring and being able to . . . trigger or support others in caring, all to a degree beyond what we had ever imagined possible."
>
> —Dennis Driver, Executive Vice President and Chief Human Resources Officer, Theravance Biopharma

A leader's first job is to inspire herself. Coming from an inspiring mindset, leaders are better positioned to activate others' inspiration. As a positive emotion, inspiration is infectious: wired for social connection, individuals have open limbic systems that are designed to pick up on the emotions of others. Thus, inspiration naturally begets inspiration and is scalable through social interaction. And leaders have a unique opportunity to direct that inspiration in ways to increase positive impact. Because others look to them for cues on how to feel and act at work, a leader's inspiration has a greater opportunity to go viral. This is true both in "front of the room" leadership moments and in everyday interactions.

INSPIRATION FROM LEADERSHIP AT THE FRONT OF THE ROOM

We often think of inspiring leadership as a great speech, a call to action, or a moving presentation. And it can be. When all eyes are on the leader, it's an opportunity to inspire. A leader who can tap into multiple styles of leadership and be authentically present in each of them can spread positive energy and excitement.

We witnessed an example of inspiring leadership a few years ago at SuccessFest, an annual conference that Peach, an athleisure retailer and InspireCorps client, organizes and presents to its salesforce. The star of the show wasn't someone you typically see at the front of the room—the head of sales or the CEO—rather, it was the chief operating officer, Derek Ohly, someone who customarily works behind the scenes to keep an organization running and doesn't always step out front and center to inspire and motivate.

When Ohly took the stage at SuccessFest before an almost entirely female audience, his vulnerability, humility, and authenticity quickly got everyone's attention. Ohly spoke from his heart, welling up a few times as he talked about his relationship with his cofounder, Janet Kraus, their vision for the company, and their mission of empowering women. He was humble, his words were heartfelt, and the audience hung on his every word. He spoke slowly, enunciating for emphasis, and used the power of the pause to draw the crowd in, feeling his hope for the future and his appreciation for how far they had come.

As Ohly described the company's growth trajectory, he used a metaphor of a sports stadium. "As of today, we've only sold four seats in a seventy-thousand-seat stadium, based on our market share," he explained. "In five years, we'll fill a section, and we'll be able to do the wave, and in ten years, we will fill all the seats in the stadium."[5] Through this visual, he helped the audience picture and experience where the company was and where it would be, thanks to their efforts. He shared with them the emotions and the energy they would all feel when they hit that next milestone. His story helped the audience capture the progress they were making, having them picture what the stadium would look like as it filled from their box seats above, looking down on their loyal customer base. He created awe.

At one point in his speech, Ohly took off his jacket and did some funny disco moves, to the delight of those in the audience. He showed his true self; his willingness to risk embarrassing himself proved his sincerity. His connection to those in the room deepened with every goofy gesture and dance step.

People were pumped! It was as if that room became the stadium. People were on their feet, cheering, ready to carry him out on their shoulders; he was heroic. They left the event feeling incredibly energized and excited for the future. They also felt a strong connection to Ohly—they would follow him anywhere!

Ohly was the epitome of the inspiring leader in that moment. He stepped up and shared his whole self with those in the audience. He was authentic and human, he was humble, and he showed agility by gracefully weaving together themes of determination, creativity, hope, and love for the audience.

INSPIRATION THROUGH EVERYDAY LEADERSHIP INTERACTIONS

Ohly had a formal event as a platform from which to voice his leadership, but that's not the only way to be an inspiring leader. Leaders can also inspire on a daily basis, in their ongoing stewardship of their organizations.

Danielle Warner, founder and CEO of Singapore-based Expat Insurance, discovered a lack of available insurance coverage for expatriates (people living outside their native country, as the American-born Warner was). Warner moved to Singapore and discovered that insurance products that were common in the United States were nearly unheard of in Singapore. And she had client business owners who were struggling to find insurance options for their businesses and employees.[6]

Warner uncovered a need and fostered a vision to develop insurance options in this marketplace, capturing a leadership position in the market by taking an unconventional approach of partnering with her clients rather than dealing with them at arm's length, as was the norm in the industry.

In all her work with clients, Warner tried to embed her team within Expat's corporate clients, so that they became "integrated," she told the British Chamber of Commerce in an interview with *Orient Magazine* a few years ago. "Our business model is totally different! With our corporate clients where we take care of their employee benefit structures we become their benefits team, like an implant. We become integrated with their team, work with the HR staff every day and try to reflect their company language and culture."[7]

Her success is also attributable to her people strategy and day-to-day leadership of the organization. One of her priorities is "creating a stable employment opportunity for my team," she says. In doing so, she builds trust that leads to longevity. "My primary responsibility is to create a safe environment and to build a culture of trust within my own team. If my team does not feel that their jobs are safe and that they have long-term prospects with us, then they will leave," she explains. Well-honed soft skills and personality are more desirable to Warner than insurance experience in the hiring process. Building relationships with clients is a higher priority than technical knowledge.

Warner's company has grown quickly by staying focused on the company's niche clients—businesses owned and operated by expats. But her skilled everyday leadership is another reason for her firm's success. She is clear about who the company's ideal client is, what they need, and how to best serve them, and that's what she is committed to pursuing.

"Being so connected to my purpose makes it easy to stay on the right path, to know what we should and should not be doing—when something is right, and when to say no," she told *Expat Living*.[8]

A LEADER'S FIRST JOB IS TO INSPIRE SELF

What is it that inspiring leaders do differently? How are they different from typical or struggling leaders? Recall that a leader's first job is to inspire self. Attending to one's own inspiration always starts with keen self-awareness. Leaders have to monitor their own levels of inspiration, starting with when it needs new and more sparks. To do that, they turn first to the inspiration engines that fuel them.

At Peach, Derek Ohly's engines were "connecting to and voicing your values and purpose" and "being vulnerable and transparent." By standing onstage and being vulnerable with the audience, sharing why he is committed to the company, his personal connection to the company's team and mission, and his vision of their success, he sparked inspiration in himself and in the audience. They felt connected to him and wanted to support the work he was doing as best they could; they became raving fans.

Danielle Warner's initial inspiration engine was "using your unique passions or qualifications to impact a situation." She found a specific opportunity in the Asian market, where insurance was relatively obscure. The lack of insurance options for her clients sparked her vision for a new firm. Once established, Warner recognized another market opportunity in how she did business. She saw that embedding employees within her clientele would make them almost indispensable, thereby making her company indispensable and more difficult to let go of. As she developed the company, the engine of "connecting to and voicing meaning and values" through purpose helped sustain her inspiration.

INSPIRING OTHERS

What a leader does matters. Their behavior is visible to followers, and thus, one of their great opportunities to share inspiration comes through role modeling. As role models, leaders can be intentional about how they demonstrate and call for inspiration. Vigilantly monitoring and maintaining their own inspiration, keeping it uppermost in their minds, and openly practicing it shows others how to do the same.

Inspiring leaders are transparent
about the importance of inspiration
to themselves and others.

Inspiring leaders are transparent about the importance of inspiration to themselves and others. You can see it in their behaviors and in how they talk about their work. For example, when Warner talks about being connected to her purpose as her guiding light for leading the business, she is demonstrating how the "connecting to and voicing values and purpose" engine drives her inspiration. This authenticity and transparency are key to effectively modeling inspiration for others.

Julia Balfour, leader of the organization that bears her name, runs an inspiring team. Her firm does print and digital marketing for its clients and is ranked as one of the fastest growing private companies in America.[9] As founder and CEO of her organization, Balfour knows that she plays a critical role in the daily inspiration of her team. Her core values, which include love, hard work, cutting-edge creativity, and a collaborative and family environment that welcomes pets and children, are evident in the workspace she has created for her employees.[10] She fills her beautiful, light-filled offices with colorful fabrics and decorations, the walls hung with framed inspiring quotes and pictures that have personal meaning aligned to her values. As a classically trained artist (Parsons and

Rhode Island School of Design), she senses how the environment around her is inspiring (or not) to herself, her clients, and her team. She also models inspiration in the way she conducts business, modeling both possibility and invincibility. "I typically will ask for things that are out of the limits of what we think is possible. For example, a client came in . . . and said 'Julia, I need a website in forty-eight hours. We have this big board meeting we're going to.'"[11] She explained that it was a big site for a large organization, and putting a site together in forty-eight hours was almost impossible. But the sense of invincibility on Balfour's team prevailed. She accepted the challenge and rallied her team to do the same. She describes: "So I got up the next morning and I met with my leads and my head of design, whom I adore, and he stated out of the gate, 'This is not possible.' And I said, 'I know. Everything that we have done before this means that this is not possible, so we have to leave behind the way we do things and completely think of this in a new way. . . . I've got you. We're gonna do the best we can do and I think this is possible.'"

Two days later, the site was up. Balfour called it "incredible." Her commitment to expanding what's possible and expecting confidence and capability to achieve is how she models inspiration for herself and her team. This modeling is a powerful way to be an inspiring leader. However, the best leaders do not stop there—they also explicitly invite others to practice inspiration with them, shoulder to shoulder.

Thought Experiment: Inspiring through Authenticity

Authenticity is a linchpin of inspiration and individuals who can develop it are likely capable of becoming inspiring leaders. Here are ten ways authenticity builds inspiration:

1. **Trust others.** Leaders build trust and inspiration by promising others to always have their back, especially when involved in a challenging or high-risk venture that could result in failure.

(continues)

2. **Be transparent and vulnerable.** Authentic leaders let others see them fully—strengths, foibles, and all. Requesting help when needed is one of the strongest leadership moves.
3. **Share your vision.** As another pathway to authenticity, leaders use storytelling to share their view of what's possible, provide meaning, and activate purpose.
4. **Discourage the enemies of inspiration.** Leaders combat negative thinking and doubt through modeling and storytelling.
5. **Be empathetic.** Another way leaders boost inspiration is by demonstrating that they sincerely care for others and offering selfless guidance.
6. **Ask questions and listen.** Leaders listen when others share information about themselves, asking open questions to understand and learn more.
7. **Create a safe environment.** When employees feel heard and not judged because they believe the leader cares about them and understands where they're coming from, the leader creates an environment conducive to possibility and invincibility.
8. **Bounce back from setbacks.** In the face of challenges and setbacks, leaders who display emotional agility and optimism are more inspiring. Not only do employees root for leaders who have been knocked down, but when they demonstrate that anyone can come back from defeat, these leaders build possibility and invincibility.
9. **Keep promises.** Leaders model inspiration through integrity, by following through on commitments and proving employees can rely on them without fail.
10. **Sponsor and mentor.** Authentic leaders invest time helping employees, advising and guiding them, and clearing the path to career advancement, and demonstrate generosity through sharing inspiration practices.

SUSTAINING INSPIRATION WITH OTHERS

As we discussed in Part III of the book, sustaining inspiration over time and in the face of day-to-day challenges that can erode it is essential for the spark to translate into inspired performance and results. The four methods introduced in Part III of the book for sustaining inspiration at the individual level can also be applied at the leadership level, as leaders model and practice sustaining inspiration with others.

RESPARK THE ENGINES

Resparking the engines in new ways and in new combinations is one way to sustain inspiration. Many stories we have shared throughout the book talk about leaders who are sparked by the "connecting to and voicing values and purpose" engine and go back to this engine regularly to sustain their connection to it. Warner talks about the importance of purpose and models this by voicing it frequently in public forums and directly to employees. This is just one example of how a leader goes back to an engine regularly and resparks inspiration for herself and others. In addition, leaders get to know the people working with them and the engines that spark *them*. We have talked about how leaders need to *know* the people who follow them. That knowledge will serve them here in selecting and introducing engines of inspiration that will particularly resonate. For example, Ohly knew that for many of the Peach entrepreneurs in the audience that advancing women's success as business owners was as important to them as the product itself. Knowing this, he activated two engines in his speech that he knew would be inspiring: "shared group mission" and "values and purpose."

DIRECT INSPIRATION TO DESIRED OUTCOMES

Directing inspiration toward desired outcomes involves activating behaviors that (1) drive to results, (2) intentionally align, (3) build connection and trust, and (4) cultivate visionary and innovative thinking. For leaders, directing behavior across these four categories happens by adopting and being agile across four leadership styles.

1. For example, when using inspiration to **drive to results**, a leader activates his or her strengths, sets aspirational goals, and charts a plan to achieve them. We refer to this style as **driver**.

2. For leaders, **intentional alignment** involves defending core values, strengthening processes, systems, and infrastructure, attending to fiduciary and regulatory responsibilities, and making sure all bases and priorities are covered. We call this leadership style **pillar**.

3. When leaders focus on building **connection and trust**, by appreciating one another's strengths and contributions and building a sense of belonging and trust, they are leading through the **advocate** style.

4. Leaders in **innovator** style advance **vision and innovation** by expressing optimism and hope, communicating a picture of what's possible and dreaming big, and envisioning a strategy to realize the dream.

What agility looks like in action is balancing and combining leadership styles in the moment. The idea of leaders using multiple styles and moving from one to another, or across them, is consistent with both seminal and newer research. In the 1960s, researchers such as Paul Hersey and Kenneth Blanchard[12] and Fred Fiedler[13] first codified typologies of different leadership styles and the idea that leaders should shift among them to be most effective across different situations. The notion of different leader styles having different impacts depending on the situation is backed up by more current research as well.[14] Our work with clients has shown us that four distinct styles are critical for leaders to access, combine, and activate according to situational demands in order to be effective and inspiring to others.

Inspiring leaders combine and blend these four styles and shift among them to expand their followers' imagination of what is possible and to empower their sense of invincibility. *Innovator* style opens up new possibilities by painting a clear picture of an imagined future—for themselves and for their followers. For example, Warner at Expat Insurance quickly recognized that insurance industry experience wouldn't give her clients the experience she wanted them to have. So, using agility to buck industry tradition, she ignored what other insurance firms did and hired employees based on their soft skills, such as empathy and their ability to connect with clients and build relationships.

Advocate style provides the trust and safety that undergirds invincibility, while also supporting risk taking to test out and explore new possibilities. For example, Warner determined that the ability to develop a personal relationship with others is more positively correlated with customer retention and satisfaction than years of insurance experience. She models this advocate style of warmth and connection both internally to those she leads and externally to her clients.

> "The most inspiring leaders have the ability to reframe like crazy—they entertain possibility. They're willing in their reframing to say, 'Ooh, imagine a world where . . . What would that be like? Let's play with it. Let's turn it around. Let's try it on. Let's experiment with it. Mentally prototype.'"
>
> —Keith Yamashita, Founder, SY Partner

Driver style models invincibility with perseverance and grit and helps followers recognize the same in themselves, inspiring them to rise to higher standards as a group. Derek Ohly activated driver style in his speech to compel his salesforce to reach higher goals together, while also modeling pillar to stay true to the Peach mission, message, and core values. *Pillar* style brings practicality to invincibility, grounding it in the *how* of both accomplishing new goals that align with the Peach structure and core mission.

Inspiring leaders produce the best results for themselves and others by being authentically agile across these four styles. It's not about acting; it's about authentically shifting how they lead, adjusting and flexing their styles to situations as needed. In some situations, agile leaders can be frank and direct; in others, more encouraging and warm. The most effective leadership response to an event or a person shifts as the situation does.

Of course, understanding what leadership response is needed begins with social and self-awareness. For example, are you demonstrating openness to different outcomes? Are you connecting with the people in the room in meaningful ways? Are you there to push boundaries or to maintain them? Recognizing your own style in the room, taking into account your strengths and your comfort level around certain activities, is a first step in being agile. Seeing the same in others is also essential.

Leaders who accurately pick up on social cues know the mood of a room, which helps them determine how they need to respond. For example, noticing that employees are seated with their arms firmly crossed could be a signal that they're expecting a confrontation. In this situation, a leader would bring a more advocate style, listening and being open to others' ideas. If everyone looks anxious, the leader knows they need reassurance about what's going on or how the company is performing and activates the innovator style to communicate hope and vision and advocate activating empathy and care. Spotting these signals can help leaders flex their responses.

GIVE YOUR INSPIRATION A BOOST: ACCOUNTABILITY, SOCIAL SUPPORT, POSITIVE RITUALS

Finally, a third way that leaders sustain their own inspiration and model this for others is through *boosting* inspiration with positive rituals, accountability, and social support.

The more that inspiration
reminders and practices are built
into the fabric of day-to-day
habits and culture, the better.

The more that inspiration reminders and practices are built into the fabric of day-to-day habits and culture, the better. One such example of a positive ritual used to sustain inspiration is described in our interview with Alexander McCobin, the CEO of Conscious Capitalism International (CCI). CCI as an organization aims to *elevate humanity through business*, inspiring all businesses—not just nonprofits—to take responsibility for bettering society through their work. While McCobin feels inspired every day by the efforts of conscientious businesses to do this, his original source of inspiration comes from his father. To remind him of this, he programs an automatic e-mail that arrives in his in-box first thing every morning about his higher purpose.[15]

To increase connection and accountability and provide regular doses of inspiration, many of our organizational clients have implemented *inspiration pulse meetings* to replace or supplement annual performance reviews. During these pulse meetings, which can happen one-on-one or with teams, leaders check in on inspiration levels, ask questions that help them understand issues that need to be addressed, and codesign next steps to boost or sustain inspiration. In addition, these pulse checks offer opportunities for in-the-moment feedback, both constructive and positive, which is a form of social support. Leaders model sustaining inspiration by prioritizing regular pulse conversations that focus on more than just the work that needs to get done—they focus on *the person behind the work* that gets done, the human pulse. CEO Bill Jennings's hospital leadership offers a novel path to accountability. He makes his priority to the patient highly public with a nameplate on his desk that—instead of bearing his name and title—is emblazoned with the question: How Does This Help the Patient?[16]

We have offered a few examples of how leaders model and practice sustainable inspiration shoulder to shoulder with those they lead—and as you can imagine, the possibilities for this are endless. We have found that leaders who prioritize the practice of inspiration for themselves understand the benefits of it and intuitively find ways to cascade it in authentic ways to those they lead.

MANAGE YOUR ENERGY: BODY, MINDSET, AND EMOTIONS

Beyond the engines, leaders must practice energy management—tuning in to their own levels of energy and, when it dips, taking action to bring it back up. In Chapter 9, we talked about many ways individuals can manage energy through their body, mindset, and emotions. Leaders, to be authentic, have to understand the importance of energy management and practice it for themselves—to model the priority of this to others. In addition, they have a platform to practice energy management shoulder-to-shoulder with those they lead. For example, Ohly—during a particularly labor-intensive period for his operations department—designed and implemented several group resets that would activate energy and positive emotions. He opened meetings with brief check-ins on how everyone was feeling and then led resets that involved stretching and energizing music. He asked his team to contribute ideas, and one of his team members came up with a metric that measured quantity of laughs in his department and tracked it as data, reporting out to the company during strategic planning. Trends show more leaders are encouraging the use of walking meetings,[17] which research shows increases creative thinking[18]—a great boost for mindset while also managing physical and emotional energy. The more that leaders understand the link between the quality of their energy and their ability to feel inspired, the more they will intentionally own and model this practice.

Leadership is an inspiration opportunity. Our wish for you, as readers, is that you will inspire yourself in service of sharing it with all those around you.

WORK IT
Inspiration Contagion

Think of an area in your work or life where you lead others.
Consider the following questions related to this area of work or life:

What engine(s) do you want to focus on, or intentionally activate, that will increase your inspiration about this area of work/life?

What opportunities (both front of the room and day to day) do you have to inspire others?

What are your desired outcomes and/or positive impact on others in this area?

Based on these desired outcomes, what leadership style or combination of styles will be most effective? What does this leadership style(s) look like for you?

Think of one way you can model your own energy management practices (e.g., reframing your mindset, taking stretch breaks, doing regular resets). How might you practice this energy management together with those you lead?

What is a new habit or positive ritual you can embed into your leadership that will help you be accountable to and sustain your inspiration over time?

What are some ways you can be transparent with others about your intentional practice of sustainable inspiration in your leadership?

CHAPTER ELEVEN

INSPIRING TEAMS

"The whole is greater than the sum of its parts."
—Aristotle

Traditionally, we've evaluated team success based on output: Is the team producing what it's supposed to produce? But a more modern way to think about teams is in terms of inspiration: How much potential do they have if they are motivated to produce and achieve more? Specifically, how *inspiring* are they? Inspiring teams collectively share possibility and invincibility to own and drive high performance. When they are inspired and inspiring, they achieve more than they ever thought possible. In the process, they make one another better, braver, and more confident.

Inspiring teams are comprised of inspiring individuals, but they are more than that. The team is its own *entity*, separate from the individual members, with its own identity, energy, dynamics, and norms. It has meaning and impact in and of itself, beyond each of its individual members. The *team entity* has influence over each of the team members in the same way a leader does.

Cliff Bogue, MD, chair of pediatrics, Yale School of Medicine, and chief medical officer, Yale New Haven Children's Hospital, says of inspiring teams he's seen in action: "[In the] intensive care unit when you have a very difficult life-and-death situation and everyone is in there, they're ready to go, they're working together. They're very focused; there's not a lot of extraneous chitchat. There's all hands on deck, let's focus, let's all work together. Everyone [is] contributing; if we need an idea, who's got an idea, let's deal with this. And they're just totally laser focused. And that's very inspiring to see a group like that come together and pull together for the patient. And being willing to do the extra work, stay the extra hours. There's not a lot of bickering; there's, 'We're focused here on this child.'"[1]

Inspiration at the team level is more complex than it is for individuals. Teams are about sharing and coordinating inspiration *across* individuals. The team should be inspired and inspiring itself, as an entity with its own identity, values, and purpose.

Richard Hackman's research on teams[2] shows that team functioning can spiral—upward or downward—as individuals on the team react to and assimilate team experiences and results. The same is true for inspiration. You can get greater gains from positive inspiration spirals, just as you can also get a negative drag on team performance from a negative inspiration spiral where levels are low or lacking. Specific attention to the team's inspiration level and trend is critical. If teams are not aware of or attuned to this, they miss an opportunity to both create upward spirals of inspiration and prevent downward spirals.

Everyone on the team has a
responsibility to be aware of their
own inspiration level as well as the
team entity's inspiration level.

Everyone on the team has a responsibility to be aware of their own inspiration level as well as the team entity's inspiration level. Building team self-awareness of inspiration levels and proactively taking steps to spark and sustain it is a responsibility they share. As Helen Russell, chief people officer at Atlassian, told us: "While a leader is key, team members need to be equally capable of inspiring one another. Leaders aren't always there, and you need the team to pick one another up when they fall and inspire one another to higher performance. A simple example is instead of just reading an interesting article over the weekend, you're the person that shares that article with the team because you want all boats to rise and inspire others' learning and growth, along with your own."[3]

To contribute to inspiration for the whole team, individual team members must grant power to the *team entity*, recognizing that, as Aristotle said, "the whole is greater than the sum of the parts."[4] Teams have to actively monitor inspiration levels and take responsibility for fueling them.

CRACKING THE CODE ON INSPIRING TEAMS

Google embarked on research to better understand teams. Specifically, its Project Aristotle dissected what makes effective teams tick. Looking at roughly 180 teams, Google researchers found that the most successful and productive ones demonstrated psychological safety—referring to teammates' comfort and security on the team. The researchers describe: "In a team with high psychological safety, teammates feel safe to take risks around their team members. They feel confident that no one on the team will embarrass or punish anyone else for admitting a mistake, asking a question, or offering a new idea."[5] Two related concepts to psychological safety, namely social sensitivity and equal talk-time during meetings, emerged in another study by scientists from Carnegie Mellon[6] as critical aspects of high-functioning teams. Social sensitivity is the intuitive ability to sense how others are feeling, often based on nonverbal cues; equality of talk time during meetings means that every voice is heard—people feel confident using their voice on the team. On the best teams, team members sensed what others on the team needed emotionally and restrained themselves from dominating discussions. Their findings align with leading academic researchers of teams, including Amy Edmondson at Harvard[7] and Jane Dutton at the University of Michigan.[8] A team that focuses only on production and loses sight of human connections, specifically the sense of safety and the importance of every member's voice, will inevitably suffer. They may achieve short-term results, but they do not build stronger capability in the process.

> The most successful and
> productive teams demonstrate
> psychological safety.

An example of social sensitivity comes from Julia Balfour's organization. Balfour's social sensitivity is based on love, which shows up in a number of ways, including their original Valentine's Day tradition.[9] She describes it as follows: "Three years ago we devised a plan for Valentine's Day . . . I had noticed that no matter your significant other situation, the office energy always seemed sad or tense. So I decided that every Valentine's Day I'd bring in a dozen roses for everyone on my team, and then the team (because they are wonderful) decided they'd all bring in a special dish to share with one another . . . and Lovesgiving was founded. Today, we have too many treats to count—tacos, pasta, homemade bread, chocolate-covered strawberries or bananas, and the list goes on and on. We may all need a nap after that, but it's all worth it because love makes the day great. Whatever your situation is today, throw a party and celebrate!"[10]

Inspiring leaders ensure all voices are heard in inspiring commitment. Steve Squinto, cofounder of Alexion, built teams where, as he described to us, "everybody leaves their ego at the door. This is not about ego, this is about solving problems and every voice counts. This is how the toughest problems will be solved." In Squinto's case, solidarity and social sensitivity were critical to his team's capabilities. He explained that his team, "data-driven guys," believed that "if you can understand the information, there is generally a solution around it. When there isn't a solution, it's because you haven't looked hard enough at every angle." So when things were really stressful, and people were losing hope, Squinto would physically gather his team in the conference room to pore through information and talk out ideas and concepts together. He recounted, while laughing, that, without fail, there would be a crisis that generally occurred when he was on a two-week vacation in Nantucket.

> "My team gets inspired in several ways, and I think some of it comes from me. It's my job to inspire them; I encourage them to be the best versions of themselves as a whole people. I'm interested in what they did this weekend, what interests them, what they care most about. Somebody's planning a wedding—how's the planning going? Those things all matter . . . I really try to make genuine relationships with each person and always foster that relationship . . . I always try to have the appropriate pulse or connection level with each person in terms of frequency and depth. Not because I need something from them right now, but because it's the right thing to do."
>
> —Brian Douglas, Chief Operating Officer, Graham Capital

The key to the team's success was Squinto's ability to help his team separate their personal identities from their ideas so that they could truly leave their egos at the door and work collaboratively, in solidarity and above individual positions and needs, to find a solution.[11]

When there is safety on the team, with social sensitivity and value for every voice, sometimes the leader's role is to step back a bit and let the team perform. Shea Gregg, MD, a trauma doctor who creates high-functioning operating room teams, told us, "I know the team is highly functional, productive, and engaged when I am not saying a word and our meetings are collaborative." Through open discussion, trust building, and compassion, he helps his team develop solutions that no one would have come up with on their own. "You open a discussion with a question," he says, "and they lead the conversation. Then you know you're successful.

Then you throw out another question, and they go." He explains that on "the most successful teams, the leader says the least."[12]

Yes, a leader needs to be present, he says, and team inspiration can be sparked by the leader, but then it's the team and their questions and probing dialogue among themselves that fuels the inspiring discussion and results in inspiring solutions.

SPARKING INSPIRATION ON TEAMS

Inspiration on teams starts with the engines, which function both at individual and team entity levels. To find the right engines for the team, you first need to know the team members and what inspires each of them. If your team members find inspiration in "vulnerability and transparency," a meeting in which you share the truth about strained finances may generate helpful discussions about how to do things differently that could boost the business's bottom line. If shared experience is important and sparks inspiration, you could encourage more collaborative work or conduct an off-site meeting and keep a pulse on how much members are working remotely.

All the engines—sparked by you, sparked by others, and sparked by situations—work for teams, in general (see the Work It at the end of this chapter for ideas on each of the engines to apply at a team level). However, some engines are especially important to build team inspiration. These include

- **Using your strengths.** Identify and acknowledge one another's strengths regularly and the strengths of the team as a collective.
- **Connecting to and voicing your values and purpose.** Clarify the purpose of the team and align it to the higher purpose of the organization and each individual's role in it.
- **Belonging.** Make sure each team member feels a connection to the group, understanding his or her role and opportunities for contribution.

- **Sharing group mission.** Teams are on missions every day to accomplish goals: ensure that the missions are shared ones, cultivating an esprit de corps to achieve them together.
- **Being vulnerable and transparent.** Cultivate a team culture of trust through social sensitivity and encouraging one another to share openly about their goals, progress and achievements, obstacles and struggles.
- **Sharing experiences.** Share experiences together, especially inspiring ones, whether it's team development, travel, meals, volunteer work, important project milestone celebrations, and so on; build a collective memory and connection to one another.
- **Seeking out environments that move us.** Finally, we have found in our own company and with many of our clients that many people are sensitive and responsive to their environment. While people's preferences for work environment and what constitutes an inspiring work space differ across individuals and teams, we know that being in emotionally moving environments can make a difference. For some, this is a more open working space, while for others this has to do with color, art, windows, and exposure to nature. Be willing to try things out, assess impact, and refine.

The responsibility for sparking inspiration on a team does not rest with the leader alone. Team members focused on sparking inspiration in their own work can and should think about ways to bring these practices and ideas to their teams. Just like at the individual level, teams need to be attuned to their collective emotional vibe. All team members should take part in monitoring the inspiration level of the team and sparking new inspiration when needed—or resparking and combining engines, one of the key ways to sustain inspiration over time (Chapter 6). As team members, individuals are attending to themselves and to the team as an entity.

SUSTAINING INSPIRATION ON TEAMS

RESPARK THE ENGINES

Resparking and combining engines is always a source of sustaining inspiration. On teams, there is often an opportunity to pack extra punch by organizing an event or experience that taps into multiple engines at once. We do this at InspireCorps by designing live team events and retreats that intentionally activate many different engines at once. As our team has multiple ties to the Cincinnati and Kentucky areas, one year, our team combined our quarterly live meeting with a trip to the 142nd Kentucky Derby at Churchill Downs racetrack. We chose this timing and venue intentionally as we knew that Churchill Downs, as an inspiring event and place in and of itself, would activate many different engines of inspiration for our team, including

- **Activating body movement and presence.** The hats, the hats, the hats! Presence at the Derby is all about the hat you sport. The more elaborate the better. Making a stunning fashion statement was a way to make yourself seen and admired. That sparked inspiration on our team, especially for Jen who specializes in presence.
- **Seeking environments that move us.** The longest continuously running sports event in the United States is run at the beautiful and historic Churchill Downs racetrack, where over two hundred thousand people descend from all across the world. The crowds, the sounds, the stunning celebration of southern culture and traditions that date back to 1875 are emotionally moving.[13]
- **Witnessing excellence.** Known as "the most exciting two minutes in sports,"[14] America's great race draws the most elite horses and jockeys. The relatively young three-year-old horses have only one chance to run this race, so every team is giving their all to win. It's a breathtaking performance.

- **Values and purpose.** Our company values include "enjoy the ride," "be bold," and "relationships first." We activated all of these by flying our whole team out for the Derby. We had great fun; we were bold in our wardrobe. We advanced our relationships on the team both at the event, through placing bets and exploring the amazing Churchill Downs, and in the hour-plus drives in a big van to and from.
- **Sharing experiences with large groups of people.** Attending the Derby had been a collective dream of ours since all three founding partners have familial and professional roots in the Bluegrass state and we even incorporated our company there. We dreamed of attending this important cultural event as a part of our Kentucky-based company experience.

Not only did this event spark inspiration for us at the time, reflecting back on it revs these engines again and again. For example, we created a video that logged our experience and watching it brings us back there, reminding us of this shared experience that moved all of us. To the extent that teams can find ways to tap into engines of great meaning to them, the payoff comes in newly sparked inspiration both at the time and, sometimes, going forward. Efforts like these to respark engines are able to inform your team of which engines are most potent. Over time, each team learns its own, specific set of go-to engines for the greatest sparks of inspiration, which then makes sustaining them over time ever more easier.

DIRECT INSPIRATION TO POSITIVE OUTCOMES

Another powerful way to sustain inspiration is to direct it toward performance and positive outcomes. When team members are collectively focused toward specific goals, they can better sustain their inspiration.

"We were really committed to wanting to serve this rather extraordinary collection of outstandingly brilliant and gifted students . . . There was a shared acknowledgment of the thing that most mattered. And so, with that, in full view of everyone's sight, everyone could train their sight to that thing and then bring not only the fullness of their gifts, but of their time, their energy, their effort to just serving these extraordinary students."

—Nicholas Lewis, Associate Dean of Student and Academic Affairs, Curtis Institute of Music

The question then becomes: How best to direct inspiration on teams toward desired positive outcomes? An illustration comes from the Orpheus Chamber Orchestra, known best because they are conductorless.[15] The group has been the subject of a Harvard Business School case study, featured in articles ranging from *The Economist* to the *New York Times* and *Fast Company*,[16] among many others, and dissected by business school professors as a model of great teamwork. Rather than having a conductor, Orpheus uses a shared leadership model with collaborative decision-making and self-governance to provide the best possible performances for their domestic and international audiences attending their seventy annual concerts.

As you read previously, there are four key categories of behaviors that, when you take action within and across them, drive positive outcomes. The same holds true for teams, as we will show with Orpheus in the examples below. Teams can best drive positive outcomes when they collectively direct sparks of inspiration to behaviors across the four categories:

1. When using inspiration to **drive to results**, team goals and roles are clear and agreed upon and members are held accountable to them. Roles reflect team member strengths and aspirations. All team members are focused on achievement and task completion. At Orpheus, being conductorless doesn't mean that no one is in charge. Their drive to achieve results is evident in the roles they assume and share: each musician has the opportunity to step into a leadership role at various times during the year, whether it's to

lead a rehearsal or to direct a performance or to serve as one of three performers on the board of trustees. The group selects the leader based on that member's interests, strengths, and level of expertise.

2. For teams, **intentional alignment** involves adopting practices that support coordination, high-integrity commitments, and communication and information sharing. The team is also self-regulating, including declining opportunities or pursuits that don't align to the larger vision and goals. Orpheus maintains alignment to its mission through clearly defined roles, where members understand and accept their personal responsibility for helping the group achieve the best sound possible. There is no conductor up front offering feedback and guidance regarding how to improve; it's up to each musician to identify how he or she can improve and help enhance and increase the orchestra's results. All the members are passionate about refining their skills and evolving and improving collectively. Musicians are encouraged to speak freely about their frustrations with themselves and one another to avoid pent-up emotions that could cloud the performances.

3. When teams are focusing on building **connection and trust**, members ask for and offer help regularly. They show concern for one another as whole people and are willing to sacrifice for others if needed, and they celebrate one another's differences. Teams high in connection and trust share love and enjoy play, thereby advancing their collaborative abilities. Orpheus members advocate for themselves and one another, requiring consensus regarding decisions before making changes or trying new approaches. The musicians decide together on who will lead them in performing a particular piece, which piece they will learn, and which guest musicians may be invited to perform with them. Using collective listening, they take individual responsibility for matching their own level of play to everyone else's, for a more harmonious sound

that enhances the overall effect. But they are also responsible for helping one another improve their respective performances, offering feedback to any musician using a two-way communication system admired by many orchestras and teams.

4. Teams that advance **vision and innovation** embrace change in the name of progress or growth, always looking for a better way or a greater opportunity. They have an impatience with the status quo and are always working to stay ahead of the curve. Visionary and innovative teams understand that experimentation is an essential part of risk management. At Orpheus, the orchestra's structure of going conductorless is an example of innovation. The innovation has caught on, so much so that companies began asking for coaching from the group, and so the Orpheus Process was trademarked and marketed to organizations seeking leadership training. Organizations ranging from IBM, Kraft Foods, Goldman Sachs, Memorial Sloan Kettering Cancer Center, and Morgan Stanley have turned to Orpheus for consulting.[17]

For teams, activating the four categories of behavior means coordinating across the team to make sure all four are utilized. Here again this involves team members being both self-aware and attending to team-level activity. Operating within the four key areas brings most teams to successful outcomes, which naturally sustains inspiration. Doing great work together and enjoying the successes that ensue keeps the flame of inspiration burning bright.

GIVE YOUR TEAM'S INSPIRATION A BOOST: ACCOUNTABILITY, SOCIAL SUPPORT, POSITIVE RITUALS

Accountability, social support, and positive rituals sustain inspiration on teams just like they do for individuals. In fact, teams offer more opportunities for accountability, support, and rituals as they are comprised of multiple people, each bringing his or her own desire for the team to succeed and history of best practices.

A great example of using accountability to boost and sustain team members' inspiration comes from Bill Jennings, president and CEO of Reading (Pennsylvania) Hospital. Jennings said in a town hall meeting at Bridgeport Hospital where he was CEO prior to Reading, in response to a question about accountability or lack thereof, that he would work with people, give people resources, give them a try, but he added, "in the end if somebody's not able to succeed with our vision [then] we would help them find success elsewhere. That day, it became the tagline for Bridgeport Hospital: 'If you're not accountable, we'll help you find success elsewhere.'"[18]

He showed us how this worked in a story about his ER department: "Our ER was broken. So I started paying attention to it. I would swing by every morning and ask the charge nurse or one of the doctors on duty to show me this board in the control room [a real-time video monitor of ER traffic]. It started with me bringing my attention to the work happening on the ground and getting curious. I'd walk over and ask, 'What's going on with Ms. [Smith]? Why has she been here for eighteen hours?' I'm not a doctor, so I can't diagnose these things, but I can ask silly questions like that, and I started doing it every morning. This practice of being in the work with them every morning was the start. Then I got the idea to have a monitor in my office . . . This allowed me to plug in, every morning, to what was happening there. I was not meddling, just being interested and asking questions."[19]

Putting the video monitor that showed ER turnaround times in his office and watching it first thing each morning allowed Jennings to ask questions and learn from his team about what he saw. It quickly became clear to him that turnaround times were a most relevant metric to indicate how well the ER was running. Then other leaders began following suit, with the chief nurse having a monitor installed in her office. Then the chief operating officer had one put up. Everyone started watching ER wait times, which caused them to improve—dramatically.[20]

Improving ER wait times turned into a competitive advantage for the hospital, thanks to Jennings's leadership. He didn't diagnose the problem or dictate solutions, which could have jeopardized psychological safety. Instead, he immersed himself in their world and asked questions to understand what was going on, bringing their voices into the conversation, and worked closely with the team on the ground to help them fix the problem. Inspiring leaders help their followers feel more confident, even invincible. They help others recognize the possibilities the future has to offer. They empower their teams to achieve more, together and individually.

Along with accountability, giving and receiving social support is another way to sustain inspiration on teams. Marisa Thalberg, global chief brand officer, Taco Bell, told us in our interview with her about how her organization focuses on building strong bonds among team members so they naturally support one another.

She told us: "Laughter and having fun is really important . . . to have a dynamic team that feels happy and comfortable coming to work . . . It's hard to sustain the energy and enthusiasm when you are in a constant state of standing in quicksand, unpredictability; it is destabilizing. We need to keep the team feeling secure and genuinely appreciated."[21]

Similarly, positive rituals on teams are supported by a strong sense of belonging and commitment among team members. As they do for individuals, and especially for athletes, positive rituals evoke positive emotions and give us more focused energy—both of which help sustain inspiration. A famous ritual Duke's basketball team holds dear provides an example. It started in the 1980s and is still current today. Mike Krzyzewski, their coach at the time, insisted that his players bend down and literally slap the floor when they go on defense. Krzyzewski told them slapping the floor would demonstrate their commitment to defensive intensity. It would affirm their pledge to one another. It would prove their readiness.[22]

Teams are so unique that each has to find the rituals that will work best for them, but we have seen examples of rituals that range from the small and playful (like sixty-second dance parties, happy hours, or dress-down days) to the more hefty in meaning (like commencement ceremonies, promotion or retirement parties, celebrating sales triumphs, or employee-of-the-month designations). Whatever the origin or nature of positive rituals, they bring positive energy and spirit to the team, boosting esprit de corps and sustaining inspiration.

MANAGING ENERGY (PHYSICAL, COGNITIVE, AND EMOTIONAL) ON TEAMS

Just like individuals, the team entity has its own physical, cognitive, and emotional energy. When one or two members of a team start to burn out, the whole team can feel the weight of it and experience the same. Likewise, when a team successfully bounces back from a setback and cultivates learning from it, they share the benefits of their collective growth mindset. Emotions, too, are shared at the team level. High-energy, positive emotions on a team go far to sustain the team's inspiration going forward.

As contagion on teams can exaggerate the impact of the energy, whether high or low, it is critical for team members to attend to their own and the team entity's energy on all three of these fronts, especially if inspiration starts to wane.

We've also covered resets as a powerful way to manage all three kinds of energy. Resets can be practiced both individually and on teams to monitor team energy and inspiration. The same resets that exist for individuals relate to teams. Below are a few examples of how resets can be applied at the team level:

- **General energy resets** can take place at the start of a meeting, especially after lunch or during the wicked 3:00 p.m. slump. They can be a pick-me-up to renew energy across the team. For example, one of our clients starts meetings by having everyone share a win or something they are grateful for. This simple, quick check-in can refresh the team's energy.

- **Pivotal resets** are useful when the team needs to shift its energy. Perhaps there's been a setback or a delay that has left the team wanting verve and inspiration. Taking time to disrupt the negativity spiral can be simple and quick. For example, just taking a few moments to have everyone stand, breathe, and listen to calming music when things are heated can change up the energy to be more supportive of inspiration.

- **Pregame resets** help teams prepare for upcoming situations that they know will be challenging or that especially need inspiration. The haka dance one of our clients created to their favorite song applies here. They performed it before every significant team event. It got them fired up and ready to meet the challenge in front of them.

In many ways sparking and sustaining inspiration on teams mirror the same processes for individuals. But healthy teams may have an advantage: the multiple members that comprise a team offer more opportunities to recognize, monitor, and pump up their collective inspiration.

WORK IT
Activating Inspiration on Teams

All teams can all be inspired through the inspiration engines. Yet, each team entity will likely lean on one or two more naturally than others. Use the tool below to take stock of how these engines operate on your team. Consider suggested ways and write in some new ways that your team can tap into each of the engines more often. Then indicate the extent to which each one sparks inspiration for your team.

Next, choose a few of the engines that are most inspiring to your team and design a reset ritual based on these to renew your energy and sustain your inspiration.

ENGINE	HOW INSPIRING IS THIS ENGINE FOR YOUR TEAM (1–5)?	WAYS TO TAP INTO THIS ENGINE MORE OFTEN (CIRCLE THE ONES YOU LIKE BEST AND ADD IN YOUR OWN)
Connecting to and Voicing Your Values and Purpose	_____	**Some examples:** Looking at the organization's values and purpose, how does your team align to it and contribute to it? Have each individual member voice his or her purpose on the team and how each member aligns to the team's and organization's purpose. Have each team member share a personal value that maps to the organization's values. A few times a year, revisit the team's purpose and do an activity together that brings the purpose to life. **What would you add?**
Using Your Strengths	_____	**Some examples:** What unique strengths does this team have that have a positive impact on the organization? Examples might be character strengths like creativity, honesty, or perseverance or specific skills and competencies. Think of specific and new ways your team can capitalize on these strengths. During team meetings, have regular check-ins identifying how the team used its strengths recently and shout-outs to individual strengths that are unique in this team. **What would you add?**

(continues)

ENGINE	HOW INSPIRING IS THIS ENGINE FOR YOUR TEAM (1–5)?	WAYS TO TAP INTO THIS ENGINE MORE OFTEN (CIRCLE THE ONES YOU LIKE BEST AND ADD IN YOUR OWN)
Progressing Toward and Achieving Success	_____	**Some examples:** Build celebrations of progress and achievements into team practices like meetings, retreats, and even performance management conversations. Focus on the progress and accomplishments that happen *together* as a team versus individual contributions. When the team experiences setbacks, discuss what was learned and how that learning can lead to progress going forward (building resilience). Looking forward, what are some of the team's wildest, biggest goals to accomplish? What legacy does the team wish to leave behind? **What would you add?**
Using Your Whole Brain with Unstructured Time	_____	**Some examples:** Just like individuals, teams need unstructured time together to solve problems. Find time as a team to do unstructured activities together that are social and fun, without set agendas or tasks to accomplish. Some teams build a cushion of time into meetings with space to have open discussions on topics without an agenda. **What would you add?**

ENGINE	HOW INSPIRING IS THIS ENGINE FOR YOUR TEAM (1–5)?	WAYS TO TAP INTO THIS ENGINE MORE OFTEN (CIRCLE THE ONES YOU LIKE BEST AND ADD IN YOUR OWN)
Developing New Perspectives	_____	**Some examples:** As a team, challenge yourselves to see something or someone in a different light or solve a problem using an unexpected approach. Use the team's diversity—on whatever dimensions are represented on the team—to invite and learn about new perspectives. Consider environment and go to a new, unexpected place to work on solving a problem. Bring in a novel speaker from a different industry or role to speak on a topic. Have the team read an article or book that offers a unique perspective. **What would you add?**
Activating Body Movement and Presence	_____	**Some examples:** Move together as a team. Try walking meetings or start meetings off with stretching to music (reset). Encourage team members to move around in meetings or discussions as needed. If conversations get heated, have everyone stand up and shake out their arms or legs as a quick break. Share best practices with one another about how to dress, stand, and speak with influential presence. **What would you add?**

ENGINE	HOW INSPIRING IS THIS ENGINE FOR YOUR TEAM (1–5)?	WAYS TO TAP INTO THIS ENGINE MORE OFTEN (CIRCLE THE ONES YOU LIKE BEST AND ADD IN YOUR OWN)
Belonging	_____	**Some examples:** Design activities during which team members get to know one another and share what they have in common. Design frequent opportunities to bring the team together for shared experiences and important conversations. Make sure that everyone is included in these. If that's not possible, be attuned and sensitive to looping in anyone who was left out so all feel included. Some teams build a tribe mentality by identifying qualities that characterize them—a team mascot, color, song, quote, and so on. These create a sense of commonality that helps everyone feel a part of something special. **What would you add?**
Admiring Our Mentors and Heroes	_____	**Some examples:** Individuals have their own mentors and heroes. It can be a powerful exercise for individual team members to identify and share those mentors and heroes and the qualities they admire most. Additionally, the team entity may have a mentor or hero specific to their mission. For example, some companies like Next Jump invite organizations in to visit and see their teams and culture in action. It can be inspiring for teams to strive toward excellence with a specific mentor or hero in mind. **What would you add?**

ENGINE	HOW INSPIRING IS THIS ENGINE FOR YOUR TEAM (1–5)?	WAYS TO TAP INTO THIS ENGINE MORE OFTEN (CIRCLE THE ONES YOU LIKE BEST AND ADD IN YOUR OWN)
Getting a Lift	_____	**Some examples:** Teams can actively lift one another up and emotionally support one another. Start meetings off with shout-outs or new insights gained from reviewing setbacks as a way to boost confidence in one another. The team, as an entity, holds each individual accountable for his or her own professional development growth. Team members coach one another, collectively, or one-on-one outside the group, to achieve goals. They see one another as supportive resources to accomplish great work together. **What would you add?**
Serving Others	_____	**Some examples:** Team members identify and articulate how they serve others within or outside the organization, making a positive difference. In addition, team members consider ways they serve and help one another (giving one another a positive lift). The team could choose a particular cause outside work that aligns to their strengths and mission, to support financially and/or through volunteer activities. **What would you add?**

(continues)

ENGINE	HOW INSPIRING IS THIS ENGINE FOR YOUR TEAM (1–5)?	WAYS TO TAP INTO THIS ENGINE MORE OFTEN (CIRCLE THE ONES YOU LIKE BEST AND ADD IN YOUR OWN)
Sharing a Group Mission	—————	**Some examples:** On a team, this engine is closely aligned to the engine "connecting to and voicing your values and purpose." For team members, a group mission is usually aligned to the team's values and purpose, but it is more specifically a way that the team takes action to have a positive result. The team can have a macromission that is more aligned to its purpose, but it can also have micromissions that are specific to shorter-term project goals. The important thing is that team members know what the missions are so they bring them together around a common goal. **What would you add?**
Being Vulnerable and Transparent	—————	**Some examples:** Willingness to be vulnerable—to expose mistakes or a need for assistance—is a great way to be true to yourself and to others. At InspireCorps, we celebrate "the beautiful oops" and build this into our team sync meetings—actually clapping and encouraging one another when we drop balls and fail. This is a way to encourage vulnerability around mistakes and learning from setbacks. **What would you add?**

ENGINE	HOW INSPIRING IS THIS ENGINE FOR YOUR TEAM (1–5)?	WAYS TO TAP INTO THIS ENGINE MORE OFTEN (CIRCLE THE ONES YOU LIKE BEST AND ADD IN YOUR OWN)
Seeking Environments That Move Us	————	**Some examples:** Individuals can craft their own environments to inspire them, and teams can do this as well. Consider where the team typically meets and how the space can be made more moving and inspiring. It may involve changing how people move and sit, changing what's hanging on the walls or how the space is used, or even moving to a new location. Individual team members can be asked to bring ideas for creating inspiring environments for meetings or retreats. **What would you add?**
Overcoming Constraints	————	**Some examples:** When the team faces setbacks or constraints, discuss how members will overcome them together. What can they learn from the setback? How can the team rely on one another for support to move forward with confidence and renewed inspiration? Constraints can be a creative challenge when viewed with a growth mindset. Some teams even build in constraints on purpose as a way to activate the team with new energy around solving a problem. **What would you add?**

(continues)

ENGINE	HOW INSPIRING IS THIS ENGINE FOR YOUR TEAM (1-5)?	WAYS TO TAP INTO THIS ENGINE MORE OFTEN (CIRCLE THE ONES YOU LIKE BEST AND ADD IN YOUR OWN)
Witnessing Excellence	————	**Some examples:** Teams benefit from witnessing the excellence of others, both within their industry and roles and outside these. One way to do this is by taking the team to watch a professional sports or cultural event. The team could also witness the excellence of other teams within the organization. Invite another team to speak about a recent win and how members successfully accomplished the project. Have individual team members share moments of excellence with one another during meetings. **What would you add?**
Using Your Unique Passions or Qualifications to Make a Difference	————	**Some examples:** This engine works well in combination with the "using your strengths" engine. Every team will have its own unique composite of strengths, skills, competencies, and qualifications. Based on this composite, is there a way that your team can make a difference within the organization like no one else can? What's the type of positive impact the team wants to have in the future? What will your team's legacy within the organization be? **What would you add?**

ENGINE	HOW INSPIRING IS THIS ENGINE FOR YOUR TEAM (1-5)?	WAYS TO TAP INTO THIS ENGINE MORE OFTEN (CIRCLE THE ONES YOU LIKE BEST AND ADD IN YOUR OWN)
Sharing Experiences with Large Groups of People		**Some examples:** Certainly, doing things together on a team can create a sense of belonging, but sharing experiences with even larger groups of people can be an exhilarating way to activate inspiration. Consider ways for the team to share experiences with large groups that will ignite inspiration—this could be company events as well as situations outside the organization. This collective consciousness can even happen in the digital arena, sharing an experience with larger groups or communities via social or online conferences. Think of creative ways to engage larger communities! **What would you add?**
Experiencing Grief, Loss, or Failure		**Some examples:** This engine aligns with transparency and vulnerability: if the team is encouraged to be open and transparent, then any team situation that involves grief, loss, or failure can be processed and learned from in a productive way. When individual team members experience grief or loss, it's important for all team members to acknowledge it in a way that is meaningful. When the team entity experiences a loss or failure, the team needs to come together to process it, discuss it, and learn from the experience. This allows the group to stay connected, continue to feel a sense of belonging, and move forward together with a renewed sense of purpose. **What would you add?**

CHAPTER TWELVE

INSPIRING ORGANIZATIONS

Many have written about President Kennedy's visit to the NASA space center in 1962, where he stopped to speak to a janitor on his tour, saying: "Hi, I'm Jack Kennedy. What are you doing?" "Well, Mr. President," the janitor responded, "I'm helping put a man on the moon."[1]

An organization has a responsibility to inspire both its employees and its clients. In today's world of dynamic global markets, it has never been more important for organizations to ignite inspiration, internally and externally. Inspiration at the organizational level is a source of competitive advantage. The way employees assess their experience as workers is the same way customers assess organizational brand. In fact, the ability of organizations to consistently inspire employees and consumers directly impacts the strength and sustainable success of their brands.

Inspiration operates at multiple levels within an organization, from the individual to the work team or business unit to entity-wide. When these levels are all aligned, they create a self-sustaining system of inspiration that propels itself. An inspiring system drives extraordinary results.

At the highest level, inspiring organizations have a purpose that sparks inspiration for all stakeholders associated with the organization—from employees to clients, vendors, board members, stockholders, and the like. Inspiration can also be found within the systems and structures that organizations put into place. For example, how the organization hires, onboards, socializes, and develops employees; how they track productivity (including offering paid time off for employee passion projects); what metrics they use to indicate success; how they celebrate milestones; and how they connect to their community are all opportunities for engines of inspiration to be sparked. Inspiration also lives in an organization's strategy—how it guides teams of individuals to collaborate for success. Finally, and perhaps most important, inspiration in organizations lives within and among its individual contributors. People in inspiring organizations feel tightly connected to one another. They lift one another up, demanding and challenging one another to greater heights.

> "There isn't anything more motivating than people who are inspired . . . Just last week, someone on my team turned down an offer for double the money because they're inspired and believe in what we're doing and their ability to impact and make a difference towards that. Getting to know each person, understanding their story and where they're going, linking that to the vision, that high-ground statement or maneuver, is literally the whole game, and it's more powerful than the biggest salaries and anything else in the world."
>
> —Alex White, Vice President of Content and Programming, Pandora

When the system is in sync, individual, team, and whole entity operations of the organization are aligned and driving one another forward. There is a reciprocal nature to the way the elements of an inspiring organization interact; one feeds the inspiration of another, which, in turn, fuels inspiration to another. For example, an organization that selects and hires people based on how their values match the organization's fosters an employee base that is sparked by a common purpose. Those employees then develop and implement structures and systems that enact the values, further fueling collective inspiration, which then binds the employees to one another ever more tightly. This constantly reinforcing system builds on itself when all the pieces are aligned to one another and toward inspiration, producing and being fueled by both possibility and invincibility. With greater vision and confidence, an inspiring organization achieves more and has greater positive impact than it otherwise could. Inspiring organizations exceed expectations.

Traditionally, organizations measure success through metrics that look at revenue, rates of turnover, profit, market share, intellectual property, and the like. Inspiring organizations excel in these areas of business success. In addition, the return on inspiration for organizations that cultivate an inspiration-driven system is an increased capability for ongoing high returns. Inspiring organizations are more innovative, productive, and responsive to market shifts; they are characterized by richer collaboration and information sharing and have greater talent magnetism—the ability to attract and retain talent (see below).

Thought Experiment: Returns on Inspiration

Our own research, along with our work with clients, has demonstrated the following advantages in an inspiring organization:

For Individuals

- ○ Visionary and strategic thinking
- ○ Better performance and results
- ○ Stronger connections and community
- ○ Purpose-driven and calling-oriented people

For Teams and Organizations

- ○ More innovative and agile
- ○ Driven to produce extraordinary results
- ○ More collaborative and rich in information sharing
- ○ Better at attracting and retaining top talent (talent magnetism)

Organizations, like individuals, have a unique inspiration fingerprint. That is, inspiration will be sparked and sustained differently depending on the organization. For example, engineering firms versus public relations firms, or retail outlets versus professional offices, all differ in how they inspire. What is common to all inspiring organizations is a strong sense of purpose—why the organization does what it does. In some cases, that purpose has to do with how it benefits others, or how it benefits us all, as in the case of Organic Valley.

DRIVEN BY A COMPELLING PURPOSE

What is now known as Organic Valley—seller of organic dairy products, vegetables, and meats—was founded more than thirty years ago by a group of seven farmers who had a commitment to healthier growing and eating and a desire support smaller family farms. The number of farms in the United States has precipitously declined in recent decades.[2] And the farms left are much larger, often squeezing out the little guy, who is at a severe competitive disadvantage.

Enter the Organic Valley co-op. Its founding co-op farmers felt inspired by a common vision to start a collaborative organization that would benefit all its members. Today, the organization consists of more than two thousand co-op farmers across North America and over nine hundred employees, based primarily at the company's headquarters in Wisconsin.

From the outset, Organic Valley's co-op farmers established a common purpose: growing and raising food in a manner that is healthier for the soil, for the animals that provide the milk and eggs, and for the people who consume the food, all while providing farmers with a living wage. That common purpose drives all decisions, fuels their continued participation in the co-op, and sustains the bonds that have formed through the years. Organic Valley hopes to pass down family farms to future generations. It is that common value that has unified the group.[3]

Although the roles of the founding farmers have evolved through the years, with George Siemon taking on the title of CEO, their values and purpose have remained the same. They proudly proclaim on their website: "We're not driven by profits; we're driven by principles. . . . Our farmers share the costs of getting their products to market, and they share the profits when the company does well. But along with everyone who works here, they share a vision of a healthier, more sustainable food system. Everything we do is a collaboration toward that goal."[4] That common purpose united a small group of farmers and continues to inspire the organization's growth and success, resulting in healthy revenue growth for the member farms.

> "One thing that I have had the benefit of seeing and learning, particularly at Organic Valley as a collaborative business, a collaborative structure, is the power of groups, of people, and the important role that inspiration can play and what one individual can do in that group and then what that group can do in a movement or culture or community."
>
> —Leslie Kruempel, Mission Executive, Organic Valley

INSPIRING ORGANIZATIONS START WITH PURPOSE

Part of what makes Organic Valley's story noteworthy is that its core values and purpose are a key source of inspiration. In fact, it would be very difficult for an organization to be inspiring without an exciting, compelling, possibility-fueled purpose that gives meaning to what it does and to those involved in its operations. Purpose is an inspiration engine that is crucial at the organization level.

The success of purposeful organizations reflects a newer perspective on how organizations can and should thrive. The purpose of for-profit organizations, versus not-for-profits, is, at their core, making money, and increasing revenue and profits requires cutting costs, innovating, increasing efficiency and productivity, and the like. Historically, success has required more of a financial focus than anything else; in today's economy, this narrow focus may hurt companies more than helping them. There's a disconnect between what individual employees need from work and what organizations are providing.

In today's economy, what author Aaron Hurst refers to as *The Purpose Economy*,[5] people connected to one another and their work through purpose drive extraordinary financial results. Individuals demand inspiration in their work, and when inspired, they give more of themselves based on traditional financial incentives alone.

> "Inspiring organizations infuse the organization's purpose and values in its structures and systems, rituals, habits, tools, and how people make decisions so they are in daily behavior, daily nudges for creating huge impact."
>
> —Bud Caddell, Founder, Nobl

The research bears this out. In *Firms of Endearment*[6] author Raj Sisodia, Franklin Olin distinguished professor of global business and Whole Foods Market research scholar in conscious capitalism at Babson College, and his colleagues found that organizations that balance the needs of all stakeholders achieve financial greatness. Sisodia and his coauthors showed that firms that balanced the needs of all stakeholders including employees, outperformed the S&P 500 by fourteen to one over a fifteen-year period. Sisodia later partnered with Dave Mackie, CEO of Whole Foods, to cofound Conscious Capitalism, which expanded on the fundamentals of *Firms of Endearment* to codify purpose as a critical aspect of a conscious company:[7] firms of endearment are purpose-driven firms.

Conscious Capitalism International (CCI) is another inspiring organization that looks to both the short term and long term—as in a fifty-year view—to translate possibility into reality, CEO Alexander McCobin said in our interview with him.[8] Part of the Conscious Capitalism credo reflects the organization's higher purpose of *elevating humanity through business*: "Conscious Capitalism is a way of thinking about capitalism and business that better reflects where we are in the human journey, the state of our world today, and the innate potential of business to make a positive impact on the world." McCobin understands that having that level of impact can't be accomplished in five, or ten, or even thirty years. That kind of change takes generations. Having such a visionary higher purpose makes it even more inspiring for those who work there and the businesses and communities they touch in their work. A *big* higher purpose can engage and inspire everyone connected to the organization.

When an organization has an inspiring purpose, it's important that all individuals within the organization know that purpose and how they personally connect to it. An organization's primary lever for driving success can create an environment where people within it feel called to the work by understanding the role they play in achieving success. At NASA in the 1960s, for example, everyone understood their common purpose as an organization: to get an American on the moon. That was never clearer than when President Kennedy went on a tour of Cape Canaveral and asked to meet the people who were committed to helping get a man on the moon by the end of the decade. As the president asked different people "What do you do here?" they responded with "I'm putting a man on the moon." Regardless of their role, their common response and responsibility demonstrated their commitment to their shared purpose.[9]

NASA was a leader in making sure all contributors understood the organization's larger purpose and were inspired to make it their own personal mission, too. While NASA certainly isn't the only organization that has successfully cascaded its larger purpose throughout all levels of the agency, inspiring individual employees and teams can be challenging. The key is making sure everyone understands the higher purpose and is aligned to it—because when inspiration is sparked within a company, it can quickly spread.

Individuals need to feel both their own sense of purpose and connected to the organization's overarching values, whether it's putting a man on the moon, providing unparalleled patient care, or selling

> "We did an employee engagement survey here in 2011, that we do every other year, and one of the results that was glaring that came out was our employees did not understand how what they did on a daily basis impacted the success of the hospital. They couldn't connect the dots. If you're a patient care tech, walking patients, bathing patients, you couldn't understand how that was helping the hospital succeed. That was a major disconnect. If you have the right worthwhile work, and you've picked the right goals, and the board is incenting me with the right goals, and a patient care tech doesn't understand how their work impacts that, that's a wipeout."
>
> —Bill Jennings, President and then CEO of Bridgeport Hospital, Bridgeport, Connecticut, now President and Chief Executive Officer, Reading Hospital

healthy food. To accomplish this requires deliberate design from organizational leadership to fortify the meaning and connection between employees and the organization itself; shifting incentive schemes to inspiration themes. Employees at Organic Valley feel a connection to selling healthy food that feeds the world while caring for the earth and the animals who provide that food. Their higher purpose inspires their work and their relationships with other member farms in the co-op.

This purpose at Organic Valley rings especially true for some members. For example, the Tranel family switched to organic, chemical-free farming and joined the Organic Valley cooperative after their patriarch, Steve, was diagnosed with cancer related to exposure to chemical pesticides. The organization's purpose attracted the Tranels to the cooperative through the strong alignment of their personal family purpose with what the organization stands for.[10]

SPARKING AND SUSTAINING INSPIRATION IN ORGANIZATIONS

If people are an organization's greatest resource, inspired people are an organization's greatest competitive advantage. An organization's job is to create conditions that drive inspiration, tilling the ground for the individuals and teams within it to spark and respark their own inspiration. As we've cited previously,[11] "inspired employees are three times more productive than dissatisfied employees, but they are rare. For most organizations, only one out of eight employees is inspired."

Clearly, the "values and purpose" engine has an enormous impact at the organizational level by cascading inspiration throughout. But it's not the only engine that can apply and reap major rewards in team and individual inspiration.

At Organic Valley, the organization was founded specifically to "overcome constraints" and "serve others," two engines of inspiration. Smaller family farms were unable to be competitive on their own, so they banded together to market collaboratively. At the core, however, was a desire to serve others. Member farmers wanted to continue to grow using techniques that didn't harm the earth or the food that was produced.

> "I'm sure you've found yourself in multiple, dull corporate boardrooms. And every single time, I always look around, and I'm like, God, these people need inspiring. I think the Internet has done a lot of awesome things for the world, but one thing it has done, it has forced a behavior of information as opposed to a behavior of inspiration, particularly inside the corporate environment. I sit inside, people spend all day writing e-mails to each other, and those e-mails are usually transactional, informational, incredibly sort of, you know, the cc-loop of life."
>
> —Paul Bennett, Chief Creative Officer, IDEO

And Organic Valley isn't alone in its reliance on multiple inspiration engines. KIND Healthy Snacks, the makers of KIND bars, also proclaims that "we're a not just for profit company," meaning the company's purpose goes beyond financial rewards. KIND has grown by tapping into multiple inspiration engines.

Daniel Lubetzsky founded the company after he went looking for a snack bar filled with whole nuts, seeds, and fruits to help him prepare for the New York Marathon in 2002, and found none. He suspected there might be a market[12] but had to overcome numerous constraints to develop, produce, and market a health bar no one had ever seen before and that cost more than other bars. The challenge of the process inspired him to keep learning and exploring how to make it work.

From the start, KIND was driven by Lubetzsky's need to do good work in the world. From an early age, Lubetzsky's father—a Holocaust survivor—taught him that the only way to combat darkness is with kindness; an astonishing lesson given his father's experiences at Dachau. His father became his mentor and hero, shaping his outlook on the world. He also heightened his son's awareness of the need for kindness to combat darkness. That perspective inspired the company and its employees.

The "serving others" engine fueled KIND thanks to Lubetsky's father's influence, which led KIND to reinvest some of the company's profits in advertising campaigns around spreading kindness, the company's core purpose.

The company's environment inspires anyone who spends time at its headquarters, which contain pieces of Lubetzsky's father's furniture—a reminder of the positive impact he had on the world.

Bain & Company focuses its culture on achievement and success aligning toward a different engine, "progressing toward and achieving success." The management consulting firm strives to attract achievement-focused employees. For people who are inspired by achievement, this can be a great match and lead to superior performance at an individual, team, and organizational level. According to William Bain, who cofounded the company in 1973, "A culture that inspires and spurs performance makes companies *3.7 times more likely to be top performers*."[13]

Known historically as an exclusive, private high-fashion brand, Chanel's release of its very public *Report to Society*[14] in June 2018 signaled a massive cultural shift. As a privately owned company, Chanel had never been required to reveal much about its internal workings to the public, so much so that secrecy had become a hallmark of the Chanel brand for 108 years. But its sudden release of a seventy-six-page document revealing Chanel's financial health, operating principles, and company mission signaled a brand reset built on transparency. The information proved inspiring to outside observers impressed with the innovation and environmental responsibility the company demonstrated, but internally as well, as employees were no longer burdened by the responsibility of silence and secrecy. Transparency as an engine of inspiration meant freedom—freedom that could only result in more collaboration and better results.

As these stories illustrate, each of these organizations activates multiple engines but they prioritize different engines at different times, based on the environment or situation. In the same way that individual and team performance can be inspiring, organizations can also inspire by using the engines. Successful organizations breed a success mindset and achievement orientation that fuels continued success.

TRANSLATE INSPIRATION ACROSS FOUR CATEGORIES TO DRIVE SUCCESS

Just as with individuals and teams, for organizations to be most effective and sustain inspiration, they need to enact behaviors that reflect their values and operate across the four categories that lead to positive outcomes: driving to results, connection and trust, intentional alignment, and vision and innovation. The most effective companies focus on all four categories simultaneously; ignoring one or more, or placing too much emphasis on some, will lead to suboptimal results.

For example, you can imagine companies that lean too heavily on vision and innovation without paying attention to intentional alignment may generate big ideas but then struggle with implementation. On the flip side, companies that focus so much on driving to results that they forget to build trust and connection with their customers or employees, can engender burnout or disloyalty. Results in those instances are never ideal.

W. L. Gore, the makers of such disparate products as Gore-Tex[15] waterproof outdoor gear, Elixir guitar strings, and Glide dental floss, demonstrates organizational agility across, and presence in, all four categories. Gore competes on its capacity for innovation. This is its strategic advantage in the market. The company's structure and culture have been studied from those who'd like to have the same results. The absence of hierarchy and traditional titles in their structure (there are no titles or ranks—just associates) are hallmarks of their unique approach. Additional practices show how they span the four categories of behavior that drive positive outcomes:

- **Vision and innovation.** Associates at W. L. Gore are encouraged to bring together products and capabilities from disparate applications to create superior products. Elixir guitar strings, for example, are made of nickel-plated steel or copper with a special patented coating (Nanoweb, Polyweb, or Optiweb). W. L. Gore has built a competitive advantage around its ability to capitalize on opportunities by using existing ideas in new ways.[16]
- **Driving to results.** Not only is W. L. Gore innovative, but its inspired culture drives individuals to make commitments to the success of its projects. Associates are not assigned tasks or projects. Rather, the company acts like a marketplace for ideas. Associates make their own commitments to projects and drive them forward to ongoing high profits.
- **Connection and trust.** W. L. Gore employees value their work relationships, for example, consulting with one another before taking action that might be damaging. Because of the importance of these work relationships, as of 2017, W. L. Gore had been on the list of the Top 100 Best Companies to work for every year for the past twenty years.[17]
- **Intentional alignment.** Fairness is one of W. L. Gore's guiding principles, with systems and processes consistent to this. The lack of hierarchy and emphasis on freedom of choice for associates is an example. They emphasize this guiding principle of fairness in their interactions with one another, suppliers, and customers. Individuals, teams, and the organization are in sync with the rest

of their guiding principles in a similar way. People have clarity of values, clarity of roles, and clarity of goals.

Organizationally and through its strategy, W. L. Gore focuses on all four categories with agility across all of them, combining them as needed and emphasizing one or more as situations demand. For example, when a project fails at W. L. Gore, they reportedly celebrate the project conclusion with beer or champagne, the same way they would have if it had succeeded. At times like that, the company leans more on connection and trust or intentional alignment for inspiration than on driving to results. Such celebrations cultivate a growth mindset and learning from setbacks. But there is always an emphasis on successful innovation and growth. They hold these priorities simultaneously and consistently with their guiding principles.

SIMULTANEOUS FOCUS ON BOTH TODAY AND TOMORROW

An organization's strategy is a directive for how it will achieve its vision. On what basis will the organization compete and thrive to realize success? Inspiring organizations have what is referred to as ambidexterity.[18] To effectively implement the organization's strategy, the leadership needs to simultaneously have one hand focused on efficiency today and the other on innovation tomorrow, pursuing both these potentially conflicting priorities.

Netflix provides a prime example of an ambidextrous organization. Over ten years, the company rolled out its DVD-by-mail service while simultaneously investing in streaming technology; it saw that streaming of movies on demand was the wave of the future. Then, as movies on demand became common and retail rentals of DVDs declined, Netflix started investing in TV and movie production.[19] And it's paying off, as Netflix now has the largest subscriber base as of 2018. Another sign of its success? The 112 Emmy nominations Netflix earned in 2018 topped HBO's count, breaking its seventeen-year winning streak.[20] As the company continues to thrive, it begs the question of what they are currently planning for the future.

PEOPLE FEEL CONNECTED, LIFT ONE ANOTHER

In inspiring organizations, people feel a sense of belonging to a tribe; they feel strong connections to other people and rely on other people to hold them accountable, to support them, and to cultivate their growth. For example, at Organic Valley, working as a cooperative with common values, the more than two thousand co-op farm members are bound by common goals and values.[21] Through their common connection to these values, members of this organization enjoy built-in opportunities to provide social support. They believe in the same guiding values and can thus identify with one another and relate.

Building a supportive culture where people lift one another up to grow was certainly the goal at Next Jump, an e-commerce company, which, in 2008, fired 50 percent of its workforce, coming out of what it refers to as its era of "brilliant jerks."[22] During this time, they started over, intentionally creating a new culture from the ground up based on a growth mindset, integrating purpose, feedback, learning, and trust at all levels. To do that, leaders focused more on relationships and hired for different traits and skills. They have identified themselves as a Deliberately Developmental Organization.[23]

As a result, Next Jump now has a more supportive, collegial culture that encourages coaching and mentoring across all levels. These shifts in Next Jump's innermost systems surely spark inspiration through engines like getting a lift, common values, shared experiences, achievement, and more. They have been so successful in this cultural turnaround that the company created a three-day immersive leadership academy where other leaders from other organizations come and learn from them.[24]

Part of the three-day academy includes a fitness component (managing energy), where identifying and fueling the physical, mental, and emotional needs of attendees is addressed. A condition for being inspired is a healthy mindset and energy level.

ESPRIT DE CORPS: LIFTING PHYSICAL, MINDSET, AND EMOTIONAL ENERGY

To be inspired, organizations need to attend to both the individual and the organizational levels, providing opportunities to boost energy and sustain inspiration. At the individual level, organizations can encourage employees to attend to their own energy. Many corporations now have in-house wellness initiatives and even design their spaces thoughtfully to promote mindfulness and balance of employees. Organizations can also offer opportunities for workers to reset their energy by stepping away from their workspace to attend conferences and courses that enhance their expertise and self-confidence, or to simply break up their day and infuse them with physical activity, such as taking a walk outside at lunch or signing up for yoga after work.

Organizations can create opportunities for energy refreshers through events, too. At InspireCorps, we schedule quarterly in-person meetings for all employees, who are geographically dispersed, so that they can come together. Not only does this provide a chance to reconnect and strengthen relationships, which foster inspiration, but we build in events and activities designed to lift everyone's spirits—boosting us physically, emotionally, and cognitively and making us even more open to new inspiration.

Similarly, Next Jump holds an annual dance competition[25] for its employees. Different locations compete with one another for the title, which provides opportunities for employees to forge relationships, work collaboratively toward a common goal, and have fun doing it. Win or lose, Next Jump teams come away feeling positive and uplifted about the experience.

THE ROLE OF THE INDIVIDUAL AND TEAMS IN INSPIRING ORGANIZATIONS

Although an organization is a separate, distinct entity from the individual contributors within it, as the building blocks of a company, individuals and teams have an opportunity to attend to their own and the organization's inspiration levels and influence them. You can ask, "How is my organization inspiring me and others?" and "Where are there cracks?" Once weak points are identified, you have the power and responsibility to influence and/or address those cracks.

At the same time, you are responsible for attending to your own levels of inspiration. You can use the workplace environment and activities to spark and respark your own engines of inspiration and institutionalize practices for sustaining inspiration. You can demand more of the organization, expecting it to be a source of inspiration and speaking up when it isn't, offering ideas and solutions proactively. Some things to consider for sustaining inspiration in organization:

- Innovate. Full stop.
- Engage others around you in being inspiring, including those above you, peers at your level, and those who are more junior employees. Seek to understand the whole organizational system, from the CEO down to the ground-floor employee. It's sometimes surprising where you find inspiration.
- Give your all. The pride you feel in yourself and from others when you fully commit to the organization's success will spark inspiration and feed your own success and that of others.
- Use your voice when needed to offer praise and encouragement and foster inspiration internally, as well as to dissent when warranted, challenging the status quo when you have better ideas.
- Start an inspiration insurrection when you feel things are lagging at the highest leadership levels; inspiration can come from the

bottom up just as well as from the top down. And research shows that division-designed culture change is more likely to work.[26]

- Know your team's purpose, mission, and function and how it fits within the larger organization's purpose and mission. Actively look for alignment and opportunities to realign.

Within your team, create a culture that is consistent with the organization's overarching culture. Be a sounding board for individual employees in need of inspiration and a place where individuals can reset. Embed and spread inspiration practices from the bottom up.

WORK IT
Scaling Inspiration

Below is an abridged version of a larger inspiration index assessment we use to inventory inspiration at our clients. Rate your organization on a scale of 1–5 on these dimensions:

Organization has an inspiring higher purpose:

____ I am inspired by my organization's higher purpose.

____ I know how my individual value and purpose align to it.

Sparking and resparking engines for all:

____ Systems and practices within my organization regularly spark my inspiration.

____ I have opportunity to spark my inspiration through my work environment and relationships.

Directing inspiration to performance:

_____ We operate in all four categories of behavior in my organization.
_____ I contribute to my organization's success.

People feel connected and lift one another up:

_____ I have found my tribe at my organization.
_____ My colleagues support me and hold me accountable to be my best.

Managing energy (physical, emotional, and cognitive):

_____ I am regularly energized by my work.
_____ My organization supports and provides opportunities to boost energy and recharge.

For any that you observe are rated 3 or lower, design a plan to boost inspiration. Use the following questions to launch your thinking and creativity:

What inspires me about my organization?

What is my organization's higher purpose? How does my personal purpose align to it?

Consider a system or process that I or my team could enact that would infuse inspiration into the organization.

EPILOGUE

"We cannot teach people anything; we can only help them discover it within themselves."

—Galileo Galilei

This book began with a story about a day in August 2012 when the three of us had a conversation that changed us. On that day, we landed on *inspiration* as being *the thing*, the resource, the X-factor— what separates a run-of-the-mill day from an extraordinary day, what distinguishes a truly meaningful and impactful career. We'll repeat here what we said in the opening because of its importance:

> In our work with clients, we have found that what will make the difference for them individually and collectively is sustainable inspiration directed toward positive impact.

What has become the great joy of our lives is bringing inspiration to our clients. Clients come to us with all kinds of requests, challenges, and pain points: struggles with culture, employee burnout, toxic communication, lack of clarity around roles, insufficient succession planning, poor strategic planning—the list goes on. We help them address these challenges by getting to the root of the specific problems. But we go beyond relieving their pain points and challenges by partnering with our clients to spark and sustain their inspiration to ensure sustainable success. We integrate the *sparks* and *flame* through the engines of inspiration into the experience and process of everything we do.

INSPIRING A BOARD

One example comes from our work with a board of directors of a major medical system. Their board was not functioning as they would like. There was dissent, factions, vying for control and resources, lack of clear strategy and common goals, and a less-than-desirable level of engagement overall.

As a starting place, we partnered to help lead a strategic planning process. We knew of the deeper issues within the board from our discovery process, so we recognized this board meeting as an opportunity to develop a strategic plan, yes, but a more important aim was to begin to produce inspiration for these individuals and for the team. We needed to break down walls (through shared experiences, vulnerability, and transparency), so they could feel a sense of unity through alignment of goals (belonging), and be excited by a compelling future together (mission and purpose)—all engines of inspiration for these board members.

On the day of the board meeting, we peppered board interactions with more engines and sustainers of inspiration: we asked each of them to share their main contributions on the board and two things that were important to them outside work. This made board members aware of one another's strengths, and it helped them see one another as whole human beings.

They learned that their teammates were parents and spouses, of course, but also dancers, woodworkers, nature lovers. Being able to see one another as whole humans helped them build connection and enabled behaviors in the connection and trust area going forward, to help sustain inspiration. We spent time showing them how to direct inspiration across the four categories of capability that are so critical to sustaining it through extraordinary performance as a board.

We subscribe to what we call 3-D learning: using mindset, body, and emotions to make learning sticky and accelerate the integration of new behaviors and insights going forward. For the board, this meant we had them on their feet, learning through active 3-D experiences. We used music to activate emotions and had them practicing leadership presence through movement, postures, and body language—and it was fun. The exercises sparked inspiration for some (physical movement and presence) and helped sustain the physical, cognitive, and emotional energy for session. We directed this inspired energy toward an immediate practical result (and an opportunity to alleviate one of their self-described pain points)—facilitating an internal decision. The dialogue that ensued was dynamic and agile; there was great participation and inclusion; and within the set time, we came to consensus and specifics on accountability in light of the decision made. Had we not produced inspiration in the room before tackling this decision, old patterns of unhealthy conflict and disengagement would have ruled. Instead, the board members got a glimpse of what was possible for them as a team, and they gained new capabilities for repeating their success. As you can imagine, when we then turned to the first phase of strategic planning, the primary impetus for the meeting, they were able to tackle it together with greater possibility and confidence.

INSPIRING A START-UP

The way we instill inspiration for our clients is also illustrated in our ongoing work with a tech start-up that engaged us soon after their launch to help develop their company values and culture. Over our years with them, meeting for live quarterly sessions and coaching a number of executives on their leadership team, we helped integrate inspiration into the very DNA of the organization.

Some of the specific work we did with them included designing their performance management and development process (as a high-frequency, in-the-moment tool that is based on goals, aspirations, and development). We created a strategic planning process for them that mapped to the non-linear nature of planning in a start-up. We trained them in recognizing and activating leadership strengths, integrating this 3-D perspective into everything they do. We instilled energy management resets as a frequent and now almost automatic practice for individuals and teams, and we integrated a system of communication that increased reliability of execution and helped them manage capacity. We codesigned a field sales communication and development strategy. We rode the wave of change with them that all start-ups inevitably face, equipping them with tools for resilience and learning in the face of setbacks, and we helped them celebrate success and integrate the practice of celebration into their culture. You can see the engines of inspiration and the sustaining practices that are inherent in all this work.

The sense of possibility and invincibility they established helped them pivot when their business needed to take a turn. Where many start-ups would have shuttered in the face of the product challenges they faced, this organization had the commitment and the capability to stay focused on their original purpose—around empowering women—while conducting a major shift in their product strategy to better fit the market. The business is now growing, with a positive return on investment, in the ways businesses usually measure it. But they are also stronger, more empowered, and more inspired than ever to succeed. They lost no members of their leadership team in their major shift; instead, there is increased pride and optimism about the future. This company measures laughter. They label themselves strengths-obsessed, and even their most remote field sales representatives have a pride and sense of belonging that is a significant strategic advantage. They are a living example of an inspiring organization, and as a result of their investment in building this foundation, we are confident they will continue to cultivate and sustain their own inspiration as the business thrives.

INSPIRING LEADERSHIP AT ALL LEVELS IN AN ORGANIZATION

One final example of how clients have integrated inspiration into their organizations comes from an ongoing leadership development effort at a biopharma research firm. Our initial engagement with them focused on performance management, where we helped them shift from a traditional, primarily deficit-focused annual performance review process to a more frequent strengths-based pulse of check-ins and feedback. This new approach keeps employees excited about their goals, aspirations, and development.

After integrating the new pulse-feedback process into their culture, they subsequently came to us seeking a plan to develop leadership skills throughout the organization. They were coming up on what they knew would be a challenging year of great opportunities and wanted to support their talent in preparation. Although they weren't asking for inspiration per se, we knew that it would be a critical resource for them at all levels to navigate successfully through these upcoming opportunities.

We partnered to design and implement a multiyear inspiration campaign comprised of live experiences, practical tools, coaching, and webinars that were tailored to various leadership levels while also touching every employee. All of our contacts with them, face-to-face and virtual, were based on building awareness and capability in the engines of inspiration—from invoking their inspiring purpose around serving others to noting achievement and progress, empowering them to overcome constraints within the organization, using their strengths, and many more. We've learned that once you are cognizant of the engines of inspiration, opportunities to bring them in and combine them are everywhere. Conversely, the engines are also a powerful diagnostic when results aren't being produced; we ask, what are the engines that are missing in this situation?

Our efforts to sustain these sparks of inspiration, while addressing their requests for culture and leader development, are designed around translating inspiration into results via the four core capabilities that drive success (driving to results, intentional alignment, connection and trust, vision and innovation). We launched the whole effort with an all-hands keynote address to the whole organization on "having your best day more often," through using and acknowledging character strengths in one another.

Then, once per quarter, we focus on one target theme driven by their strategic priorities that quarter and the company values, including what it means *at their company*, the behaviors and capabilities within it and tools and strategies to reinforce it throughout the culture. For example, in the quarter focused on directing inspiration toward driving to results, we delivered live experiences, webinars, and follow-on microtools and videos on using strengths to set and achieve aspirational goals. By activating their sense of greater possibility and invincibility, they set goals that are more ambitious and more meaningful to them. Some unique inspiration practices we baked in from the ground floor included having all employees take a character strengths assessment and using strengths-based language in their team meetings and interactions, tracking and celebrating progress and achievement in their work, and giving and receiving aspirational feedback. In addition, we introduced the inspiration sustainer of *energy management* via resets with music and walking meetings, showing them how to practice individually and on teams as a proactive way to get focused and boost energy.

This multiyear partnership is already yielding desirable results. The organization is better poised to navigate the turbulence inherent in their industry. We see new connections being built across the organization promoting unity and belonging among leaders who sometimes feel siloed away from other parts of the organization. Leaders are understanding how to embrace and lead change for themselves and their groups, rather than be discouraged or frustrated by it. We trained everyone to be a leader and that a leader's first job is to inspire one's self. As a result, individual contributors—leading from where they stand—are taking greater ownership of their roles and their contributions to the company's success.

Over time, we've realized that although clients want the pain points alleviated, a faster and more sustainable path to drive success—and what they really want and need—is more inspiration in their organizations. To know the most powerful leverage points to start, we use our Inspiration Index to assess their strengths and opportunities at individual, team, and organization levels to better spark and sustain inspiration entity-wide.

As we interviewed leaders, we heard again and again how seriously people take their own inspiration and their responsibility to inspire others in today's world of work. Inspiration is the common denominator that integrates for people what they care about the most in their work and their lives outside work. It's something we collectively experience as human beings and, therefore, connects us all.

When we work with our clients, we start with what we envision is possible for them when they activate inspiration as a resource throughout their organization. Of course, this inherently addresses the pain points along the way. But addressing the pain is not enough; we want our clients to thrive and flourish in inspiration. We want the same for you.

We trust this book has been a discovery process for you, that from the stories and leaders we featured, the Work It activities and tools provided, you've experienced:

- Ways that you get inspired,
- How to spark your own inspiration more often,
- Practices to sustain your inspiration over time, making it stronger like a muscle, and
- Creating plans to bring inspiration to your team and organization.

Our hope is that this book activates in you new ideas about what's **possible** for you, your team, your organization, along with a sense of **invincibility** to achieve it.

ACKNOWLEDGMENTS

Our greatest gratitude goes to the inspired ones—the subjects of the many stories and quotes that validate and animate the content of this book. We launched this project with exploratory interviews about inspiration; over time, as we conducted more and more of them, we had rich, illustrative data from which to develop our framework and thinking. The people we interviewed gave us insight into who they are, who they were as children, what lights them up, what drags them down, and how they respark and rise. They shared generously, and our work is better for it. Each of them brings inspiration into the world through their work in unique and powerful ways. We offer great thanks for all we learned from those who sat with us for interviews, with special gratitude to Carmen Erian, Janet Patti, and Robin Stern, our first three interviewees.

Along with insights from interviews, this book conveys stories and descriptions of research from people we did not interview personally but who contributed to this work nonetheless. To the business and cultural leaders we profile in this book, we offer thanks for your leadership and commitment to doing good. You show the world what business can be and do to make all of our lives better. We have learned from you, and we know others will continue to do the same. We are also grateful to the many social and psychological scientists whose research we stand on and feature throughout the book. We love science! (You can tell by the number of citations and endnotes.) We love it because those scientists' work gives us deep knowledge, which is firm ground to stand on as we build our models of inspiration from our own data. For this we are grateful. We share your ongoing quest for new and insightful understanding.

This book simply could not have happened without the faith, love, and support of our InspireCorps team. They are our practice and training ground for our ideas, frameworks, and tools and for actually understanding how inspiration works. Not to mention, it's really difficult to build a business and write a book at the same time. The amazing Gabi Joyce, Laura Campbell, Judy Dobai, Serina Capuano, and Katie Giasullo helped us make writing happen and keep writing a priority. They took on extra when needed, provided amazing moral support and encouragement, and tested and challenged ideas with us. They celebrated our progress along the way. It takes a village to write a book; they are our village. We love you, team. We are more grateful than we can say for all you bring to who we are and what we do.

We are especially grateful to our book team. While we have a lot to say about things, none of us was very familiar with the book writing or publishing process. We got a lot of critical support. That started with Angie Morgan and Courtney Lynch of Lead Star who led us to the key members of our team. Our team captain from the start was our agent Esmond Harmsworth. He has consistently and ardently advanced our work from the very start. He provided brilliant early stage input when our ideas were still forming, he offered insightful and sharp edits to our book proposal, and he has been our guide and great supporter through the whole process. Thank you, Esmond. We are also grateful to our editor Dan Ambrosio at Da Capo. From our first conversation with him, Dan understood what *Dare to Inspire* is about and the impact and contribution we want it to make. He believes in us. He gets us. We're grateful for his stewardship in getting our message out to the world. Thank you to Marcia Layton Turner for helping us accelerate the process. We offer our thanks as well to the rest of the Da Capo/Hachette team. The legal reviewers, copy editor, book designers, and marketing experts have been great guides.

Allison shares her gratitude for her incredible support team: to Paul, Adrian, and Isaac—you are my spark, my flame, my source of joy and strength. I feel so lucky to be on this journey of life with you. Thank you to my parents for your love: you have always encouraged me to try new things and experiment, from building forts to starting a soap-carving business as a child. My sisters, Amy and Angela, I can't think of anyone else I've laughed or cried harder with—I love you, always. Thank you to my extended family for your encouragement: Mike, Ximena, Big Steve, Little Steve, David, Reshma, Bucky, Eleni, Briley, Aidan, Leah, and cousins from New York and Kentucky to Ecuador. To my dearest friends—you know who you are—thanks for making life so much fun. And with deep gratitude to the teachers, mentors, and institutions who ignited my fierce love of learning and passion for inspiring others: Walt Gander, Dick Aylor, Bill Bornschein, Christian Jernstedt, Shelby Gratham, Joy Kenseth, Janet Patti, Kentucky Country Day School, Dartmouth College, the Yale Center for Emotional Intelligence, and the Coaches Training Institute.

Sandy offers special thanks to her students and her family: my students are the sparks of inspiration in my teaching and in my research. Working with them gives me new ideas about my own work and brings me unbridled joy. I also get to test-drive lots of material on them in class (and they provide great feedback!). My family is also critical to any success I enjoy. Mom and Dad are my cheerleaders extraordinaire. My sister Suzanne was a keen reviewer of early drafts of the work and is always a great support. Her husband, Mark, is an adviser to our firm and a personal coach to me; everyone should be as lucky as I am to have a big brother like him. Kevin, Michelle, Katie, and Jonathan round out the home team. Thanks, everybody, for being on board. I love you all.

Jen shares deep gratitude for her family and support systems: first, I wish to thank my family for supporting my continued growth, always. Thank you for having my back when I most need it and for loving and believing in me always. Thank you, Theo B., my love, for being the hottest, sparkiest, and most sustaining source of inspiration and learning in my life. Thank you to Jim for his friendship and love. Finally, thank you to the powerful women leaders and mentors who have crossed and lit my path: Zoë Chance, Molly Nagler, Jessica Brahaney Cain, Randie Flaig,

Frances Garfield, Joan Bronston, Nina Baron, Eileen Cummings, Rebecca Guerra, Julie Brewer, Kelly Conklin, Amy Wrzesniewski, Janet Kraus, Carrie Christiansen, Laura Campbell, Christa Doran, and Julia Balfour. *Non nobis solum* (not for ourselves alone are we born): you shaped me and made me more.

Finally, this book was created over many long hours with the three of us connected on Zoom, writing in Google Docs. We live in three different cities, so most of the work was done remotely. There were many times when we literally had six hands in a single Google document, typing over each others' sentences, while we were talking it through on Zoom. We recognize for some that sounds like a miserable fate, but for us, it was pure joy being able to collaborate so smoothly. These two pieces of technology were instrumental in bringing our three voices together to generate this work. We are grateful.

APPENDIX A

Road Map to Spark, Sustain, and Scale Inspiration

STEP 1: ENVISIONING INSPIRATION

Identify an area where you could use more inspiration (invincibility + possibility):

If you were inspired in this area, what positive outcomes would you be looking for? (For you? For others? For your impact?)

STEP 2: SPARKING INSPIRATION | "A LEADER'S FIRST JOB IS TO INSPIRE SELF."

When you first read through Chapters 3, 4, and 5, what engines resonated with you the most? What are the engines you reliably use now that work well for you?

In this area where you are seeking more inspiration, what other engines might be useful to consider to spark it?

STEP 3: SUSTAINING INSPIRATION THROUGH INTENTIONAL PRACTICE | "THE KEY TO SUSTAINING THE SPARK IS TURNING IT INTO A FLAME."

How will you revisit the engines or combine new engines that spark your inspiration on a regular basis?

What actions can you take to direct your inspiration toward your desired outcomes across four categories?

Drive to results

Intentional alignment

Connection and trust

Vision and innovation

How will you monitor and manage your physical, emotional, and mental energy to keep your energy high and bounce back quickly from setbacks?

How will you boost your inspiration when needed?

What positive rituals can you create and practice?

Who will you look to for social support?

How and with whom will you introduce accountability for your plan?

STEP 4: SCALING INSPIRATION TO TEAMS AND ORGANIZATION | "DARE TO INSPIRE. INSPIRED PEOPLE DRIVE SUCCESS."

How can you be a leader in generating and sustaining inspiration at work?

How will you actively model your inspiration practice as a leader and expect the same from others?

What would greater inspiration on your team look like? How can you keep inspiration top of mind for the team?

What engines are most potent for your team?

How can you help to create psychological safety?

What does social sensitivity look like for your team?

How will you and the team make sure every voice gets heard?

What practices in the four categories should the team implement to direct inspiration toward desired outcomes?

What is inspiring about your organization?

How does the organization's purpose connect with your own?

How can you contribute to the success of your organization through the four categories that direct inspiration toward desired outcomes?

What system or process could you impact and help infuse inspiration into the organization?

APPENDIX B

What Inspiration Is Not

lthough inspiration shares some common themes with creativity, motivation, flow, and even awe, it is distinctly different in key ways. Traditional conceptions of inspiration overlap with other concepts we know are important, although inspiration is distinctive.

- **Creativity**—is the use of imagination or original ideas to create something; inventiveness.[1] Creativity is one possible outcome when you are inspired, but there are many other outcomes of inspiration as well (e.g., increased energy, agility in thinking and acting, strategic thinking, motivation and engagement, alignment to purpose and work, meaning and satisfaction in relationships).
- **Flow**—is the mental state in which a person performing an activity is fully immersed in a feeling of energized focus, full involvement, and enjoyment in the activity. In essence, flow is characterized by complete absorption in what one is doing where there is a lost sense of time. In flow, one is fully consumed in the process of being challenged. One can feel inspired to do an activity that puts oneself in a state of flow, and being in a state of flow can help us sustain inspiration over time. But flow is something in and of itself.

- **Motivation or drive**—is the general desire or willingness of someone to do something. Motivation is an outcome of inspiration. These concepts are related but not the same. Many things besides inspiration can motivate us (consider fear or guilt), and inspiration has multiple other outcomes from it in addition to greater motivation or drive.

- **Awe**—is a feeling of reverential respect mixed with fear or wonder. Awe, like spirituality, reminds us just how small we are in relation to a larger sense of space or time. We often feel a sense of awe in the presence of natural wonders or when witnessing incredible feats of creativity or performance.[2] Feelings of awe can lead to feelings of inspiration or be experienced alongside inspiration; however, awe itself is more passive. It is about taking in the experience around you. In contrast, inspiration drives you to new thinking or taking action in a new way.

- **Engagement**—is a term used in organizations that refers to the emotional commitment the *employee* has to the organization and its goals, or how much they care about their work and their company.[3] Engagement can be an outcome of inspiration and is often used in the workplace to describe employees' commitment and connection to their work. Employees who feel inspired will naturally be more engaged in their work. As with motivation, engagement has other sources than inspiration; inspiration has other outcomes.

- **Morality**—is a sense of decency, virtue, or rightness. We tend to focus on the positive side of inspiration—inspired to do good, to be good. But the combination of possibility and invincibility that comprise inspiration are not limited to virtuous acts. Morally reprehensible leaders may be inspired and inspirational, even toward indecent priorities. Inspiration should not be confused with goodness. However, our focus in this book will be on positive, righteous inspiration.

- **Grit**—is defined by researchers as a combination of passion and persistence applied toward longer term goals in life.[4] A key aspect of it is the ability to persevere through difficult times and obstacles. The of engine of "overcoming obstacles" can ignite sparks of inspiration; however, the experience of inspiration itself is less about pushing through and more about capitalizing on the feelings of possibility and invincibility.

None of these concepts carries the distinct combination of possibility and invincibility that define positive, sustainable inspiration and that give it the power to transform us and move us to action.

APPENDIX C

Table of Inspiration Engines

SPARKED
BY YOU

♡ VALUES AND PURPOSE

💪 ACTIVATING STRENGTHS

🏆 ACHIEVEMENTS

💭 UNSTRUCTURED TIME

💡 NEW PERSPECTIVES

💪 BODY MOVEMENT & PRESENCE

**SPARKED
BY OTHERS**

BELONGING

MENTORS & HEROES

GETTING A LIFT

SERVING OTHERS

SHARED MISSION

VULNERABILITY

**SPARKED
BY SITUATIONS**

ENVIRONMENTS THAT MOVE US

OVERCOMING CONSTRAINTS

WITNESSING EXCELLENCE

MAKING A DIFFERENCE

SHARED GROUP EXPERIENCES

GRIEF, LOSS, OR FAILURE

NOTES

PART I: UNDERSTANDING INSPIRATION

Chapter 1: What Is Inspiration and Why Does It Matter?

1. Jessica Pryce-Jones, *Happiness at Work: Maximizing Your Psychological Capital for Success* (Hoboken, NJ: John Wiley & Sons, 2011).

1. "Taj Mahal Facts," http://www.softschools.com/facts/wonders_of_the_world /taj_mahal_facts/91/ (accessed June 2, 2019).

2. "Taj Mahal Story," Taj Mahal, https://www.tajmahal.org.uk/story.html (accessed February 1, 2017).

3. Ibid.

4. Ibid.

5. History.com editors, "Taj Mahal," History, August 21, 2018, https://www .history.com/topics/taj-mahal (accessed February 1, 2017).

6. Ibid.

7. "Cost of the Taj Mahal," Landmarks of the World, https://www.wonders-of -the-world.net/Taj-Mahal/Cost-of-the-Taj-Mahal.php (accessed February 1, 2017).

8. Eric Garton and Michael C. Mankins, "Engaging Your Employees Is Good, but Don't Stop There," *Harvard Business Review,* December 9, 2015, https://hbr.org /2015/12/engaging-your-employees-is-good-but-dont-stop-there (accessed March 15, 2016).

9. Eric Garton, "The Case for Investing More in Your People," *Harvard Business Review,* September 4, 2017, https://hbr.org/2017/09/the-case-for-investing-more-in -people (accessed September 17, 2017).

10. "Word History: Breathing Life into 'Inspire'," Merriam Webster, https://www .merriam-webster.com/words-at-play/the-origins-of-inspire (accessed February 1, 2017).

11. Paul D. Holzer interview by Sandra Spataro, January 13, 2018.

12. Christina Maslach and Michael P. Leiter, "Understanding the burnout experience: Recent research and its implications for psychiatry," *World Psychiatry* 15, no. 2 (2016): 103–111.

13. Jennifer Tombaugh interview by Jen Grace Baron, April 8, 2019.

14. NPR/TED staff, "How Do You 'Design' Trust between Strangers?," TED Radio Hour, NPR, May 20, 2016, https://www.npr.org/templates/transcript/transcript.php?storyId=478563991 (accessed on February 1, 2017).

15. Aaron Hurst, *The Purpose Economy: How Your Desire for Impact, Personal Growth and Community Is Changing the World* (Boise, ID: Elevate, 2016).

16. "Co-working: The New Way to Work," *CBS News*, April 15, 2018, CBS News, https://www.cbsnews.com/news/co-working-the-new-way-to-work/ (accessed on February 1, 2017).

17. Ibid.

18. "Taj Mahal: An Epitome of True Love and Beauty," *The India Review*, August 14, 2018, http://www.theindiareview.com/140818_01/ (accessed June 3, 2019).

19. Eric Garton, "What If Companies Managed People as Carefully as They Managed Money?," *Harvard Business Review*, May 24, 2017, https://hbr.org/2017/05/what-if-companies-managed-people-as-carefully-as-they-manage-money (accessed on June 15, 2017).

20. Barbara L. Fredrickson, "The Role of Positive Emotions in Positive Psychology: The Broaden-and-Build Theory of Positive Emotions," *American Psychologist* 56, no. 3 (2001): 218–226.

21. Barbara L. Fredrickson, "What Good Are Positive Emotions?," *Review of General Psychology* 2, no. 3 (1998): 300–319.

22. Sarah Whitten, "Unicorn Frappuccino Bumped Up Starbucks' Sales, More Quirky Drinks to Come," April 27, 2017, CNBC, https://www.cnbc.com/2017/04/27/unicorn-frappuccino-bumped-up-starbucks-sales-more-quirky-drinks-to-come.html (accessed on June 1, 2017).

23. Daniel Goleman, Richard E. Boyatzis, and Annie McKee, *Primal Leadership: Unleashing the Power of Emotional Intelligence* (Boston: Harvard Business Review Press, 2013).

24. Andrea Goulet interview by Allison A. Holzer, July 1, 2016.

25. Blake Mycoskie, "How I Did It: The TOMS Story," *Entrepreneur*, September 20, 2011, https://www.entrepreneur.com/article/220350 (accessed on June 13, 2017).

26. Ibid.

27. Ibid.

28. Dennis Green, "Amazon Takes on FEDEx and UPS with New Delivery Service," *Business Insider*, October 5, 2017, https://www.inc.com/business-insider/amazon-launches-delivery-service-seller-flex-rival-ups-fedex-2017.html (accessed June 3, 2019).

29. Ibid.

30. "A Truly Human Organization," Barry-Wehmiller International, https://www.barrywehmiller.com/our-culture (accessed on June 1, 2017).

31. William Fricks, "Barry-Wehmiller International: Easing the Manufacturing Processes from Raw Materials to Products," Manufacturing Technology Insights, https://consulting-service.manufacturingtechnologyinsights.com/vendor/barryweh

miller-international-easing-the-manufacturing-processes-from-raw-materials-to
-products-cid-25-mid-13.html (accessed on June 2, 2017).

32. Ed Catmull, *Creativity, Inc.: Overcoming the Unseen Forces That Stand in the Way of True Inspiration* (New York: Random House, 2014), 195, https://www.amazon.com
/Creativity-Inc-Overcoming-Unseen-Inspiration/dp/0812993012.

33. "SAS Celebrates 20th Year as One of Fortune's Best US Workplaces," SAS, March 9, 2017, https://www.sas.com/hu_hu/news/press-releases/2017/march/great
-workplace-US-Fortune-2017.html (accessed on December 12, 2018).

34. Ibid.

Chapter 2: Truths about Inspiration

1. "Meet Barrington," Experience Aviation, http://www.experienceaviation.org
/index.php?option=com_content&view=article&id=61&Itemid=100 (accessed October 15, 2017).

2. Barrington Irving interview by Allison A. Holzer and Jen Grace Baron, December 10, 2018.

3. "2012 Emerging Explorer: Barrington Irving," *National Geographic,* https://
www.nationalgeographic.org/find-explorers/barrington-irving (accessed on October 15, 2018).

4. Ken Kaye, "Record-Breaking Pilot Urges Students to Soar," *Sun Sentinel* (Palm Beach, FL), December 12, 2014, http://www.sun-sentinel.com/local/palm-beach
/fl-barrington-irving-oxbridge-20141212-story.html (accessed on October 17, 2017).

5. "Barrington Irving: Young Pilot Promotes Aviation Careers," Avjobs Weekly, May 20, 2019, https://www.avjobs.com/avjobsweekly/newsletters/Pilot-Promotes
-Aviation-Careers.asp (accessed on November 1, 2018).

6. "Barrington Irving & World Flight Adventure," Florida Memorial University, fmuniv.edu. http://www.fmuniv.edu/about/our-history/barrington-irving-world-flight
-adventure/ (accessed on October 1, 2017).

7. Kaye, "Record-Breaking Pilot Urges Students to Soar."

8. Ibid.

9. "If I Can Do It, Anyone Can," About Us, Experience Aviation, http://www
.experienceaviation.org/about-us.html (accessed on November 1, 2017).

10. Barrington Irving interview by Allison A. Holzer and Jen Grace Baron, December 10, 2018.

11. Kaye, "Record-Breaking Pilot Urges Students to Soar."

12. Elaine Hatfield, John T. Cacioppo, and Richard L. Rapson, "Emotional Contagion," *Current Directions in Psychological Science* 2, no. 3 (1993): 96–100.

13. "Steven Spielberg on How Lawrence of Arabia Inspired Him to Make Movies," American Film Institute, December 27, 2012, https://www.youtube.com/watch?v
=ayJLeVDOCZ0 (accessed on October 4, 2018).

14. Jennifer M. Talarico, Dorthe Berntsen, and David C. Rubin, "Positive Emotions Enhance Recall of Peripheral Details," *Cognition and Emotion* 23, no. 2 (2009): 380–398.

15. Shea Gregg interview by Allison A. Holzer, January 5, 2017.

16. Joe Kasper interview by Jen Grace Baron, October 24, 2018.

17. Devika Bulchandani interview by Laura Campbell and Jen Grace Baron, January 7, 2018.

18. Derek Ohly interview by Allison A. Holzer and Jen Grace Baron, April 10, 2017.

19. Hajo Adam and Adam D. Galinsky, "Enclothed Cognition," *Journal of Experimental Social Psychology* 48, no. 4 (2012): 918–925.

20. Jer Clifton interview by Jen Grace Baron, August 23, 2018.

21. Jenna Bell interview by Jen Grace Baron, July 10, 2018.

22. Chuck Firlotte interview by Jen Grace Baron, April 23, 2018.

23. Keith Yamashita interview by Sandra Spataro, June 27, 2017.

24. Raymond D. Fowler, Martin EP Seligman, and Gerald P. Koocher, "The APA 1998 Annual Report," *American Psychologist* 54, no. 8 (1999): 537–568.

25. Martin E. P. Seligman, *Flourish: A Visionary New Understanding of Happiness and Well-Being* (New York: Simon & Schuster, 2012).

26. Cal Newport, *Deep Work: Rules for Focused Success in a Distracted World* (London: Hachette UK, 2016).

27. Brian Parkinson and Gwenda Simons, "Affecting Others: Social Appraisal and Emotion Contagion in Everyday Decision Making," *Personality and Social Psychology Bulletin* 35, no. 8 (2009): 1071–1084.

28. Jonas T. Kaplan and Marco Iacoboni, "Getting a Grip on Other Minds: Mirror Neurons, Intention Understanding, and Cognitive Empathy," *Social Neuroscience* 1, no. 3–4 (2006): 175–183.

29. Laurie Carr, Marco Iacoboni, Marie-Charlotte Dubeau, John C. Mazziotta, and Gian Luigi Lenzi, "Neural Mechanisms of Empathy in Humans: A Relay from Neural Systems for Imitation to Limbic Areas," *Proceedings of the National Academy of Sciences* 100, no. 9 (2003): 5497–5502.

PART II: SPARKING INSPIRATION

1. Barbara L. Fredrickson, "The Role of Positive Emotions in Positive Psychology: The Broaden-and-Build Theory of Positive Emotions," *American Psychologist* 56, no. 3 (2001): 218.

Chapter 3: Sparked by YOU

1. Chris Hughes, "Meet the Culinary Rebel behind LA's Hottest Tacos," *Coastal Living*, https://www.coastalliving.com/food/kitchen-assistant/wes-avila-guerrilla-tacos-los-angeles-california (retrieved January 22, 2019).

2. Mandalit del Barco, "'Guerrilla Tacos': Street Food with a High-End Pedigree," NPR, November 2, 2017, https://www.npr.org/sections/thesalt/2017/11/02/561417108/guerrilla-tacos-street-food-with-a-high-end-pedigree (accessed on July 2, 2018).

3. Wes Avila interview by Allison A. Holzer, January 21, 2019.

4. Ibid.

5. Del Barco, "'Guerrilla Tacos': Street Food with a High-End Pedigree."

6. Ibid.

7. Ibid.

8. Wes Avila interview by Allison A. Holzer, January 21, 2019.

9. Aaron Hurst, *The Purpose Economy: How Your Desire for Impact, Personal Growth and Community Is Changing the World* (Boise, ID: Elevate, 2016).

10. Katherine Brooks, "Job, Career, Calling: Key to Happiness and Meaning at Work?," *Psychology Today*, June 29, 2012, https://www.psychologytoday.com/blog /career-transitions/201206/job-career-calling-key-happiness-and-meaning-work (accessed on September 15, 2018).

11. David Stuart, "'Job Crafting': The Great Opportunity in the Job You Already Have," *Forbes*, June 20, 2013, https://www.forbes.com/sites/groupthink/2013/06/20 /job-crafting-the-great-opportunity-in-the-job-you-already-have/#65c915f325df (accessed on September 15, 2018).

12. Wes Avila interview by Allison A. Holzer, January 21, 2019.

13. Christopher Peterson and Martin E. P. Seligman, *Character Strengths and Virtues: A Handbook and Classification,* vol. 1 (New York: Oxford University Press, 2004).

14. Susan Peppercorn, "The Benefits of Using Your Strengths at Work," Positive Workplace Partners, https://positiveworkplacepartners.com/the-benefits-of-using -your-strengths-at-work/ (accessed on December 22, 2018).

15. Justin M. Berg, Jane E. Dutton, and Amy Wrzesniewski, "What Is Job Crafting and Why Does It Matter?," Center for Positive Organizational Scholarship, revised August 1, 2008, https://positiveorgs.bus.umich.edu/wp-content/uploads/What-is -Job-Crafting-and-Why-Does-it-Matter1.pdf. The job crafting workbook is located at https://positiveorgs.bus.umich.edu/cpo-tools/job-crafting-exercise/.

16. Amy Wrzesniewski, Clark McCauley, Paul Rozin, and Barry Schwartz, "Jobs, careers, and callings: People's relations to their work," *Journal of Research in Personality* 31, no. 1 (1997): 21–33.

17. Martin E. P. Seligman, *Flourish: A Visionary New Understanding of Happiness and Well-being* (New York: Simon & Schuster, 2012).

18. Richard M. Ryan and Edward L. Deci, "Self-Determination Theory and the Facilitation of Intrinsic Motivation, Social Development, and Well-Being," *American Psychologist* 55, no. 1 (2000): 68.

19. Gary Garfield interview by Jen Grace Baron, October 24, 2017.

20. Tom Kolditz interview by Jen Grace Baron, October 24, 2017.

21. Bill Jennings interview by Laura Campbell and Allison A. Holzer, April 4, 2018.

22. Manda Mahoney, "The Subconscious Mind of the Consumer (and How to Reach It)," Working Knowledge: Business Research for Business Leaders, Harvard Business School, January 13, 2003, https://hbswk.hbs.edu/item/the-subconscious -mind-of-the-consumer-and-how-to-reach-it.

23. Christian Jernstedt interview by Allison A. Holzer, October 10, 2016.

24. Nancy Andreasen, "Secrets of the Creative Brain," *The Atlantic*, July–August 2014, https://www.theatlantic.com/magazine/archive/2014/07/secrets-of-the-creative -brain/372299/ (accessed on June 14, 2018).

25. Richard E. Boyatzis, Kylie Rochford, and Anthony I. Jack, "Antagonistic neural Networks Underlying Differentiated Leadership Roles," *Frontiers in Human Neuroscience* 8, article 114 (2014). Note: Richard Boyatzis, a researcher who writes about the neurology of emotions, notes that activating a part of the brain called the task-positive

network will inhibit another part of the brain responsible for openness to new ideas, called the default mode network. Unstructured time encourages the default mode network to emerge.

26. Wes Avila interview by Allison A. Holzer, January 21, 2019.

27. Tom Dente, "From Déjà Vu to Vuja De: The Importance of New Perspectives" (blog), Humentum, https://www.humentum.org/blog/d%C3%A9j%C3%A0-vu-vuja-de-importance-new-perspectives (accessed on July 7, 2018).

28. "From Bike to Flight," Who Were Wilbur & Orville, Smithsonian National Air and Space Museum, https://airandspace.si.edu/exhibitions/wright-brothers/online/who/1895/biketoflight.cfm (accessed on August 12, 2018).

29. Matt Rosoff, "The Only Reason the Mac Looks Like It Does Is Because Steve Jobs Dropped in on a Course Taught by This Former Monk," *Business Insider,* March 8, 2016, http://www.businessinsider.com/robert-palladino-calligraphy-class-inspired-steve-jobs-2016-3 (accessed on August 1, 2017).

30. Hannah Steinberg, Elizabeth A. Sykes, Tim Moss, Susan Lowery, Nick Le-Boutillier, and Alison Dewey, "Exercise Enhances Creativity Independently of Mood," *British Journal of Sports Medicine* 31, no. 3 (1997): 240–245.

31. Justin Rhodes, "Why Do I Think Better after I Exercise?," *Scientific American,* July 2013, https://www.scientificamerican.com/article/why-do-you-think-better-after-walk-exercise/ (accessed on August 17, 2018).

32. "Johnson & Johnson Human Performance Institute Invests in the Future of Wellbeing with New $18 Million Facility in Lake Nona Medical City," Johnson & Johnson, https://www.jnj.com/media-center/press-releases/johnson-johnson-human-performance-institute-invests-in-the-future-of-wellbeing-with-new-18-million-facility-in-lake-nona-medical-city (accessed on December 20, 2018).

33. Vivian Giang, "What 11 Highly Successful People Do to Stay in Shape," *Business Insider,* November 11, 2013, http://www.businessinsider.com/workout-routines-of-highly-successful-people-2013-11 (accessed on August 17, 2018).

34. "Guide to Walking Meetings," Feet First, http://www.feetfirst.org/walk-and-maps/walking-meetings (accessed on August 15, 2018).

35. Emily Peck, "Why Walking Meetings Can Be Better Than Sitting Meetings," Huffington Post, updated December 6, 2017, http://www.huffingtonpostcom/2015/04/09/walking-meetings-at-linke_n_7035258.html (accessed on August 15, 2018).

Chapter 4: Sparked by OTHERS

1. Rebecca Thomas, "Malala Yousafzai: Her Father's Daughter," BBC, November 6, 2015, https://www.bbc.com/news/entertainment-arts-34637751 (accessed on August 3, 2018).

2. "Malala Yousafzai: Biographical," The Nobel Prize, 2014, https://www.nobelprize.org/nobel_prizes/peace/laureates/2014/yousafzai-bio.html (accessed on August 3, 2018).

3. "Malala: Like Father, Like Daughter," *Telegraph* (London), https://www.telegraph.co.uk/film/he-named-me-malala/malala-father-daughter-relationship/ (accessed on August 3, 2018).

4. Becky Little, "Malala's Dad Says His Daughter Is Unstoppable," *National Geographic*, February 26, 2016, https://news.nationalgeographic.com/2016/02/160226-he -named-me-malala-ziauddin-yousafzai-interview/ (accessed on August 3, 2018).

5. Ibid.

6. Dennis Driver interview by Jen Grace Baron, March 14, 2019.

7. George E. Vaillant, *Aging Well: Surprising Guideposts to a Happier Life from the Landmark Study of Adult Development* (Boston: Little, Brown, 2008).

8. Liz Mineo, "Good Genes Are Nice, but Joy Is Better," *Harvard Gazette*, https:// news.harvard.edu/gazette/story/2017/04/over-nearly-80-years-harvard-study-has -been-showing-how-to-live-a-healthy-and-happy-life/ (accessed on August 20, 2018).

9. J. Holt-Lunstad, T. B. Smith, T. B. and J. B. Layton, "Social Relationships and Mortality Risk: A Meta-Analytic Review," *PLoS Medicine* 7, no. 7 (2010): e1000316.

10. Dan Buettner, *The Blue Zones: 9 Lessons for Living Longer from the People Who've Lived the Longest* (Washington, DC: National Geographic Books, 2012).

11. Barrington Irving interview by Allison A. Holzer and Jen Grace Baron, December 10, 2018.

12. George R. Goethals and Scott T. Allison, "Making Heroes: The Construction of Courage, Competence, and Virtue," in *Advances in Experimental Social Psychology*, vol. 46, eds. Mark Zanna and James Olson (San Diego: Academic Press, 2012), 183–235.

13. Michael Allen, "Female Mentors Help Retain Female Students," *Physics World* 30, no. 7 (2017): 10.

14. Amy Wrzesniewski interview by Sandra Spataro and Allison A. Holzer, December 14, 2016.

15. Adelle Platon, "Common Recalls the Time He Gave Advice to a Young Rapper Who Turned Out to Be Chance The Rapper," *Billboard*, April 20, 2017, https://www billboard.com/articles/columns/hip-hop/7767808/time-100-most-influential-people -common-chance-the-rapper (accessed on August 15, 2017).

16. Will Kenton, "Oprah Effect," Investopedia, https://www.investopedia.com /terms/o/oprah-effect.asp (accessed on August 3, 2017).

17. Entrepreneurs' Organization, https://www.eonetwork.org/ (accessed on August 20, 2018).

18. "An elite ecosystem of entrepreneurs," Plug and Play, https://www.plugand playtechcenter.com/startups/ (accessed on October 1, 2018).

19. Michael Olmstead interview by Jen Grace Baron, April 30, 2019.

20. Maggie Doyne, "Our History," BlinkNow, https://blinknow.org/pages/our -history (accessed on August 20, 2018).

21. Ibid.

22. Ibid.

23. Michael Baroody interview by Allison A. Holzer, November 21, 2017.

24. Ibid.

25. Roy F. Baumeister, Kathleen D. Vohs, Jennifer L. Aaker, and Emily N. Garbinsky, "Some Key Differences Between a Happy Life and a Meaningful life," *Journal of Positive Psychology* 8, no. 6 (2013): 505–516.

26. Aristotle, "Chapter 8: Loving Is More of the Essence of Friendship Than Being Loved," Book 8, Nicomachean Ethics, Internet Sacred Text Archive, https://www.sacred-texts.com/cla/ari/nico/nico089.htm (accessed on August 21, 2018).

27. Netta Weinstein and Richard M. Ryan, "When Helping Helps: Autonomous Motivation for Prosocial Behavior and Its Influence on Well-Being for the Helper and Recipient," *Journal of Personality and Social Psychology* 98, no. 2 (2010): 222–244.

28. Zoë Chance and Michael Norton, "I Give Therefore I Have: Charitable Donations and Subjective Wealth," in *Advances in Consumer Research*, vol. 38, eds. Darren W. Dahl, Gita V. Johar, and Stijn M. J. van Osselaer (Duluth, MN: Association for Consumer Research, 2011).

29. Adam M. Grant, Elizabeth M. Campbell, Grace Chen, Keenan Cottone, David Lapedis, and Karen Lee, "Impact and the Art of Motivation Maintenance: The Effects of Contact with Beneficiaries on Persistence Behavior," *Organizational Behavior and Human Decision Processes* 103, no. 1 (2007): 53–67.

30. Sebastian Junger, *Tribe: On Homecoming and Belonging* (London: Hachette UK, 2016).

31. John E. Mathieu, Tonia S. Heffner, Gerald F. Goodwin, Eduardo Salas, and Janis A. Cannon-Bowers, "The Influence of Shared Mental Models on Team Process and Performance," *Journal of Applied Psychology* 85, no. 2 (2000): 273–283.

32. Amy Wrzesniewski, "Finding Positive Meaning in Work," in *Positive Organizational Scholarship: Foundations of a New Discipline,* eds. Kim S. Cameron, Jane E. Dutton, and Robert E. Quinn (San Francisco: Berrett-Koehler, 2003), 296–308.

33. Marissa Thalberg interview by Allison A. Holzer and Laura Campbell, June 8, 2017.

34. Tom Kolditz interview by Jen Grace Baron, October 19, 2017.

35. Ibid.

36. Michael Paulson, "'Hamilton' Producers and Actors Reach Deal on Sharing Profits," *New York Times,* April 15, 2016, https://www.nytimes.com/2016/04/16/theater/hamilton-producers-and-actors-reach-deal-on-sharing-profits.html.

37. "Transtheoretical Model," Pro-change Behavior Systems, https://www.prochange.com/transtheoretical-model-of-behavior-change (accessed on August 15, 2018).

38. Brené Brown, *Daring Greatly: How the Courage to Be Vulnerable Transforms the Way We Live, Love, Parent, and Lead* (New York: Penguin, 2015).

39. Bruce J. Avolio and William L. Gardner, "Authentic Leadership Development: Getting to the Root of Positive Forms of Leadership," *Leadership Quarterly* 16, no. 3 (2005): 315–338.

40. Emma Seppälä, "What Bosses Gain by Being Vulnerable," *Harvard Business Review,* December 11, 2014, https://hbr.org/2014/12/what-bosses-gain-by-being-vulnerable.

41. Will Yacowitz, "Why Being Vulnerable Doesn't Mean You're Being Weak," *Inc.,* December 16, 2014, https://www.inc.com/will-yakowicz/why-being-vulnerable-is-a-good-idea.html (accessed on September 20, 2018).

42. Margaret Greenberg, personal communication, February 22, 2017.

Chapter 5: Sparked by SITUATIONS

1. Robin P. Zander, "Charles Best, Donors Choose—A Purpose Driven Company," Vimeo, October 27, 2017, https://vimeo.com/240183506 (accessed on July 5, 2018).

2. Ibid.

3. Charles Best interview by Allison A. Holzer, July 22, 2018.

4. "See Our Impact Nationwide since Our Start in 2000," DonorsChoose.org, https://www.donorschoose.org/about/impact.html (accessed on January 5, 2019).

5. Gregory N. Bratman, Gretchen C. Daily, Benjamin J. Levy, and James J. Gross, "The Benefits of Nature Experience: Improved Affect and Cognition," *Landscape and Urban Planning* 138 (2015): 41–50.

6. Ibid.

7. Allison Aubrey, "Forest Bathing: A Retreat to Nature Can Boost Immunity and Mood," NPR, July 17, 2017, https://www.npr.org/sections/health-shots/2017/07/17/536676954/forest-bathing-a-retreat-to-nature-can-boost-immunity-and-mood (accessed on July 20, 2018).

8. Daniel J. Levitin, "Hit the Reset Button in Your Brain," *New York Times*, August 9, 2014, https://www.nytimes.com/2014/08/10/opinion/sunday/hit-the-reset-button-in-your-brain.html (accessed on July 2, 2018).

9. Howard Schultz and Joanne Gordon, *Onward: How Starbucks Fought for Its Life without Losing Its Soul* (New York: Rodale Books, 2012).

10. Ed Catmull, *Creativity, Inc.: Overcoming the Unseen Forces That Stand in the Way of True Inspiration* (New York: Random House, 2014), https://www.amazon.com/Creativity-Inc-Overcoming-Unseen-Inspiration/dp/0812993012.

11. Cat Overman, "Sanctuary: An Artist's Oasis," Zillow, May 4, 2016, https://www.zillow.com/blog/sanctuary-an-artists-oasis-197089/ (accessed on July 5, 2018).

12. Angela Duckworth, *Grit: The Power of Passion and Perseverance*, vol. 124 (New York: Scribner, 2016).

13. Karen Reivich and Andrew Shatté, *The Resilience Factor: 7 Essential Skills for Overcoming Life's Inevitable Obstacles* (New York: Broadway Books, 2002).

14. Richard M. Ryan and Edward L. Deci, "Self-Determination Theory and the Facilitation of Intrinsic Motivation, Social Development, and Well-Being," *American Psychologist* 55, no. 1 (2000): 68–78.

15. Malcolm Gladwell, *David and Goliath: Underdogs, Misfits, and the Art of Battling Giants* (London: Hachette UK, 2013).

16. Dan P. McAdams, *The Redemptive Self: Stories Americans Live By* (New York: Oxford University Press, 2013).

17. Steve Squinto interview by Laura Campbell, November 15, 2017.

18. Sara B. Algoe and Jonathan Haidt, "Witnessing Excellence in Action: The 'Other-Praising' Emotions of Elevation, Gratitude, and Admiration," *Journal of Positive Psychology* 4, no. 2 (2009): 105–127.

19. Jennifer E. Stellar, Neha John-Henderson, Craig L. Anderson, Amie M. Gordon, Galen D. McNeil, and Dacher Keltner, "Positive Affect and Markers of Inflammation: Discrete Positive Emotions Predict Lower Levels of Inflammatory Cytokines," *Emotion* 15, no. 2 (2015): 129–133.

20. Xin Hu, Jianwen Yu, Mengdi Song, Chun Yu, Fei Wang, Pei Sun, Daifa Wang, and Dan Zhang, "EEG correlates of ten positive emotions," *Frontiers in Human Neuroscience* 11, article 26 (2017): 1368–1378.

21. John O'Donohue, "The Inner Landscape of Beauty," *On Being* (podcast), Public Radio Exchange, originally aired February 28, 2008, updated August 31, 2017, https:// onbeing.org/programs/john-odonohue-the-inner-landscape-of-beauty-aug2017/ (accessed on July 20, 2018).

22. Temple Grandin, "Making Slaughterhouses More Humane for Cattle, Pigs, and Sheep," *Annual Review Animal Bioscience* 1, no. 1 (2013): 491–512.

23. Temple Grandin, *Thinking in Pictures: And Other Reports from My Life with Autism* (New York: Vintage, 2006).

24. Temple Grandin, "Cattle vocalizations Are Associated with Handling and Equipment Problems at Beef Slaughter Plants," *Applied Animal Behaviour Science* 71, no. 3 (2001): 191–201.

25. Ryan Bell, "Temple Grandin, Killing Them Softly at Slaughterhouses for 30 Years," *National Geographic*, August 19, 2015, https://www.nationalgeographic.com /people-and-culture/food/the-plate/2015/08/19/temple-grandin-killing-them-softly -at-slaughterhouses-for-30-years/ (accessed on November 15, 2018).

26. "Salva's Story," Water for South Sudan, https://www.waterforsouthsudan.org /salvas-story/ (accessed on November 15, 2018).

27. Matt Weinberger, "This Is Why Steve Jobs Got Fired from Apple—and How He Came Back to Save the Company," *Business Insider*, July 31, 2017, https://www .businessinsider.com/steve-jobs-apple-fired-returned-2017-7#in-june-of-1997-an -anonymous-party-sold-15-million-apple-shares-in-a-single-transaction-the-move -caused-apple-shares-to-dip-to-a-12-year-low-over-that-july-4th-weekend-jobs-had -convinced-the-board-to-name-him-interim-ceo-and-fire-amelio-14.

28. Apple's Evolution: The Return of Jobs, the Apple Revolution: 10 Key Moments, *Time*, http://content.time.com/time/specials/packages/article/0,28804,1873486 _1873491_1873461,00.html.

29. Ibid.

30. Erica J. Boothby, Margaret S. Clark, and John A. Bargh, "Shared Experiences Are Amplified," *Psychological Science* 25, no. 12 (2014): 2209–2216.

31. Nathaniel Rakich, "How Many Fans Does Each MLB Team Have?," Baseballot (blog), July 17, 2014, baseballot.blogspot.com. http://baseballot.blogspot.com/2014/07 /how-many-fans-does-each-mlb-team-have.html (accessed on November 20, 2018).

32. John Troan, "Philadelphia Eagles," Football @ JT-SW.com, updated January 13, 2019, http://www.jt-sw.com/football/pro/teams.nsf/histories/eagles (accessed on November 20, 2018).

33. Christopher G. Davis, Susan Nolen-Hoeksema, and Judith Larson, "Making Sense of Loss and Benefiting from the Experience: Two Construals of Meaning," *Journal of Personality and Social Psychology* 75, no. 2 (1998): 561–574.

34. Dr. Leah Osowiecki interview by Allison A. Holzer, June 5, 2019.

35. Mike Isaac, "Her Husband's Death Motivates Sheryl Sandberg to Write Another Book," *New York Times*, August 1, 2018, https://www.nytimes.com/2016/08/01

/technology/her-husbands-death-motivates-sheryl-sandberg-to-write-another-book
.html (accessed on June 5, 2019).

36. Joe Kasper interview by Jen Grace Baron, August 24, 2018.

37. Lawrence G. Calhoun and Richard G. Tedeschi, "The Foundations of Post-traumatic Growth: An Expanded Framework," in *Handbook of Posttraumatic Growth: Research and Practice*, eds. Lawrence G. Calhoun and Richard G. Tedeschi (New York: Psychology Press, 2014), 3–23.

38. Jenna Bell, "A Journey of the Heart," Grapefruit and Tattoos, https://grape
fruitandtattoos.com/ (accessed on November 1, 2018).

39. Jenna Bell interview by Jen Grace Baron, May 1, 2018.

40. Whitney Johnson, "Stacy London: Getting Fired Was Just What She Needed" (blog), January 17, 2017, https://whitneyjohnson.com/stacy-london/ (accessed on May 15, 2018).

41. "Watch Bennis Commenting on How to Make One's Organization Dancing," Freedom, Inc., October 27, 2010, https://freedomincbook.com/2011/07/02/warren-bennis-on-how-leaders-can-be-creative/ (accessed on December 21, 2018).

Chapter 6: Respark the Engines

1. Edward Delman, "How Lin-Manuel Miranda Shapes History," *The Atlantic*, September 2015, https://www.theatlantic.com/entertainment/archive/2015/09/lin-manuel-miranda-hamilton/408019/ (accessed on June 3, 2019).

2. Jane Levere, "Historic Manhattan Home That Inspired Miranda to Write 'Hamilton' Offers Special Cocoa Exhibition," *Forbes*, April 30, 2017, https://www.forbes.com/sites/janelevere/2017/04/30/historic-manhattan-home-that-inspired-miranda-to-write-hamilton-offers-special-cocoa-exhibition/#3a613aaf427d (accessed on December 1, 2018).

3. "Lindsey Vonn Interview," *Elle,* https://www.elle.com/life-love/a41344/lindsey-vonn-interview-rolex/ (accessed on July 1, 2018).

4. Ibid.

5. Barbara O'Brien, "The Buddhist Earth Witness Mudra," Learn Religions, March 4, 2019, https://www.learnreligions.com/earth-witness-449958 learnreligions.com (accessed on June 3, 2019).

6. Bill Bornschein interview by Allison A. Holzer, April 13, 2017.

7. Partho Burman, "An Assamese Who Created a Woodland in a River Island Is the Forest Man of India," *The Weekend Leader*, April 27, 2015, theweekendleader.com., http://www.theweekendleader.com/Heroism/2155/forest-maker.html (accessed on November 2, 2018).

8. David Beard, "Meet the Man Who Single-Handedly Planted a Forest in India," *Mother Jones*, September 5, 2018, https://www.motherjones.com/media/2018/09/recharge-newsletter-18-india-jadav-payeng-forest/ (accessed on December 18, 2018).

9. "30-Year Journey from Tribal Boy to Forest Man," *Times of India*, updated August 3, 2014, https://timesofindia.indiatimes.com/home/environment/developmental-issues/30-year-journey-from-tribal-boy-to-Forest-Man/articleshow/39510215.cms (accessed on November 2, 2018).

10. Laura Batten and Tricia Robertson, "3 to Be Honored for Contributions to Music, Medicine, Humanities," *Morning Star* (Wilmington, NC), March 17, 1993, Google Newspaper Archive, https://news.google.com/newspapers?id=964sAAAAIBAJ&sjid=wRQEAAAAIBAJ&pg=3069,637510&dq=dr-robert-muller&hl=en (accessed on November 20, 2018).

11. Janet Patti interview by Allison A. Holzer, October 12, 2016.

12. Denis Stamaris, "UN Official Says Life Should Be 1st Alliance," *Spokane Daily Chronicle,* October 25, 1976, Google Newspaper Archive, https://news.google.com/newspapers?id=zE9OAAAAIBAJ&sjid=4_gDAAAAIBAJ&pg=5855,1807329&dq=dr-robert-muller&hl=en (accessed on November 20, 2018).

13. Janet Patti interview by Allison A. Holzer, October 12, 2016.

14. Ibid.

15. Ibid.

16. Susan Adams, "The Coffee Cult: How Dutch Bros. Is Turning Its 'Bro-istas' into Wealthy Franchisees," *Forbes,* https://www.forbes.com/sites/susanadams/2016/06/15/the-coffee-cult-how-dutch-bros-is-turning-its-bro-istas-into-wealthy-franchisees/#1b3fec763694 (accessed on November 3, 2018).

17. Ibid.

18. Dutch Bros. Coffee, "Because of You: Since 1992," https://www.dutchbros.com/our-story.

Chapter 7: Direct Inspiration to Desired Outcomes

1. CEO Genome, https://ceogenome.com/ (accessed on February 1, 2019).

2. Elena Botelho, Kim Powell, Stephen Kincaid, and Dina Wang, "What Sets Successful CEOs Apart," *Harvard Business Review,* May–June 2017, 70–77, https://hbr.org/2017/05/what-sets-successful-ceos-apart.

3. Elena Botelho and Kim Powell, *The CEO Next Door: The 4 Behaviors That Transform Ordinary People into World Class Leaders* (New York: Currency, 2018).

4. David Ulrich, Norm Smallwood, and Kate Sweetman, *The Leadership Code: 5 Rules to Lead By* (Boston: Harvard Business Press, 2009).

5. NPR/TED staff, "How Do You 'Design' Trust between Strangers?," TED Radio Hour, NPR, May 20, 2016, https://www.npr.org/templates/transcript/transcript.php?storyId=478563991 (accessed on February 1, 2017).

6. Kirk J. Schneider, James F. T. Bugental, and J. Fraser Pierson, eds., *The Handbook of Humanistic Psychology: Leading Edges in Theory, Research, and Practice* (Thousand Oaks, CA: Sage, 2001).

7. J. Richard Hackman, "Why Teams Don't Work," in *Theory and Research on Small Groups,* eds. R. Scot Tindale, Linda Heath, John Edwards, Emil J. Posavac, Fred B. Bryant, Yolanda Suarez-Balcazar, Eaaron Henderson-King, and Judith Myers (Boston: Springer, 2002), 245–267.

8. Martin E. P. Seligman, *Flourish: A Visionary New Understanding of Happiness and Well-Being* (New York: Simon & Schuster, 2012).

9. James E. Maddux, "Self-Efficacy Theory," in *Self-Efficacy, Adaptation, and Adjustment: Theory, Research, and Application,* ed. James Maddux (Boston: Springer, 1995), 3–33.

10. Teresa Amabile and Steven Kramer, *The Progress Principle: Using Small Wins to Ignite Joy, Engagement, and Creativity at Work* (Boston: Harvard Business Review Press, 2011).

11. Pamela Engel, "Here's the Real Story of the 'Cool Runnings' Bobsled Team That the Movie Got Wrong," *Business Insider,* February 6, 2014, https://www.business insider.com/the-real-story-of-the-cool-runnings-bobsled-team-2014-2.

12. George Fitch, "The Real Cool Runnings," ESPN UK, February 5, 2014, http://en.espn.co.uk/olympic-sports/sport/story/280229.html (accessed on February 1, 2019).

13. Ibid.

14. Rhiannon Walker, "On This Day: Rosa Parks Refused to Give Up Her Bus Seat, Igniting the Civil Rights Movement," The Undefeated, December 1, 2016, https://theundefeated.com/features/on-this-day-rosa-parks-refused-to-give-up-her-bus-seat-igniting-the-civil-rights-movement/ (accessed on February 2, 2019).

15. Ariel Schwartz, "Bill and Melinda Gates on How They Work Together for Good," *Fast Company,* March 19, 2014, https://www.fastcompany.com/3027896/bill-and-melinda-gates-on-how-they-work-together-for-good (accessed on February 4, 2019).

16. Ben Lillie, "Married and Working Together to Solve Inequality: Bill and Melinda Gates at TED2014," TED Blog, March 18, 2014, https://blog.ted.com/married-and-working-together-to-solve-inequality-bill-and-melinda-gates-at-ted2014/ (accessed on February 12, 2019).

17. Christine Lagorio-Chafkin, "This Billion-Dollar Founder Says Hiring Refugees Isn't a Political Act," *Inc.,* June 2018.

18. Ibid.

19. Ryan Grenoble, "Chobani Hires Refugees and Treats Them Well: That Makes a Lot of People Angry," Huffington Post, November 1, 2016, https://www.huffingtonpost.com/entry/chobani-ceo-refugee-immigrant-hamdi-ulukaya_us_58189ac4e4b0990edc336cab (accessed on February 12, 2019).

Chapter 8: Give Your Inspiration a Boost

1. David G. Allan, "Ben Franklin's '13 Virtues' Path to Personal Perfection," CNN, March 1, 2018, https://www.cnn.com/2018/03/01/health/13-virtues-wisdom-project/index.html (accessed on November 18, 2018).

2. "In 1726, at the age of 20, Benjamin Franklin created a system to develop his character," thirteenvirtues.com/ (accessed on October 2, 2018).

3. Eames Yates, "A Navy SEAL Commander Explains Why You Should Make Your Bed Every Single Day," *Business Insider,* https://www.businessinsider.com/navy-seal-commander-explains-why-you-should-make-your-bed-2017-4 (accessed on October 5, 2018).

4. M. L. Rose, "What Does Michael Phelps Do Before a Race?," Livestrong, https://www.livestrong.com/article/1002130-michael-phelps-before-race/ (accessed on June 1, 2019).

5. Neal Tarparia, "Kick the Chair: How Standing Cut Our Meeting Times by 25%," *Forbes,* June 19, 2014, https://www.forbes.com/sites/groupthink/2014/06/19/kick

-the-chair-how-standing-cut-our-meeting-times-by-25/#238d8ad135fe (accessed on October 8, 2018).

6. Lisa Evans, "Why Sharing Your Progress Makes You More Likely to Accomplish Your Goals," *Fast Company*, June 19, 2015, https://www.fastcompany.com/3047432 /why-sharing-your-progress-makes-you-more-likely-to-accomplish-your-goals (accessed on October 3, 2018).

7. Angela Jia Kim interview by Laura Campbell, January 8, 2018.

8. Entrepreneurs' Organization, www.eonetwork.org/ (accessed on October 15, 2018).

9. IVY: The Social University, https://www.ivy.com/about (accessed on March 17, 2019).

10. Melanie Pritchard, "Executive Coaching: The Fortune 500's Best Kept Secret," LinkedIn, June 16, 2016, https://www.linkedin.com/pulse/executive-coaching -fortune-500s-best-kept-secret-melanie-pritchard/ (accessed on October 13, 2018).

11. Anthony M. Grant, Linley Curtayne, and Geraldine Burton, "Executive Coaching Enhances Goal Attainment, Resilience and Workplace Well-Being: A Randomised Controlled Study," *Journal of Positive Psychology* 4, no. 5 (2009): 396–407.

12. David R. Caruso and Peter Salovey, *The Emotionally Intelligent Manager: How to Develop and Use the Four Key Emotional Skills of Leadership* (Hoboken, NJ: John Wiley & Sons, 2004).

13. Daniel Goleman, "The Emotional Intelligence of Leaders," *Leader to Leader* 1998, no. 10 (1998): 20–26.

14. Randolph M. Nesse, "Evolutionary Explanations of Emotions," *Human Nature* 1, no. 3 (1990): 261–289; Robert Plutchik, "The Nature of Emotions: Human Emotions Have Deep Evolutionary Roots, a Fact That May Explain Their Complexity and Provide Tools for Clinical Practice," *American Scientist* 89, no. 4 (2001): 344–350; and Peter Salovey and John D. Mayer, "Emotional Intelligence," *Imagination, Cognition and Personality* 9, no. 3 (1990): 185–211.

15. Susan David and Christina Congleton, "Emotional Agility," *Harvard Business Review*, November 2013, 125–131.

16. Salovey and Mayer, "Emotional Intelligence."

17. Susan E. Rivers, Marc A. Brackett, Maria R. Reyes, Nicole A. Elbertson, and Peter Salovey, "Improving the Social and Emotional Climate of Classrooms: A Clustered Randomized Controlled Trial Testing the RULER Approach," *Prevention Science* 14, no. 1 (2013): 77–87.

18. "The Mood Meter App Is Here," Yale Center for Emotional Intelligence, http://ei.yale.edu/mood-meter-app/ (accessed on December 15, 2018).

19. Carol Dweck, "Carol Dweck Revisits the Growth Mindset," *Education Week* 35, no. 5 (2015): 20–24.

20. Paul Rozin and Edward B. Royzman, "Negativity Bias, Negativity Dominance, and Contagion," *Personality and Social Psychology Review* 5, no. 4 (2001): 296–320.

21. S. F. Dingfelder, "Our Stories, Ourselves," *Monitor on Psychology* 42, no. 1 (2011): 42–43.

22. Daniel T. Gilbert and Timothy D. Wilson, "Prospection: Experiencing the Future," *Science* 317, no. 5843 (2007): 1351–1354.

23. Kristin D. Neff, "Does Self-Compassion Entail Reduced Self-Judgment, Isolation, and Over-Identification? A Response to Muris, Otgaar, and Petrocchi," *Mindfulness* 7, no. 3 (2016): 791–797.

24. Anthony D. Mancini, George A. Bonanno, and Andrew E. Clark, "Stepping Off the Hedonic Treadmill," *Journal of Individual Differences* 32, no. 1 (2011): 144–152; and Ed Diener, Richard E. Lucas, and Christie Napa Scollon, "Beyond the Hedonic Treadmill: Revising the Adaptation Theory of Well-Being," in *The Science of Well-Being*, Social Indicators Research Series, vol. 37, ed. Ed Diener (Dordrecht, Netherlands: Springer, 2009), 103–118.

25. "Can't Sleep? Blame Your Screen Time," Daily Life, January 9, 2014, http://www.dailylife.com.au/health-and-fitness/dl-wellbeing/cant-sleep-blame-your-screen-time-20140109-30jcc.html; "Why Electronics May Stimulate You before Bed," National Sleep Foundation, https://www.sleepfoundation.org/articles/why-electronics-may-stimulate-you-bed; Caitlyn Fuller, Eric Lehman, Steven Hicks, and Marsha B. Novick, "Bedtime Use of Technology and Associated Sleep Problems in Children," *Global Pediatric Health* 4 (2017), https://www.ncbi.nlm.nih.gov/pmc/articles/PMC5669315/; Nina Schroder, "How to Reduce Screen Time in the Digital Age," National Alliance on Mental Illness, August 10, 2018, https://www.nami.org/Blogs/NAMI-Blog/August-2018/How-to-Reduce-Screen-Time-in-the-Digital-Age.

26. Neil Pasricha, "Why You Need an Untouchable Day Every Week," *Harvard Business Review*, March 16, 2018, https://hbr.org/2018/03/why-you-need-an-untouchable-day-every-week.

Chapter 9: Manage Your Energy: Body, Mindset, and Emotions

1. Jim Loehr and Tony Schwartz, *The Power of Full Engagement: Managing Energy, Not Time, Is the Key to High Performance and Personal Renewal* (New York: Simon & Schuster, 2003).

2. Vitalius Tumonis, Mykolas Šavelskis, and Inga Žalytė, "Judicial Decision-Making from an Empirical Perspective," *Baltic Journal of Law & Politics* 6, no. 1 (2013): 140–162.

3. Ibid.

4. Angela Haupt, "Food and Mood: 6 Ways Your Diet Affects How You Feel," *U.S. News & World Report*, August 31, 2011, https://health.usnews.com/health-news/diet-fitness/diet/articles/2011/08/31/food-and-mood-6-ways-your-diet-affects-how-you-feel (accessed on November 15, 2018).

5. Albert C. Yang, Norden E. Huang, Chung-Kang Peng, and Shih-Jen Tsai, "Do Seasons Have an Influence on the Incidence of Depression? The Use of an Internet Search Engine Query Data as a Proxy of Human Affect," *PloS One* 5, no. 10 (2010): e13728.

6. David Morgan, "Arianna Huffington: Better Sleep Improves Every Aspect of Our Lives," CBS News, https://www.cbsnews.com/news/arianna-huffington-better-sleep-improves-every-aspect-of-our-lives/ (accessed on November 3, 2018).

7. Justin McCarthy and Alyssa Brown, "Getting More Sleep Linked to Higher Well-Being," March 2, 2015, Gallup News, https://news.gallup.com/poll/181583/getting-sleep-linked-higher.aspx (accessed on December 21, 2018).

8. Carol S. Dweck, *Mindset: The New Psychology of Success* (New York: Random House Digital, 2008).

9. Mike Wooldridge, "Mandela Death: How He Survived 27 Years in Prison," BBC, https://www.bbc.com/news/world-africa-23618727 (accessed on November 2, 2018).

10. Deborah Berecz, "Madiba Mindset: What Can We Learn from Nelson Mandela?," Berecz & Associates, December 5, 2013, https://familyresolutions.us/2013/12/05/madiba-mindset-what-can-we-learn-from-nelson-mandela/ (accessed on November 1, 2018).

11. Marc A. Brackett and Nicole A. Katulak, "Emotional Intelligence in the Classroom: Skill-Based Training for Teachers and Students," in *Applying Emotional Intelligence: A Practitioner's Guide,* eds. Joseph Ciarrochi and John D. Mayer (New York: Psychology Press, 2007), 1–27.

12. Peter Salovey and John D. Mayer, "Emotional Intelligence," *Imagination, Cognition and Personality* 9, no. 3 (1990): 185–211.

13. Susan David and Christina Congleton, "Emotional Agility," *Harvard Business Review,* November 2013, 125–131.

14. "The 001 Experience," DoubleOone, https://www.doubleoone.com/ (accessed on December 20, 2018).

15. "The Mood Meter App Is Here," Yale Center for Emotional Intelligence, http://ei.yale.edu/mood-meter-app/ (accessed on December 15, 2018).

16. Michael Finn, "How to Reduce Stress Like a Navy SEAL," Gear Patrol, https://gearpatrol.com/2018/04/22/box-breathing-navy-seals/ (accessed on November 5, 2018).

17. "About Our App," Smiling Mind, https://www.smilingmind.com.au/smiling-mind-app/ (accessed on December 19, 2018).

18. Ana Gotter, "Box Breathing," Healthline, https://www.healthline.com/health/box-breathing#steps (accessed on November 20, 2018).

19. "The Haka," Team All Blacks, www.allblacks.com/Teams/Haka (accessed on November 22, 2018).

PART IV: SCALING INSPIRATION

1. Eric Garton, "What If Companies Managed People as Carefully as They Managed Money?," *Harvard Business Review,* May 24, 2017, https://hbr.org/2017/05/what-if-companies-managed-people-as-carefully-as-they-manage-money (accessed on June 15, 2017).

Chapter 10: Inspiring Leaders

1. Jack Zenger, Joseph Folkman, and Scott Edinger, *The Inspiring Leader* (Mill Valley, CA: Kantola Productions, 2009).

2. Jack Zenger and Joseph Folkman, "What Inspiring Leaders Do," *Harvard Business Review,* June 20, 2013, https://hbr.org/2013/06/what-inspiring-leaders-do.

3. Eric Garton and Michael C. Mankins, "Engaging Your Employees Is Good, but Don't Stop There," *Harvard Business Review,* December 9, 2015, https://hbr.org/2015/12/engaging-your-employees-is-good-but-dont-stop-there (accessed on January 15, 2019).

4. Zach Guy and Taylor G. Pentz, "Millennial Employment through Maslow's Eyes," *Career Planning and Adult Development Journal* 33, no. 2 (2017): 22.

5. Derek Ohly interview by Allison A. Holzer and Jen Grace Baron, July 6, 2016.

6. "Excerpts from Dear Ms Expat: Danielle Warner," Lifestyle, Expat Choice, January 9, 2018, https://www.expatchoice.asia/travel/excerpts-dear-ms-expat-danielle -warner (accessed on June 3, 2019).

7. Lucy Haydon, "In Focus: Danielle Warner," *Orient Magazine*, September 14, 2016, 16–23, https://issuu.com/orient_magazine/docs/issue_59_full_book.

8. Susannah Jaffer, "Inspiring Entrepreneur Stories: Danielle Warner," *Expat Living*, July 13, 2017.

9. "Julia Balfour: About," Julia Balfour: An Integrated Agency, https://www.julia balfour.com/about/ (accessed on December 15, 2019).

10. Julia Balfour interview by Jen Grace Baron, November 9, 2018.

11. Ibid.

12. P. Hersey and K. H. Blanchard, *Management of Organizational Behavior: Utilizing Human Resources* (Englewood Cliffs, NJ: Prentice Hall, 1969).

13. Fred E. Fiedler, "A Theory of Leadership Effectiveness," in *Advances in Experimental Social Psychology*, vol. 1, ed. Leonard Berkowitz (New York: Academic Press, 1964), 149–190.

14. Daniel Goleman, "Leadership That Gets Results," *Harvard Business Review*, March–April 2000, 4–17.

15. Alexander McCobin interview by Allison A. Holzer, December 17, 2018.

16. Bill Jennings interview by Laura Campbell and Allison A. Holzer, April 4, 2018.

17. Russell Clayton, Christopher Thomas, and Jack Smothers, "How to Do Walking Meetings Right," *Harvard Business Review*, August 5, 2015.

18. Marily Oppezzo and Daniel L. Schwartz, "Give your ideas some legs: The positive effect of walking on creative thinking," *Journal of Experimental Psychology: Learning, Memory, and Cognition* 40, no. 4 (2014): 1142–1152.

Chapter 11: Inspiring Teams

1. Cliff Bogue interview by Jen Grace Baron, February 9, 2019.

2. J. Richard Hackman, "Why Teams Don't Work," in *Theory and Research on Small Groups*, eds. R. Scot Tindale, Linda Heath, John Edwards, Emil J. Posavac, Fred B. Bryant, Yolanda Suarez-Balcazar, Eaaron Henderson-King, and Judith Myers (Boston: Springer, 2002), 245–267.

3. Helen Russell interview by Jen Grace Baron, March 12, 2019.

4. Re:Work editors, "Guide: Understand Team Effectiveness," Google, https:// rework.withgoogle.com/guides/understanding-team-effectiveness/steps/introduction / (accessed on January 31, 2019).

5. Ibid.

6. Anita Williams Woolley, Christopher F. Chabris, Alex Pentland, Nada Hashmi, and Thomas W. Malone, "Evidence for a Collective Intelligence Factor in the Performance of Human Groups," *Science* 330, no. 6004 (2010): 686–688.

7. Amy C. Edmondson, *Teaming: How Organizations Learn, Innovate, and Compete in the Knowledge Economy* (Hoboken, NJ: John Wiley & Sons, 2012).

8. Jane E. Dutton, *Energize Your Workplace: How to Create and Sustain High-Quality Connections at Work*, vol. 39 (San Francisco: Jossey-Bass, 2003).

9. "Julia Balfour: About," Julia Balfour: An Integrated Agency, https://www.juliabalfour.com/about/ (accessed on December 15, 2019).

10. Julia Balfour interview by Jen Grace Baron, December 15, 2018.

11. Steve Squinto interview by Laura Campbell, November 15, 2017.

12. Shea Gregg interview by Allison A. Holzer, January 5, 2017.

13. "Kentucky Derby History," History & Tradition, Kentucky Derby: Woodford Reserve, https://www.kentuckyderby.com/history/kentucky-derby-history (accessed on June 3, 2019).

14. Ibid.

15. Edith Luc, "The 8 Leadership Principles of Orpheus, the Conductor-Less Chamber Orchestra," Le blogue d' Edith Luc, December 11, 2011, http://blogue.edithluc.com/the-8-leadership-principles-of-orpheus-the-conductor-less-chamber-orchestra/?lang=en Blogue.edithluc.com (accessed on March 1, 2019).

16. Ron Lieber, "Leadership Ensemble," *Fast Company*, May 2000, https://www.fastcompany.com/39214/leadership-ensemble (accessed on March 15, 2019).

17. BBS, "#MBALecture: A Case of Shared Leadership by the Orpheus Chamber Orchestra," University of Bologna Business School, April 16, 2015, https://www.bbs.unibo.eu/hp/orpheus-post/ (accessed on March 14, 2019).

18. Bill Jennings interview by Laura Campbell and Allison A. Holzer, April 4, 2018.

19. Ibid.

20. Ibid.

21. Marissa Thalberg interview by Allison A. Holzer and Laura Campbell, June 8, 2017.

22. Ben Shpigel, "Duke Turns Up the Heat with a Slap of the Floor," *New York Times*, March 28, 2015, https://www.nytimes.com/2015/03/29/sports/ncaabasketball/duke-turns-up-the-heat-with-a-slap-of-the-floor.html (accessed on January 18, 2019).

Chapter 12: Inspiring Organizations

1. John Nemo, "What a NASA Janitor Can Teach Us about Living a Bigger Life," The Business Journals, https://www.bizjournals.com/bizjournals/how-to/growth-strategies/2014/12/what-a-nasa-janitor-can-teach-us.html (accessed on February 2, 2019).

2. Roberto Ferdman, "The Decline of the Small American Family Farm in One Chart," *Washington Post*, September 16, 2014, https://www.washingtonpost.com/news/wonk/wp/2014/09/16/the-decline-of-the-small-american-family-farm-in-one-chart/?utm_term=.2144a0ad3be3 (accessed on February 10, 2019).

3. Ibid.

4. Organic Valley, https://www.organicvalley.coop/about-us/organic-food-co-op/ (accessed on June 3, 2019).

5. Aaron Hurst, *The Purpose Economy: How Your Desire for Impact, Personal Growth and Community Is Changing the World* (Boise, ID: Elevate, 2016).

6. Rajendra Sisodia, David Wolfe, and Jagdish N. Sheth, *Firms of Endearment: How World-Class Companies Profit from Passion and Purpose* (Saddle River, NJ: Prentice Hall, 2003).

7. John Mackey and Rajendra Sisodia, *Conscious Capitalism: Liberating the Heroic Spirit of Business* (Boston: Harvard Business Press, 2014).

8. Alexander McCobin interview by Allison A. Holzer, December 12, 2018.

9. Nemo, "What a NASA Janitor Can Teach Us about Living a Bigger Life."

10. Joan Tranel interview by Leslie Kruempel, February 15, 2019.

11. Eric Garton, "What If Companies Managed People as Carefully as They Managed Money?," *Harvard Business Review,* May 24, 2017, https://hbr.org/2017/05/what-if-companies-managed-people-as-carefully-as-they-manage-money (accessed on June 15, 2017).

12. Gabe Friedman, "How a Holocaust Legacy Helped Launch Kind Bars," *Times of Israel,* October 25, 2015, https://www.timesofisrael.com/how-a-holocaust-legacy-helped-launch-kind-bars/ (accessed on February 3, 2019).

13. "Winning Culture," Bain & Company, https://www.bain.com/consulting-services/organization/winning-culture/ (accessed on February 15, 2019).

14. Chanel, *Report to Society,* 2018, http://services.chanel.com/i18n/en_US/pdf/Chanel_CSR_0305_Proof_180620_for_web.pdf (accessed February 2, 2019).

15. Gary Hamel, "Innovation Democracy: W. L. Gore's Original Management Model," Management Innovation eXchange, September 23, 2010, https://www.managementexchange.com/story/innovation-democracy-wl-gores-original-management-model (accessed on Feb 2, 2019).

16. Ibid.

17. "Gore Marks 20th Year on 100 Best Companies to Work For® List" (press release), March 9, 2017, https://www.gore.com/news-events/press-release/enterprise-press-release-fortune-100-list-2017-us (accessed on February 15, 2019).

18. James G. March, "Exploration and Exploitation in Organizational Learning," *Organization Science* 2, no. 1 (1991): 71–87.

19. Sam Cook, "60+ Netflix Statistics and Facts Stats That the Company's Dominance," Comparitech, updated March 14, 2019, https://www.comparitech.com/blog/vpn-privacy/netflix-statistics-facts-figures/ (accessed on May 23, 2019).

20. Zach Epstein, "Netflix 2018 Emmy Nominations: The Full List of Netflix's 112 Emmy Noms," BGR, July 13, 2018, https://bgr.com/2018/07/13/2018-emmy-nominations-complete-list-netflix-112-noms/ (accessed on June 3, 2019).

21. "Organic Valley Ends Year Standing Strong with 2,000 Farm Families," Organic Valley, December 20, 2016, https://www.organicvalley.coop/newspress/organic-valley-ends-year-standing-strong-2000-farm-families/ (accessed on June 3, 2019).

22. "Next Jump Origins," Next Jump, https://www.nextjump.com/next-jump-origins/ (accessed on June 2, 2019).

23. Robert Kegan and Lisa Laskow Lahey, *An Everyone Culture: Becoming a Deliberately Developmental Organization* (Boston: Harvard Business Review Press, 2016).

24. Next Jump Leadership Academy, http://www.nextjump.com/academy/ (accessed on February 15, 2019).

25. Next Jump 2018 Dance Competition video, https://www.youtube.com/watch?v=hh2yAQLTf2I (accessed on February 14, 2019).

26. Bryan Walker and Sarah Soule, "Changing Company Culture Requires a Movement, Not a Mandate," *Harvard Business Review*, June 30, 2017, 2–6.

Appendix B

1. Elliot Samuel Paul and Scott Barry Kaufman, eds., *The Philosophy of Creativity: New Essays* (Oxford, UK: Oxford University Press, 2014).

2. Dacher Keltner and Jonathan Haidt, "Approaching Awe, a Moral, Spiritual, and Aesthetic Emotion," *Cognition and Emotion* 17, no. 2 (2003): 297–314.

3. William H. Macey and Benjamin Schneider, "The Meaning of Employee Engagement," *Industrial and Organizational Psychology* 1, no. 1 (2008): 3–30.

4. Angela L. Duckworth, Christopher Peterson, Michael D. Matthews, and Dennis R. Kelly, "Grit: Perseverance and Passion for Long-Term Goals," *Journal of Personality and Social Psychology* 92, no. 6 (2007): 1087–1101.

INDEX